EACL Joint Workshop of LINGVIS & UNCLH 2012

Visualization of Linguistic Patterns and Uncovering Language History from Multilingual Resources

Held at the 13th Conference of the European Chapter of the Association for Computational Linguistics (EACL 2012)

Avignon, France
23-24 April 2012

ISBN: 978-1-62276-471-6

Printed from e-media with permission by:

Curran Associates, Inc.
57 Morehouse Lane
Red Hook, NY 12571

Printed by Curran Associates, Inc. (2013)

For permission requests, please contact the Association for Computational Linguistics at the address below.

Association for Computational Linguistics
209 N. Eighth Street
Stroudsburg, Pennsylvania 18360

Phone: 1-570-476-8006
Fax: 1-570-476-0860

acl@aclweb.org

Additional copies of this publication are available from:

Curran Associates, Inc.
57 Morehouse Lane
Red Hook, NY 12571 USA
Phone: 845-758-0400
Fax: 845-758-2634
Email: curran@proceedings.com
Web: www.proceedings.com

Organizers:

LINGVIS:
Miriam Butt (University of Konstanz)
Sheelagh Carpendale (University of Calgary)
Gerald Penn (University of Toronto)

UNCLH:
Jelena Prokić (LMU Munich)
Michael Cysouw (LMU Munich)
Thomas Mayer (LMU Munich)
Steven Moran (LMU Munich)

Program Committee:

Quentin Atkinson (University of Auckland)
Christopher Collins (University of Ontario)
Chris Culy (University of Tübingen)
Dan Dediu (MPI Nijmegen)
Michael Dunn (MPI Nijmegen)
Sheila Embleton (York University, Toronto)
Simon Greenhill (University of Auckland)
Harald Hammarström (University of Nijmegen)
Annette Hautli (University of Konstanz)
Wilbert Heeringa (Meertens Institute, Amsterdam)
Gerhard Heyer (University of Leipzig)
Eric Holman (UCLA)
Gerhard Jäger (University of Tübingen)
Daniel Keim (University of Konstanz)
Tibor Kiss (University of Bochum)
Jonas Kuhn (University of Stuttgart)
John Nerbonne (University of Groningen)
Anke Lüdeling (Humboldt University, Berlin)
Don Ringe (University of Pennsylvania)
Christian Rohrdantz (University of Konstanz)
Tandy Warnow (University of Texas at Austin)
Søren Wichmann (EVA MPI, Leipzig)

Invited Speakers:

Daniela Oelke (University of Konstanz)
Grzegorz Kondrak (University of Alberta)

Table of Contents

Conference Program

Introduction
Miriam Butt, Jelena Prokić, Thomas Mayer and Michael Cysouw

Monday, April 23, 2012

9:00	Invited talk by Christopher Collins
10:00	Coffee break
10:30	*Lexical Semantics and Distribution of Suffixes - A Visual Analysis* Christian Rohrdantz, Andreas Niekler, Annette Hautli, Miriam Butt and Daniel A. Keim
11:15	*Looking at word meaning. An interactive visualization of Semantic Vector Spaces for Dutch synsets* Kris Heylen, Dirk Speelman and Dirk Geeraerts
12:00	*First steps in checking and comparing Princeton WordNet and Estonian Wordnet* Ahti Lohk, Kadri Vare and Leo Võhandu
12:30	Lunch break
14:30	*Visualising Typological Relationships: Plotting WALS with Heat Maps* Richard Littauer, Rory Turnbull and Alexis Palmer
15:00	*Automating Second Language Acquisition Research: Integrating Information Visualisation and Machine Learning* Helen Yannakoudakis, Ted Briscoe and Theodora Alexopoulou
15:30	*Visualising Linguistic Evolution in Academic Discourse* Verena Lyding, Ekaterina Lapshinova-Koltunski, Stefania Degaetano-Ortlieb, Henrik Dittmann and Chris Culy
16:15	*The Potential of Visual Analytics for Computational Linguistics (Invited talk)* Daniela Oelke
17:15	Discussion

Tuesday, April 24, 2012

9:00	*Similarity Patterns in Words (Invited talk)* Grzegorz Kondrak
10:30	Coffee break
10:30	*Language comparison through sparse multilingual word alignment* Thomas Mayer and Michael Cysouw
11:00	*Recovering dialect geography from an unaligned comparable corpus* Yves Scherrer
11:30	*Detecting Shibboleths* Jelena Prokić, Çağrı Cöltekin and John Nerbonne
12:00	*Estimating and visualizing language similarities using weighted alignment and force-directed graph layout* Gerhard Jäger
12:30	Lunch break
14:30	*Explorations in creole research with phylogenetic tools* Aymeric Daval-Markussen and Peter Bakker
15:00	*Tracking the dynamics of kinship and social category terms with AustKin II* Patrick McConvell and Laurent Dousset
15:30	Coffee break
16:00	*Using context and phonetic features in models of etymological sound change* Hannes Wettig, Kirill Reshetnikov and Roman Yangarber
16:30	*LexStat: Automatic Detection of Cognates in Multilingual Wordlists* Johann-Mattis List
17:00	Discussion

Visualization of Linguistic Patterns and Uncovering Language History from Multilingual Resources

Miriam Butt[1] **Jelena Prokić**[2] **Thomas Mayer**[2] **Michael Cysouw**[3]
[1]Department of Linguistics, University of Konstanz
[2]Research Unit Quantitative Language Comparison, LMU Munich
[3]Research Center Deutscher Sprachatlas, Philipp University of Marburg

1 Introduction

The LINGVIS and UNCLH (Visualization of Linguistic Patterns & Uncovering Language History from Multilingual Resources) were originally conceived of as two separate workshops. Due to perceived similarities in content, the two workshops were combined and organized jointly.

The overal aim of the joint workshop was to explore how methods developed in computational linguistics, statistics and computer science can help linguists in exploring various language phenomena. The workshop focused particularly on two topics: 1) visualization of linguistic patterns (LINGVIS); 2) usage of multilingual resources in computational historical linguistics (UNCLH).

2 LINGVIS

The overall goal of the first half of the workshop was to bring together researchers working within the emerging subfield of computational linguistics — using methods established within Computer Science in the fields of Information Visualization (InfoVis) and Visual Analytics in conjunction with methodology and analyses from theoretical and computational linguistics. Despite the fact that statistical methods for language analysis have proliferated in the last two decades, computational linguistics has so far only marginally availed itself of techniques from InfoVis and Visual Analytics (e.g., Honkela et al. (1995); Neumann et al. (2007); Collins et al. (2009); Collins (2010); Mayer et al. (2010a); Mayer et al. (2010b); Rohrdantz et al. (2011)). The need to integrate methods from InfoVis and Visual Analytics arises particularly with respect to situations in which the amount of data to be analyzed is huge and the interactions between relevant features are complex. Both of these situations hold for much of current (computational) linguistic analysis. The usual methods of statistical analysis do not allow for quick and easy grasp and interpretation of the patterns discovered through statistical processing and an integration of innovative visualization techniques has become imperative.

The overall aim of the first half of the workshop was thus to draw attention to this need and to the newly emerging type of work that is beginning to respond to the need. The workshop succeeded in bringing together researchers interesting in combining techniques and methodology from theoretical and computational linguistics with InfoVis and Visual Analytics.

Three of the papers in the workshop focused on the investigation and visualization of lexical semantics. Rohrdantz et al. present a diachronic study of fairly recently coined derivational suffixes (*-gate, -geddon, -athon*) as used in newspaper corpora across several languages. Their analysis is able to pin-point systematic differences in contextual use as well as some first clues as to how and why certain new coinages spread better than others. Heylen et al. point out that methods such as those used in Rohrdantz et al., while producing interesting results, are essentially black boxes for the researchers — it is not clear exactly what is being calculated. Their paper presents some first steps towards making the black box more transparent. In particular, they take a close look at individual tokens and their semantic use with respect to Dutch synsets. Crucially, they anticipate an interactive visualization that will allow linguistically informed lexicogra-

Proceedings of the EACL 2012 Joint Workshop of LINGVIS & UNCLH, pages 1–6,
Avignon, France, April 23 - 24 2012.

phers to work with the available data and patterns. A slightly different take on synset relations is presented by Lohk et al., who use visualization methods to help identify errors in WordNets across different languages.

Understanding differences and relatedness between languages or types of a language is the subject of another three papers. Littauer et al. use data from the WALS (World Atlas of Language Structures; Dryer and Haspelmath (2011)) to model language relatedness via heat maps. They overcome two difficulties: one is the sparseness of the WALS data; another is that WALS does not directly contain information about possible effects of language contact. Littauer et al. attempt to model the latter by taking geographical information about languages into account (neighboring languages and their structure). A different kind of language relatedness is investigated by Yannakoudakis et al., who look at learner corpora and develop tools that allow an assessment of learner competence with respect to various linguistic features found in the corpora. The number of relevant features is large and many of them are interdependent or interact. Thus, the amount and complexity of the data present a classic case of complex data sets that are virtually impossible to analyze well without the application of visualization methods. Finally, Lyding et al. take academic texts and investigate the use of modality across academic registers and across time in order to identify whether the academic language used in different subfields (or adjacent fields) of an academic field has an effect on the language use of that field.

3 UNCLH

The second half of the workshop focused on the usage of multilingual resources in computational historical linguistics. In the past 20 years, the application of quantitative methods in historical linguistics has received increasing attention among linguists (Dunn et al., 2005; Heggarty et al., 2010; McMahon and McMahon, 2006), computational linguists (Kondrak, 2001; Hall and Klein, 2010) and evolutionary anthropologists (Gray and Atkinson, 2003). Due to the application of these quantitative methods, the field of historical linguistics is undergoing a renaissance. One of the main problems that researchers face is the limited amount of suitable *comparative* data, often falling back on relatively restricted 'Swadesh type' wordlists. One solution is to use synchronic data, like dictionaries or texts, which are available for many languages. For example, in Kondrak (2001), vocabularies of four Algonquian languages were used in the task of automatic cognate identification. Another solution employed by Snyder et al. (2010) is to apply a non-parametric Bayesian framework to two non-parallel texts in the task of text deciphering. Although very promising, these approaches have so far only received modest attention. Thus, many questions and challenges in the automatization of language resources in computational historical linguistics remain open and ripe for investigation.

In dialectological studies, there is a long tradition, starting with Séguy (1971), in which language varieties are grouped together on the basis of their similarity with respect to certain properties. Later work in this area has incorporated methods of string alignment for a quantitative comparison of individual words to obtain an average measure of the similarity of languages. This line of research became known as dialectometry. Unlike traditional dialectology which is based on the analysis of individual items, dialectometry shifts focus on the aggregate level of differences. Most of the work done so far in dialectometry is based on the carefully selected wordlists and problems with the limited amount of suitable data (i.e. computer readable and comparable across dialects) are also present in this field.

This workshop brings together researchers interested in computational approaches that uncover sound correspondences and sound changes, automatic identification of cognates across languages and language comparison based both on wordlists and parallel texts. First, Wettig et al. investigate the sound correspondences in cognate sets in a sample of Uralic languages. Then, List's contribution to the volume introduces a novel method for automatic cognate detection in multilingual wordlists which combines various previous approaches for string comparison. The paper by Mayer & Cysouw presents a first step to use parallel texts for a quantitative comparison of languages. The papers by Scherrer and Prokić et al. both are in the spirit of the dialectometric line of research. Further, Jäger reports on quantifying language similarity via phonetic alignment of core vocabulary items. Finally, some of the papers presented in this workshop deal with further topics in quantitative language comparison, like the application of phylogenetic methods in creole research in the paper by Daval-Markussen & Bakker, and the study of the evolution of the Australian kinship terms reported on in the paper by McConvell & Dousset.

In the next section, we give a brief introduction into the papers presented in this workshop, ordered according to the program of the oral presentations at the workshop.

4 Papers

Christian Rohrdantz, Andreas Niekler, Annette Hautli, Miriam Butt and Daniel A. Keim ('Lexical Semantics and Distribution of Suffixes — A Visual Analysis) present a quantitative cross-linguistic investigation of the lexical semantic content expressed by three suffixes originating in English: *-gate, -geddon* and *-athon*. Using data from newspapers, they look at the distribution and lexical semantic usage of these morphemes across several languages and also across time, with a time-depth of 20 years for English. Using techniques from InfoVis and Visual Analytics is crucial for the analysis as the occurrence of these suffixes in the available corpora is comparatively rare and it is only by dint of processing and visualizing huge amounts of data that a clear pattern can begin to emerge.

Kris Heylen, Dirk Speelman and Dirk Geeraerts ('Looking at Word Meaning. An Interactive Visualization of Semantic Vector Spaces for Dutch synsets') focus on the pervasive use of Semantic Vector Spaces (SVS) in statistical NLP as a standard technique for the automatic modeling of lexical semantics. They take on the fact that while the method appears to work fairly well (though they criticize the standardly available evaluation measures via some created gold standard), it is in fact quite unclear how it captures word meaning. That is, the standard technology can be seen as a black box. In order to find a way of providing some transparency to the method, they explore the way an SVS structures the individual occurrences of words with respect to the occurrences of 476 Dutch nouns. These were grouped into 214 synsets in previous work. This paper looks at a token-by-token similarity matrix in conjunction with a visualization that uses the Google Chart Tools and compares the results with previous work, especially in light of different uses in different versions of Dutch.

Ahti Lohk, Kadri Vare and Leo Võhandu ('First Steps in Checking and Comparing Princeton WordNet and Estonian WordNet') use visualization methods to compare two existing WordNets (English and Estonian) in order to identify errors and semantic inconsistencies that are a result of the manual coding. Their method opens up a potentially interesting way of automatically checking for inconsistencies and errors not only at a fairly basic and surface level, but by working with the lexical semantic classification of the words in question.

Richard Littauer, Rory Turnbull and Alexis Palmer ('Visualizing Typological Relationships: Plotting WALS with Heat Maps') present a novel way of visualizing relationships between languages. The paper is based on data extracted from the World Atlas of Language Structures (WALS), which is the most complete set of typological and digitized data available to date, but which presents two challenges: 1) it actually has very low coverage both in terms of languages represented and in terms of feature description for each language; 2) areal effects are not coded for. While the authors find a way to overcome the first challenge, the paper's real contribution lies in proposing a method for overcoming the second challenge. In particular, the typological data is filtered by geographical proximity and then displayed by means of heat maps, which reflect the strength of similarity between languages for different linguistic features. Thus, the data should allow one to be able to ascertain areal typological effects via a single integrated visualization.

Helen Yannakoudakis, Ted Briscoe and Theodora Alexopoulou ('Automatic Second Language Acquisition Research: Integrating Information Visualisation and Machine Learning') look at yet another domain of application. They show how data-driven approaches to learner corpora can support Second Language Acquisition (SLA) research when integrated with visualization tools. Learner corpora are interesting because their analysis requires a good understanding of a complex set of interacting linguistic features across corpora with different distributional patterns (since each corpus potentially diverges from the standard form of the language by a different set of features). The paper presents a visual user interface which supports the investigation of a set of linguistic features discriminating between pass and fail exam scripts. The system displays directed graphs to model interactions between features and supports exploratory search over a set of learner texts. A very useful result for SLA is the proposal of a new method for empirically quantifying the linguistic abilities that characterize different levels of language learning.

Verena Lyding, Ekaterina Lapshinova-Koltunski, Stefania Degaetano-Ortlieb, Henrik Dittmann and Chris Culy ('Visualizing Linguistic Evolution in Academic Discourse') describe methods for visualizing diachronic language changes in academic writing. In particular, they look at the use of modality across different academic subfields and investigate whether adjacent subfields affect the use of language in a given academic subfield. Their findings potentially provide crucial information for further NLP tasks such as automatic text classification.

Grzegorz Kondrak's invited contribution ('Similarity Patterns in Words') sketches a number of the author's research projects on diachronic linguistics. He first discusses computational techniques for implementing several steps of the comparative method. These techniques include algorithms that deal with a wide range of problems: pairwise and multiple string alignment, calculation of phonetic similarity between two strings, automatic extraction of recurrent sound correspondences, quantification of semantic similarity between two words, identification of sets of cognates and building of phylogenetic trees. In the second part, Kondrak sketches several NLP projects that directly benefitted from his research on diachronic linguistics: statistical machine translation, word alignment, identification of confusable drug names, transliteration, grapheme-to-phoneme conversion, letter-phoneme alignment and mapping of annotations.

Thomas Mayer and Michael Cysouw ('Language Comparison through Sparse Multilingual Word Alignment') present a novel approach on how to calculate similarities among languages with the help of massively parallel texts. Instead of comparing languages pairwise they suggest a simultaneous analysis of languages with respect to their co-occurrence statistics for individual words on the sentence level. These statistics are then used to group words into clusters which are considered to be partial (or 'sparse') alignments. These alignments then serve as the basis for the similarity count where languages are taken to be more similar the more words they share in the various alignments, regardless of the actual form of the words. In order to cope with the computationally demanding multilingual analysis they introduce a sparse matrix representation of the co-occurrence statistics.

Yves Scherrer ('Recovering Dialect Geography from an Unaligned Comparable Corpus') proposes a simple metric of dialect distance, based on the ratio between identical word pairs and cognate word pairs occurring in two texts. Scherrer proceeds from a multidialectal corpus and applies techniques from machine translation in order to extract identical words and cognate words. The dialect distance is defined as as function of the number of cognate word pairs and identical word pairs. Different variations of this metric are tested on a corpus containing comparable texts from different Swiss German dialects and evaluated on the basis of spatial autocorrelation measures.

Jelena Prokić, Çağrı Cöltekin and John Nerbonne ('Detecting Shibboleths') propose a generalization of the well-known precision and recall scores to deal with the case of detecting distinctive, characteristic variants in dialect groups, in case the analysis is based on numerical difference scores. This method starts from the data that has already been divided into groups using cluster analyses, correspondence analysis or any other technique that can identify groups of language varieties based on linguistic or extra-linguistic factors (e.g. geography or social properties). The method seeks items that differ minimally within a group but differ a great deal with respect to elements outside it. They demonstrate the effectiveness of their approach using Dutch and German dialect data, identifying those words that show low variation within a given dialect area, and high variation outside a given area.

Gerhard Jäger ('Estimating and Visualizing Language Similarities Using Weighted Alignment and Force-Directed Graph Layout') reports several studies to quantify language similarity via phonetic alignment of core vocabulary items (taken from the Automated Similarity Judgement Program data base). Jäger compares several string comparison measures based on Levenshtein distance and based on Needleman-Wunsch similarity score. He also tests two normalization functions, one based on the average score and the other based on the informatic theoretic similarity measure. The pairwise similarity between all languages are analyzed and visualized using the CLANS software, a force directed graph layout that does not assume an underlying tree structure of the data.

Aymeric Daval-Markussen and Peter Bakker ('Explorations in Creole Research with Phylogenetic Tools') employ phylogenetic tools to investigate and visualize the relationship of creole languages to other (non-)creole languages on the basis of structural features. Using the morphosyntactic features described in the monograph on Comparative Creole Syntax (Holm and Patrick, 2007), they create phylogenetic trees and networks for the languages in the sample, which show the similarity between the various languages with respect to the grammatical features investigated. Their results lend support to the universalist approach which assumes that creoles show creole-specific characteristics, possibly due to restructuring universals. They also apply their methodology to the comparison of creole languages to other languages, on the basis of typological features from the *World Atlas of Language Structures*. Their findings confirm the hypothesis that creole languages form a synchronically distinguishable subgroup among the world's languages.

Patrick McConvell and Laurent Dousset ('Tracking the Dynamics of Kinship and Social Category Terms with AustKin II') give an overview of their ongoing work on kinship and social category terms in Australian languages. They describe the AustKin I database which allows for the reconstruction of older kinship systems as well as the visualization of patterns and changes. In particular, their method reconstructs so-called 'Kariera' kinship systems for the proto-languages in Australia. This supports earlier hypotheses about the primordial world social organization from which Dravidian-Kariera systems are considered to have evolved. They also report on more recent work within the AustKin II project which is devoted to the co-evoluation of marriage and social category systems.

Hannes Wettig, Kirill Reshetnikov and Roman Yangarber ('Using Context and Phonetic Features in Models of Etymological Sound Change') present a novel method for a context-sensitive alignment of cognate words, which relies on the information theoretic concept of Minimum Description Length to decide on the most compact representation of the data given the model. Starting with an initial random alignment for each word pair, their algorithm iteratively rebuilds decision trees for each feature and realigns the corpus while monotonically decreasing the cost function until convergence. They also introduce a novel test for the quality of the models where one word pair is omitted from the training phase. The rules that have been learned are then used to guess one word from the other in the pair. The Levenshtein distance of the correct and the guessed word is then computed to give an idea of how good the model actually learned the regularities in the sound correspondences.

Johann-Mattis List ('LexStat: Automatic Detection of Cognates in Multilingual Wordlists') presents a new method for automatic cognate detection in multilingual wordlists. He combines different approaches to sequence comparison in historical linguistics and evolutionary biology into a new framework which closely models central aspects of the comparative method. The input sequences, i.e. words, are converted to sound classes and their sonority profiles are determined. In step 2, a permutation method is used to create language specific scoring schemes. In step 3, the pairwise distances between all word pairs, based on the language-specific scoring schemes, are computed. In step 4, the sequences are clustered into cognate sets whose average distance is beyond a certain threshold. The method is tested on 9 multilingual wordlists.

5 Final remarks

The breadth and depth of the research collected in this workshop more than testify to the scope and possibilities for applying new methods that combine quantitative methods with not only a sophisticated linguistic understanding of language phenomena, but also with visualization methods coming out of the Computer Science fields of InfoVis and Visual Analytics. The papers in the workshop addressed how the emerging new body of work can provide advances and new insights for questions pertaining to theoretical linguistics (lexical semantics, derivational morphology, historical linguistics, dialectology and typology) and applied linguistic fields such as second language acquisition and statistical NLP.

6 Acknowledgments

We are indebted to the members of the program committee of the workshop for their effort in thoroughly reviewing the papers: Quentin Atkinson, Christopher Collins, Chris Culy, Dan Dediu, Michael Dunn, Sheila Embleton, Simon Greenhill, Harald Hammarström, Annette Hautli, Wilbert Heeringa, Gerhard Heyer, Eric Holman, Gerhard Jäger, Daniel Keim, Tibor Kiss, Jonas Kuhn, Anke Lüdeling, Steven Moran, John Nerbonne, Gerald Penn, Don Ringe, Christian Rohrdantz, Tandy Warnow, Søren Wichmann.

We also thank the organizers of the EACL 2012 conference for their help in setting up the joint workshop.

References

Christopher Collins, Sheelagh Carpendale, and Gerald Penn. 2009. Docuburst: Visualizing document content using language structure. *Computer Graphics Forum (Proceedings of Eurographics/IEEE-VGTC Symposium on Visualization (EuroVis '09))*, 28(3):1039–1046.

Christopher Collins. 2010. *Interactive Visualizations of Natural Language*. Ph.D. thesis, University of Toronto.

Matthew S. Dryer and Martin Haspelmath, editors. 2011. *The World Atlas of Language Structures Online*. Max Planck Digital Library, Munich, 2011 edition.

Michael Dunn, Angela Terrill, Ger Resnik, Robert A. Foley, and Stephen C. Levinson. 2005. Structural phylogenetics and the reconstruction of ancient language history. *Science*, 309(5743):2072–2075.

Russell Gray and Quentin Atkinson. 2003. Language-tree divergence times support the Anatolian theory of Indo-European origins. *Nature*, 426:435–439.

David LW Hall and Dan Klein. 2010. Finding cognate groups using phylogenies. In *Proceedings of the Association for Computational Linguistics*.

Paul Heggarty, Warren Maguire, and April McMahon. 2010. Splits or waves? trees or webs? how divergence measures and network analysis can unravel language histories. In *Philosophical Transactions of the Royal Society (B)*, volume 365, pages 3829–3843.

John Holm and Peter L. Patrick, editors. 2007. *Comparative Creole Syntax*. London: Battlebridge.

Timo Honkela, Ville Pulkki, and Teuvo Kohonen. 1995. Contextual relations of words in grimm tales, analyzed by self-organizing map. In *Proceedings of International Conference on Artificial Neural Networks (ICANN-95)*, pages 3–7.

Grzegorz Kondrak. 2001. Identifying cognates by phonetic and semantic similarity. In *Proceedings of the North American Chapter of the Association of Computational Linguistics*.

Thomas Mayer, Christian Rohrdantz, Miriam Butt, Frans Plank, and Daniel A. Keim. 2010a. Visualizing vowel harmony. *Linguistic Issues in Language Technology (LiLT)*, 2(4).

Thomas Mayer, Christian Rohrdantz, Frans Plank, Peter Bak, Miriam Butt, and Daniel A. Keim. 2010b. Consonant co-occurrence in stems across languages: Automatic analysis and visualization of a phonotactic constraint. In *Proceedings of the 2010 Workshop on NLP and Linguistics: Finding the Common Ground, ACL 2010*, pages 70–78.

April McMahon and Robert McMahon. 2006. *Language Classification by Numbers*. OUP.

Petra Neumann, Annie Tat, Torre Zuk, and Sheelagh Carpendale. 2007. Keystrokes: Personalizing typed text with visualization. In *Proceedings of Eurographics IEEE VGTC Symposium on Visualization*.

Christian Rohrdantz, Annette Hautli, Thomas Mayer, Miriam Butt, Daniel A. Keim, and Frans Plank. 2011. Towards tracking semantic change by visual analytics. In *Proceedings of the 49th Annual Meeting of the Association for Computational Linguistics (Short Papers)*, pages 305–310. Portland, Oregon.

Jean Séguy. 1971. La relation entre la distance spatiale et la distance lexicale. *Revue de Linguistique Romane*, 35(138):335–357.

Benjamin Snyder, Regina Barzilay, and Kevin Knight. 2010. A statistical model for lost language decipherment. In *Proceedings of the Association for Computational Linguistics*.

Lexical Semantics and Distribution of Suffixes — A Visual Analysis

Christian Rohrdantz[1] **Andreas Niekler**[2] **Annette Hautli**[1] **Miriam Butt**[1] **Daniel A. Keim**[1]

[1] University of Konstanz
first.last@uni-konstanz.de

[2]Leipzig University of Applied Sciences
aniekler@fbm.htwk-leipzig.de

Abstract

We present a quantitative investigation of the cross-linguistic usage of some (relatively) newly minted derivational morphemes. In particular, we examine the lexical semantic content expressed by three suffixes originating in English: *-gate*, *-geddon* and *-athon*. Using data from newspapers, we look at the distribution and lexical semantic usage of these morphemes not only within English, but across several languages and also across time, with a time-depth of 20 years. The occurrence of these suffixes in available corpora are comparatively rare, however, by investigating huge amounts of data, we are able to arrive at interesting insights into the distribution, meaning and spread of the suffixes. Processing and understanding the huge amounts of data is accomplished via visualization methods that allow the presentation of an overall distributional picture, with further details and different types of perspectives available on demand.

1 Introduction

It is well-known that parts of a compound can begin to lead an additional life as derivational suffixes, or even as stand-alone items. A famous example is *burger*, which is now used to denote a food-item (e.g., *burger, cheese burger, veggie burger*) and is originally from the word *Hamburger*, which designates a person from the German city of Hamburg. These morphemes are generally known as *cranberry morphemes* (because of the prolific use of *cran*). Some other examples are *-(o)nomics, -(o)mat* or *(o)rama*.

While it is well-known that this morphological process exists, it is less clear what conditions trigger it and how the coinage "catches" on to become a regular part of a language. Given the current availability of huge amounts of digital data, we decided to investigate whether we could gain an insight into the use and spread of some of these morphemes via quantitative methods, thereby confirming our intuitions.

Furthermore, we decided to focus not just on the use of the cranberry morphemes in their language of origin, but also on their use and spread in other languages. In particular, we want to model the contexts in which these suffixes are used to coin new words and how these neologisms transport to other languages. We chose to look at the following three morphemes: *-gate*, *-geddon* and *-athon* because they tend to be used in "newsworthy" contexts and are therefore likely to appear in newswire and newspaper corpora, which are available to us in large amounts.

This paper describes work in progress, where we visually analyze the lexical semantics and use of the three suffixes *-gate*, *-geddon* and *-athon*. We were able to add some time-depth to our investigation via an analysis of the New York Times corpus from 1987–2007. This means that while we cannot pin-point the first occurrence and further spread of the morpheme uses, we can gain some idea as to their historical development.

Given that the amount of data we analyze is huge, we use methods from Visual Analytics in order to make the vast amount of information generated from the computational models easily accessible to the human eye and mind.

We proceed as follows: After a review of related work in Section 2, we describe our study in Section 3 and discuss the visual analysis in Section 4. In a case study we compare the meaning of

Proceedings of the EACL 2012 Joint Workshop of LINGVIS & UNCLH, pages 7–15,
Avignon, France, April 23 - 24 2012.

words with the suffix *-gate* to other semantically related words (4.1) based on an optimized topic model. We also develop, customize and apply visualizations to investigate the productivity of new suffixes and their spread across news sources and languages (4.2). We conclude with Section 5.

2 Related Work

As already mentioned, the coinage and spread of new suffixes is well-known in theoretical linguistics. However, linguists are generally not sure what effects exactly are involved in the process (Baayen, 1992; Plag, 1999). We are not aware of any other computational work on cranberry morphemes. Work by Lüdeling and Evert (2005) on the German non-medical suffix *-itis* is closest to this paper; however, the type of the morpheme investigated is different and their focus is mainly on productivity. We concentrate more on the lexical semantic content of the suffixes, look at them across languages in bigger corpora to investigate their distribution and use and provide a layer of visual analysis.

One question we asked ourselves is whether we could predict from the context the likelihood of the suffixes *-gate*, *-geddon* and *-athon* and whether one can identify the lexical semantic content of the suffixes more precisely. This task can be formulated as a topic modeling problem for which we chose to employ Latent Dirichlet Allocation (LDA) (Blei et al., 2003). It has recently been used to perform word sense induction from small word contexts (e.g. Brody (2009)) and has also proven successful when detecting changes in word meanings over time on small word contexts in diachronic corpora (Rohrdantz et al., 2011).

We applied an optimized topic model and combined the statistical results with methods from Visual Analytics. Visual Analytics is based on the tight coupling of algorithms for automatic data analysis and interactive visual components (Thomas and Cook, 2005; Keim et al., 2010). The idea is to exploit human perceptive abilities to support the detection of interesting patterns (see Card et al. (1999) for details). Examples for visualizations used previously to investigate linguistic questions are Mayer et al. (2010a) on vowel harmony, Mayer et al. (2010b) on consonant patterns, Honkela et al. (1995) on syntactic categories, Rohrdantz et al. (2011) on lexical semantics across time.

We also used visualizations to look at cross-linguistic use and productivity of the suffixes. Prominent theoretical work on the productivity of morphemes has been done by Baayen (1992) and Plag (1999), most computational approaches have worked on English due to the availability of large enough corpora (Nishimoto, 2004). To the best of our knowledge, no large-scale quantitative study has been performed which takes into account both the diachronic as well as the cross-linguistic dimension of the development.

3 Our Approach

3.1 Research Questions & Analysis Tasks

The object of research are three productive suffixes, namely *-gate*, *geddon* and *-athon*. What these suffixes have in common is that they trigger neologisms in various languages and all of them seem to carry some lexical semantic information. Whereas *-gate*, which was coined by the *Watergate* affair, is used for scandalous events or affairs, *-geddon* seems to denote a similar concept but more of a disastrous event, building on its original use in the bible. Usually, *-athon*, coming from *marathon*, denotes a long-lasting event. We assume that the lexical semantic content of these suffixes can be modeled with standard topic models.

3.2 Data & Statistics

Our investigations are based on two different data sets, one is a diachronic news corpus, the New York Times Annotated Corpus[1] containing 1.8 million newspaper articles from 1987 to 2007. To generate the second data set, we performed an online scan of the EMM news service,[2] which links to multilingual news articles from all over the world and enriches them with metada (Atkinson and der Goot, 2009; Krstajic et al., 2010). Between May 2009 and January 2012, we scanned about eleven million news articles in English, German and French.

For both data sources, we extract a context of 25 words before and after the word under investigation, together with its timestamp. In the case of the EMM data, we also save information on the news source, the source country and the language of the article. In a manual postprocessing step, we

[1]http://www.ldc.upenn.edu/

[2]http://emm.newsexplorer.eu/

clean the dataset from words ending in the suffixes by coincidence, many of which are proper names of persons and locations.

From the EMM metadata, we can attribute the employment of the suffixes to the countries they were used in. Table 1 shows the figures for the *-gate* suffix, what language it was used in, and its country of origin. We can see that the suffix was used in many countries and different world regions between May 2009 and January 2012.

Lang.	**Country**
English	GB (1142), USA (840), Ireland (364), Pakistan (275), South Africa (190), India (131), Australia (129), Canada (117), Zimbabwe (73)
French	France (2089), Switzerland (429), Belgium (108), Senegal (30)
German	Germany (493), Switzerland (151), Austria (151)

Table 1: Usage of the suffix *-gate* in different languages/countries. For each language only the countries with the most occurrences are listed.

Among the total 7,500 *-gate* appearances, *Rubygate* – the affair of Italian's ex prime minister Silvio Berlusconi with an under-aged girl from Morocco – was the most frequent word with 1558 matches, followed by *Angolagate* with 1025 matches and *Climategate* with 752 matches. The NYT corpus has 1,000 matches of *-gate* words, the top ones were *Iraqgate* with 148, *Travelgate* with 122, and *Irangate* with 105 matches. The frequency of *-geddon* and *-athon* was much lower.

3.3 Topic Modeling

The task of the topic modeling in this paper is to discover meaning relationships between our the suffixes and semantically related words, i.e. we want to determine from the word contexts whether *-gate* words share context features with words such as *scandal* or *affair*. For this task, we use LDA, which describes a generative hierarchical Bayesian model that relates the words and documents within a corpus through a latent variable. The interpretation of this latent variable could be seen as topics that are responsible for the usage of words within the documents. Within the LDA framework we can describe the generation of a document by the following process

1. draw K multinomials $\phi_k \propto Dir(\beta_k)$, one for each topic k
2. for each document d, $d = 1, \ldots, D$
   (a) draw multinomial $\theta_d \propto Dir(\alpha_d)$
   (b) for each word w_{dn} in document d, $n = 1, \ldots, N_d$
      i. draw a topic $z_{dn} \propto Multinomial(\theta_d)$
      ii. draw a word w_{dn} from $p(w_{dn}|\phi_{z_{dn}})$, the multinomial probability conditioned on topic z_{dn}

Following this generative process we identify the hidden variables for every document in a corpus by computing the posterior distribution:

$$p(\theta, \phi, \mathbf{z}|\mathbf{w}, \alpha, \beta) = \frac{p(\theta, \phi, \mathbf{z}, \mathbf{w}|\alpha, \beta)}{p(\mathbf{w}|\alpha, \beta)}. \quad (1)$$

Exact inference for this posterior distribution is not tractable and we use collapsed Gibbs sampling as in Griffiths and Steyver (2004). We compute the posterior distribution over all variables and model parameters instead of inferring θ and ϕ directly. The Gibbs sampling procedure samples a topic z_{dn} for each word in all documents of the corpus. This procedure is iterated until the approximated posterior distribution does not change the likelihood of the model with more iterations. As a result we get a sampled topic z_{dn} for each word in the corpus and can trace θ and ϕ. For our problem we can use the counts of z_{dn}, the count of words belonging to a topic, for each document in combination with the timestamps to see which word in question appears how often in a specific topic in which time slice. This allows us to observe the usage of a word within a certain timespan. The hidden variable ϕ can be interpreted as a matrix having the conditional probability $p(w_i|z_k)$ at the matrix position $\phi_{i,k}$. This means that every column vector in ϕ is a probability distribution over the whole vocabulary. These distributions can be seen as topics since they describe a mixture of words with exact probabilities. Having those distributions at hand we can analyze which words occur significantly often in the same topic or semantic context.

The purpose of the LDA model is to analyze the latent structure of the passages extracted from the NYT corpus. We decided to use the contexts of *Watergate, scandal, affair, crisis, controversy* in combination with the suffix *-gate*. We can then

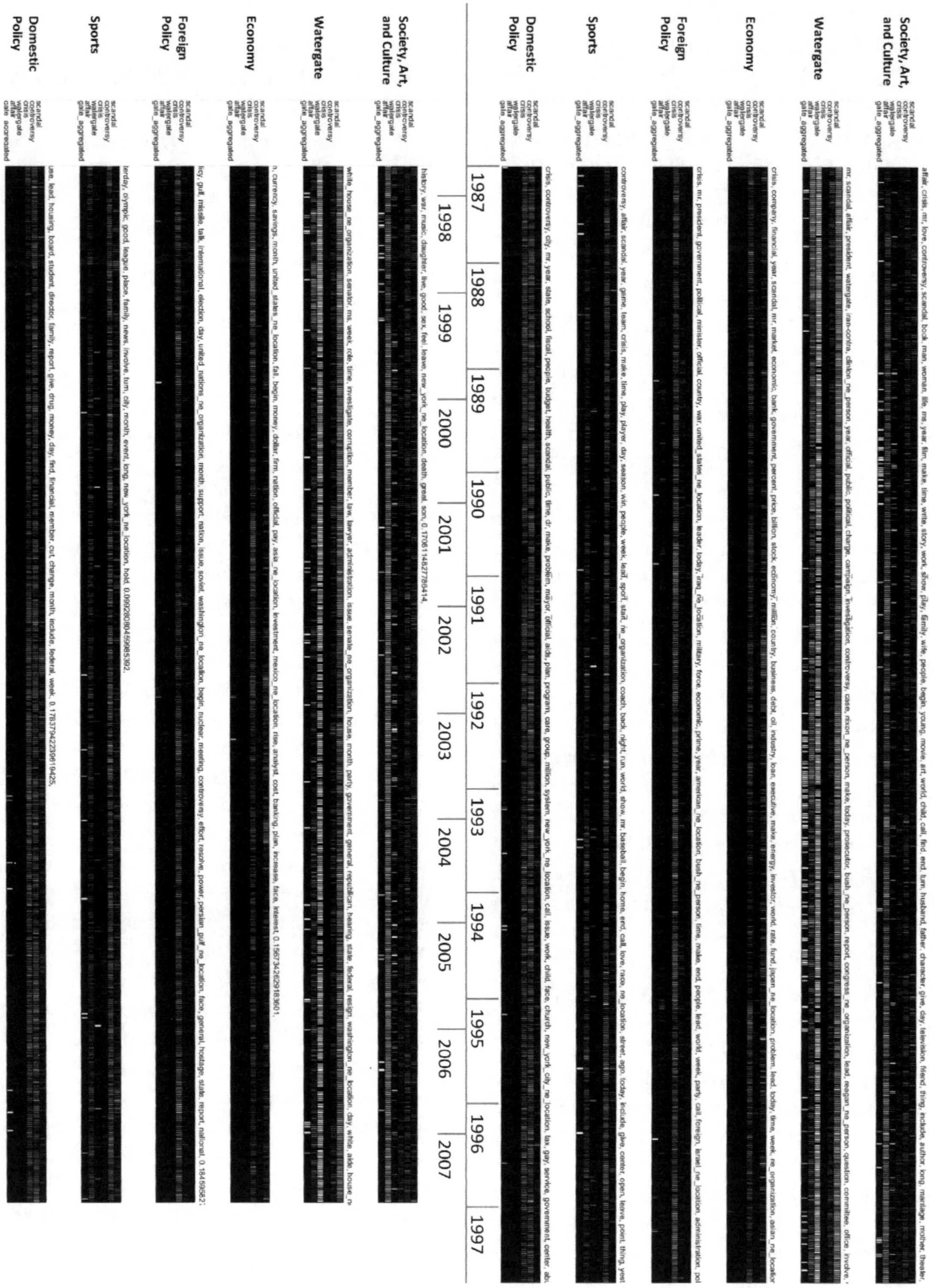

Figure 1: The diachronic distribution of the words under investigation over the 6 topics learned from the New York Times Corpus.

see where these terms co-occur and hence what the semantic context is. We infer a model which consists of six topics under the assumption that if the word senses of the six words given above do not overlap at all, there should not be more than six senses to analyze. The fixed parameter K in the model leads us to an optimization problem of the hyper-parameter β. The hyper-parameter α is not as important as β since it scales the topic per document mixture. For that reason we do not optimize α explicitly. We rather estimate the optimal value after optimizing the value for β. Since the β parameter is of crucial impact to the generation of the hidden variable ϕ and thus the topics, we need to find the optimal hyper-parameter that generalizes the model to the given data. Most approaches show that one can optimize the model for fixed parameters α and β when testing models with different values for K as in (Griffiths and Steyver, 2004). Since we are fixing K we must test the dataset for an optimal model given different values for β. This can be done by utilizing the model perplexity (Blei et al., 2003) and thus maximizing the likelihood of a test dataset from the same corpus.

In our experiment we used a relatively small number of topics and we expected a large number of words aligned to a topic.

4 Visual Analytics

4.1 Topic Modeling

The topics extracted from the NYT corpus by the model described in Section 3.3 was further investigated with respect to the correlation between the lexical semantic content of the suffixed words and a development over time. For this purpose we designed a pixel visualization (see Figure 1), mapping the data facets to the visual variables as follows: The data is divided according to the topics mapping each topic to one horizontal band. The descriptive words of a topic as found by LDA are listed above its band. In addition, each topic is manually assigned an interpretive label. These labels are at the far left of a topic band.

Each topic band is further subdivided according to the words under investigation. Under the label "gate-aggregated", all words with *-gate* suffixes (except *Watergate*) are summarized. The bands are aligned with a time axis and vertically divided into cells, each cell representing one week of data. The cell color indicates whether the corresponding word under investigation occurred within the corresponding topic in the corresponding week. The black color means that there was no such occurrence, whereas the brightest white is assigned to the cell of the week where most occurrences (*max*) of a word under investigation are found, independent from the topic. Other occurrence counts are colored in grey tones according to a linear mapping into the normalized color range from black=0 to white=*max*. Note that the normalization depends on the word under investigation, i.e. is relative to its maximal occurrence.

In Figure 1, the data has to be split into two chunks to fit the page. The upper part shows the years from 1987 to 1997 and the lower part from 1997 to 2007. There are several possibilities for user interaction: A semantic zoom allows the data to be displayed in different levels of time granularity, e.g. day, week, month, year. By mousing over a cell, the underlying text passages are displayed in a tooltip.

Findings Figure 1 shows that the topics are dominated by different words under investigation, i.e. the words under investigation cannot be clearly separated into self-contained meanings. This mixture indicates that the words under investigation have similar meanings, but that in different contexts they are used in different combinations:

1. Society, Art, and Culture: This seems to be the most general topic with the broadest usage of the words under investigation. The descriptive terms show that it is a lot about interpersonal relations and dominated by "affair". In 1989/1990 the play *Mastergate* becomes visible in the "gate-aggregated" band.

2. Economy: This topic is strongly related to "crisis" and apart from the moderate frequency of "scandal", other words are rarely used in this context. Apparently, financial scandals were usually not described attaching the suffix "-gate" in the years between 1987 and 2007.

3. Foreign Policy: This is another topic dominated by "crisis", with moderate occurrences of "controversy". Some "gate-words" also appear.

4. Sports: Here, "controversy" is the dominating element, with a raised frequency of "affair" and small frequency of "scandal". Again, "gate-words" appear from time to time, with a slightly increased frequency towards the end.

5. Domestic Politics: The dominant words are "controversy" and "crisis". It's noteworthy that "controversy" is a lot more frequent here than for Foreign Policy. Especially in the last years "gate-words" appeared from time to time.

In sum, we find that there are preferred contexts in which *-gate* is used, namely mainly in topics to do with society, art and culture and that topics to do with the economy, *-gate* is hardly used. The lexical semantic content of *-gate* seems to be most closely linked to the word *affair*.

4.2 Productivity

The cases of suffixation presented above should also be considered from the standpoint of morphological productivity. For Baayen (1992), morphological productivity is a complex phenomenon in which factors like the structure of the language, its processing complexities and social conventions mingle. Whereas he focuses on the the correlation between productivity and frequency, we can take into account another variable for productivity. In particular, we can consider the number of newspapers that use a certain term. This will normalize the measures usually taken in that a term like "Watergate", which is highly frequent and mentioned in a variety of sources is more productive than a term that occurs frequently, but only in one source. Using this methodology we can at least partly circumvent the problem of productivity effects that are merely based on the specific style of one particular newspaper.

First, we visually evaluate the productivity of the different suffixes plotting the sum of different coinages against time, see Figure 2. As can be expected, in all three cases there is a steeper slope in the beginning of the monitored period. This is an artifact because all older coinages that had been around before the monitoring started will be observed for the first time. As more time passes all plots show a linear overall trend, indicating that the rate with which new coinages appear remains somewhat constant. Yet, there are some local oscillations in the rate that become more visible in the plots of *-geddon-* and *-athon*-coinages, which are in general much more infrequent than *-gate*-coinages. It can be concluded that over the last two and a half years the suffixes kept their rate of productivity in English, German, and French newswire texts fairly constant.

To investigate the cross-linguistic productivity of the new coinages we customized a visualization with the Tableau software.[3] Figure 3 shows the appearances of the 15 most frequent *-gate*-coinages across the three languages over time. Along the y-axis the data is divided according to *-gate*-coinages and languages, whereas the x-axis encodes the time. Whenever a certain coinage appears in a certain language at a certain point in time, a colored triangle is plotted to the corresponding position. The color redundantly encodes the language for easier interpretation.

Figure 3 shows many interesting patterns. The most salient patterns can be summarized as:

1. No language barrier: The top *-gate*-coinages belong to scandals that are of international interest and once they are coined in English they immediately spread to the other languages, see *Rubygate*, *Climategate*, *Cablegate*, *Antennagate*, and *Crashgate*. Only in the case of *Angolagate* and *Karachigate* there is a certain delay in the spread, possibly due to the fact that it was coined in French first and initially did not achieve the same attention as coinages in English.

2. Pertinacity partly depends on language: Some *-gate*-coinages re-appear over and over again only in individual languages. This especially holds for words that were coined before the monitoring started, e.g. *Sachsgate*, *Oilgate*, *Troopergate*, and *Travelgate* which all persist in English. Examples can be found for other languages, e.g. *Angolagate* for French. Interestingly, in German *Nipplegate* persists over the whole monitored period, but only in German, and even outperforms its German spelling *Nippelgate*.

3. Some coinages are special: Some of the recent coinages such as *Memogate*, *Asiagate*, and *Weinergate* reach an extremely high frequency within very short time ranges, but can be found almost exclusively in English. These will be subject of further investigation in Section 4.2.1. It has to be noted that many of the infrequent coinages appear only once and are never adopted.

4.2.1 Spread across News Sources and Countries

Figure 3 clearly shows that *Memogate* is heavily mentioned within English speaking news

[3] http://www.tableausoftware.com/

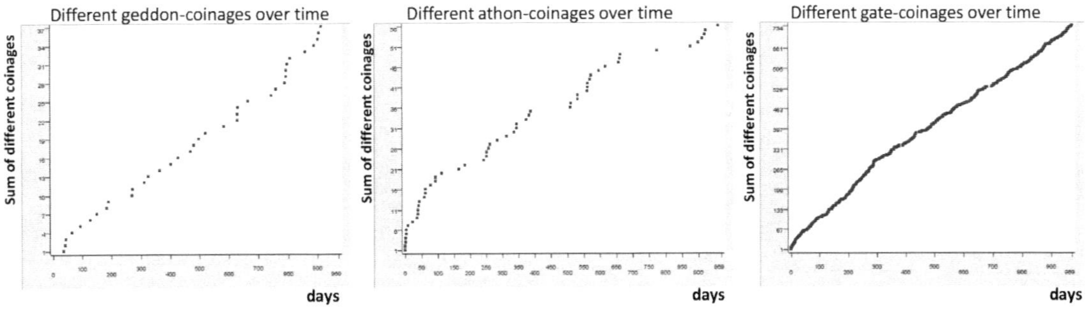

Figure 2: The number of different coinages containing the suffixes under investigation (on the y-axis) plotted against the number of days passed during the monitoring process (on the x-axis)

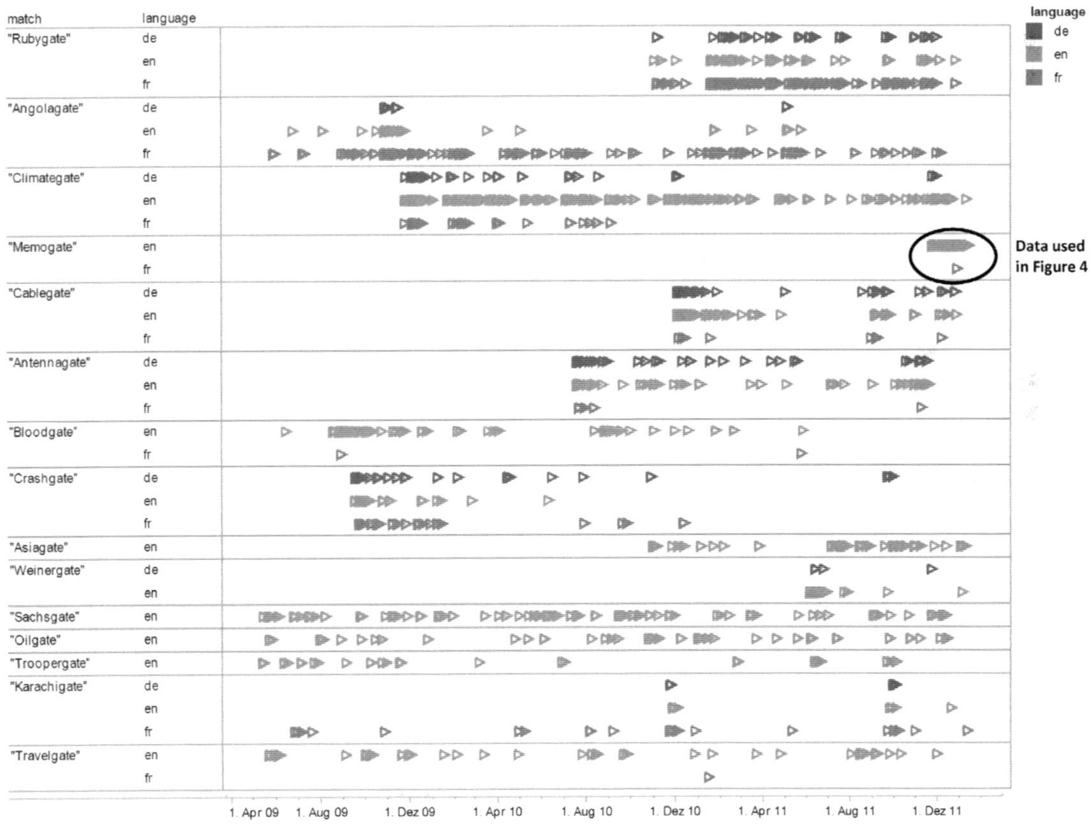

Figure 3: The appearances of the 15 most frequent *-gate* coinages over time and across the different languages

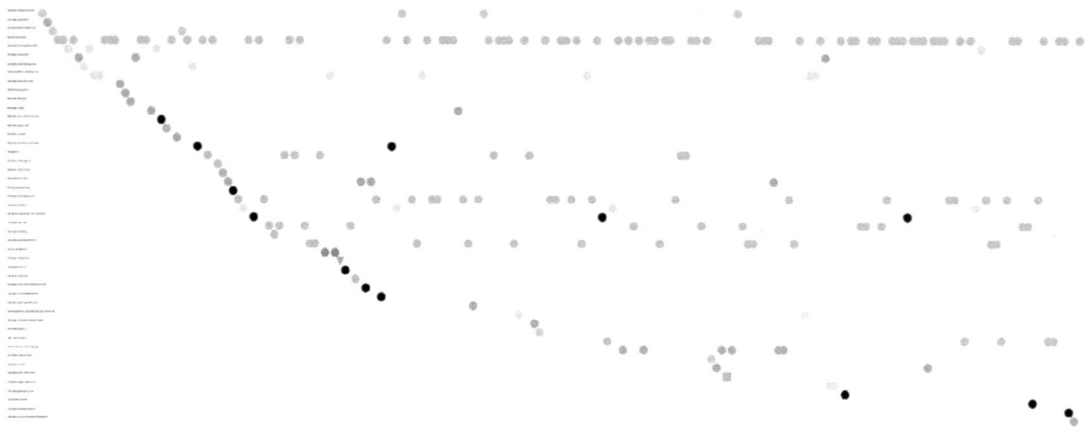

Figure 4: Detailed analysis of the *Memogate* cluster highlighted in Figure 3 using alternative visual mappings: Sequence of spread over different countries and news sources.

sources within a short time range. We developed a further visualization that shows how these mentions sequentially distribute over different news sources and countries. In Figure 4 each article mentioning *Memogate* is represented by a colored icon. The y-axis position encodes the news source, the x-axis position encodes the temporal order of the occurrences. Note that exact time differences are omitted to make the display more compact. The shape of an icon indicates the language of the article; Circles (English) heavily dominate. The color encodes the country of origin of the news source, here green (Pakistan), yellow (India), and purple (USA) dominate.

Findings: While the first three mentions of *Memogate* could be found in British and American Newspapers, early on it was adopted by *http://tribune.com.pk/* in Pakistan (fourth line from the top) and used so heavily that it kept being adopted and became constantly used by further sources from Pakistan and also India. Apparently, individual sources may have a huge influence on the spread of a new coinage.

5 Future work and conclusion

We have presented initial experiments with respect to the application of topic modeling and visualization to gain a better understanding of developments in morphological coinage and lexical semantics. We investigated three relatively new productive suffixes, namely *-gate*, *-geddon*, and *-athon* based on their occurrences in newswire data. Even though our data set was huge, the occurrences of the suffixes are comparatively rare and so we only had enough data for *-gate* to investigate the contexts it occurs in with an optimized topic modeling. The results indicate that it is used in broader contexts than *affair*, with which it is most related. Different domains of usage could be distinguished, even though a clear development over time could not be detected based the NYT corpus. Investigating the multilingual newswire data it became evident that all three suffixes under investigation have a relatively stable rate of appearance. Many more different *-gate*-coinages could be found, though. We could observe that *-gate* was usually attached to one specific single event, and especially in many of the less frequent coinages the suffix was combined with proper names of persons, institutions, or locations. In contrast, *-athon* and *-mageddon* coinages seem to be easier to generalize. For example, the two most widely spread coinages *Snowmageddon* and *Carmageddon*, while initially referring to a certain snow storm and a certain traffic jam, have been applied to further such events and can be found listed in resources such as the Urban Dictionary.[4]

In conclusion, we demonstrated that visual analyses can help to gain insight and generate new hypotheses about the behavior of the distribution and use of new morphemes. In our future research we aim to investigate how much the success of a certain coinage depends on the event as such and its news dynamics, and what role linguistic features like e.g. phonology (two vs. three syllables, etc.) might play.

[4]http://www.urbandictionary.com/define.php?term=Carmageddon

Acknowledgments

This work has partly been funded by the Research Initiative "Computational Analysis of Linguistic Development" at the University of Konstanz and by the German Research Society (DFG) under the grant GK-1042, Explorative Analysis and Visualization of Large Information Spaces, Konstanz. The authors would like to thank Volker Rehberg for his programming support and Thomas Mayer for comments on previous versions of the paper.

References

Martin Atkinson and Erik Van der Goot. 2009. Near real time information mining in multilingual news. In Juan Quemada, Gonzalo León, Yoëlle S. Maarek, and Wolfgang Nejdl, editors, *Proceedings of the 18th International Conference on World Wide Web, WWW 2009, Madrid, Spain, April 20-24, 2009*, pages 1153–1154.

R. Harald Baayen. 1992. On frequency, transparency, and productivity. *Yearbook of Morphology*, pages 181–208.

David M. Blei, Andrew Y. Ng, and Michael I. Jordan. 2003. Latent dirichlet allocation. *Journal of Machine Learning Research*, 3:993–1022.

Samuel Brody and Mirella Lapata. 2009. Bayesian word sense induction. In *Proceedings of the 12th Conference of the European Chapter of the Association for Computational Linguistics*, EACL '09, pages 103–111, Stroudsburg, PA, USA. Association for Computational Linguistics.

Stuart K. Card, Jock D. Mackinlay, and Ben Shneiderman, editors. 1999. *Readings in information visualization: using vision to think*. Morgan Kaufmann Publishers Inc., San Francisco, CA, USA.

Thomas L. Griffiths and Mark Steyver. 2004. Finding scientific topics. In *Proceedings of the National Academy of Sciences 101*, pages 5228–5235.

Timo Honkela, Ville Pulkki, and Teuvo Kohonen. 1995. Contextual relations of words in grimm tales, analyzed by self-organizing map. In *Proceedings of International Conference on Artificial Neural Networks (ICANN-95)*, pages 3–7.

Daniel A. Keim, Joern Kohlhammer, Geoffrey Ellis, and Florian Mansmann, editors. 2010. *Mastering The Information Age - Solving Problems with Visual Analytics*. Goslar: Eurographics.

Milos Krstajic, Florian Mansmann, Andreas Stoffel, Martin Atkinson, and Daniel A. Keim. 2010. Processing Online News Streams for Large-Scale Semantic Analysis. In *Proceedings of the 1st International Workshop on Data Engineering meets the Semantic Web (DESWeb 2010)*.

Anke Lüdeling and Stefan Evert. 2005. The emergence of productive non-medical *-itis*. corpus evidence and qualitative analysis. In S. Kepser and M. Reis, editors, *Linguistic Evidence. Empirical, Theoretical, and Computational Perspectives*, pages 351–370. Berlin: Mouton de Gruyter.

Thomas Mayer, Christian Rohrdantz, Miriam Butt, Frans Plank, and Daniel Keim. 2010a. Visualizing vowel harmony. *Journal of Linguistic Issues in Language Technology (LiLT)*, 4(2).

Thomas Mayer, Christian Rohrdantz, Frans Plank, Peter Bak, Miriam Butt, and Daniel A. Keim. 2010b. Consonant co-occurrence in stems across languages: Automatic analysis and visualization of a phonotactic constraint. In *Proceedings of the ACL 2010 Workshop on NLP and Linguistics: Finding the Common Ground (NLPLING 2010)*, pages 67–75.

Eiji Nishimoto. 2004. Defining new words in corpus data: Productivity of english suffixes in the british national corpus. In *26th Annual Meeting of the Cognitive Science Society*.

Ingo Plag. 1999. *Morphological productivity. Structural constraints in English derivation*. Berlin/New York: Mouton de Gruyter.

Christian Rohrdantz, Annette Hautli, Thomas Mayer, Miriam Butt, Daniel A. Keim, and Frans Plank. 2011. Towards tracking semantic change by visual analytics. In *Proceedings of the 49th Annual Meeting of the Association for Computational Linguistics: Human Langauge Technologies (ACL-HLT '11): shortpapers*, pages 305–310, Portland, Oregon. Association for Computational Linguistics.

James J. Thomas and Kristin A. Cook. 2005. *Illuminating the Path The Research and Development Agenda for Visual Analytics*. National Visualization and Analytics Center.

Looking at word meaning.
An interactive visualization of Semantic Vector Spaces for Dutch synsets

Kris Heylen, Dirk Speelman and **Dirk Geeraerts**
QLVL, University of Leuven
Blijde-Inkomsstraat 21/3308, 3000 Leuven (Belgium)
{kris.heylen, dirk.speelman, dirk.geeraerts}@arts.kuleuven.be

Abstract

In statistical NLP, Semantic Vector Spaces (SVS) are the standard technique for the automatic modeling of lexical semantics. However, it is largely unclear how these black-box techniques exactly capture word meaning. To explore the way an SVS structures the individual occurrences of words, we use a non-parametric MDS solution of a token-by-token similarity matrix. The MDS solution is visualized in an interactive plot with the Google Chart Tools. As a case study, we look at the occurrences of 476 Dutch nouns grouped in 214 synsets.

1 Introduction

In the last twenty years, distributional models of semantics have become the standard way of modeling lexical semantics in statistical NLP. These models, aka Semantic Vector Spaces (SVSs) or Word Spaces, capture word meaning in terms of frequency distributions of words over co-occurring context words in a large corpus. The basic assumption of the approach is that words occurring in similar contexts will have a similar meaning. Speficic implementations of this general idea have been developed for a wide variety of computational linguistic tasks, including Thesaurus extraction and Word Sense Disambiguation, Question answering and the modeling of human behavior in psycholinguistic experiments (see Turney and Pantel (2010) for a general overview of applications and speficic models). In recent years, Semantic Vector Spaces have also seen applications in more traditional domains of linguistics, like diachronic lexical studies (Sagi et al., 2009; Cook and Stevenson, 2010; Rohrdantz et al., 2011) , or the study of lexical variation (Peirsman et al., 2010). In this paper, we want to show how Semantic Vector Spaces can further aid the linguistic analysis of lexical semantics, provided that they are made accessible to lexicologists and lexicographers through a visualization of their output.

Although all applications mentioned above assume that distributional models can capture word meaning to some extent, most of them use SVSs only in an indirect, black-box way, without analyzing which semantic properties and relations actually manifest themselves in the models. This is mainly a consequence of the task-based evaluation paradigm prevalent in Computational Linguistics: the researchers address a specific task for which there is a pre-defined gold standard; they implement a model with some new features, that usually stem from a fairly intuitive, commonsense reasoning of why some feature might benefit the task at hand; the new model is then tested against the gold standard data and there is an evaluation in terms of precision, recall and F-score. In rare cases, there is also an error analysis that leads to hypotheses about semantic characteristics that are not yet properly modeled. Yet hardly ever, there is in-depth analysis of which semantics the tested model actually captures. Even though task-based evaluation and shared test data sets are vital to the objective comparison of computational approaches, they are, in our opinion, not sufficient to assess whether the phenomenon of lexical semantics is modeled adequately from a linguistic perspective. This lack of linguistic insight into the functioning of SVSs is also bemoaned in the community itself. For example, Baroni and Lenci (2011) say that "To gain a real insight into the

Proceedings of the EACL 2012 Joint Workshop of LINGVIS & UNCLH, pages 16–24,
Avignon, France, April 23 - 24 2012. ©2012 Association for Computational Linguistics

abilities of DSMs (*Distributional Semantic Models*, A/N) to address lexical semantics, existing benchmarks must be complemented with a more intrinsically oriented approach, to perform direct tests on the specific aspects of lexical knowledge captured by the models". They go on to present their own lexical database that is similar to WordNet, but includes some additional semantic relations. They propose researchers test their model against the database to find out which of the encoded relations it can detect. However, such an analysis still boils down to checking whether a model can replicate pre-defined structuralist semantic relations, which themselves represent a quite impoverished take on lexical semantics, at least from a linguistic perspective. In this paper, we want to argue that a more linguistically adequate investigation of how SVSs capture lexical semantics, should take a step back from the evalution-against-gold-standard paradigm and do a direct and unbiased analysis of the output of SVS models. Such an analysis should compare the SVS way of structuring semantics to the rich descriptive and theoretic models of lexical semantics that have been developed in Linguistics proper (see Geeraerts (2010b) for an overview of different research traditions). Such an in-depth, manual analyis has to be done by skilled lexicologists and lexicographers. But would linguists, that are traditionally seen as not very computationally oriented, be interested in doing what many Computational Linguists consider to be tedious manual analysis? The answer, we think, is yes. The last decade has seen a clear *empirical turn* in Linguistics that has led linguists to embrace advanced statistical analyses of large amounts of corpus data to substantiate their theoretical hypotheses (see e.g. Geeraerts (2010a) and other contributions in Glynn and Fischer (2010) on research in semantics). SVSs would be an ideal addition to those linguists' methodological repertoire. This creates the potential for a win-win situation: Computational linguists get an in-depth evaluation of their models, while theoretical linguists get a new tool for doing large scale empirical analyses of word meaning. Of course, one cannot just hand over a large matrix of word similaties (the raw output of an SVS) and ask a lexicologist what kind of semantics is "in there". Instead, a linguist needs an intuitive interface to explore the semantic structure captured by an SVS. In this paper, we aim to present exactly that: an interactive visualization of a Semantic Vector Space Model that allows a lexicologist or lexicographer to inspect how the model structures the uses of words.

2 Token versus Type level

SVSs can model lexical semantics on two levels:

1. the type level: aggregating over all occurrences of a word, giving a representation of a word's general semantics.

2. the token level: representing the semantics of each individual occurrence of a word.

The type-level models are mostly used to retrieve semantic relations *between* words, e.g. synonyms in the task of thesaurus extraction. Token-level models are typically used to distinguish between the different meanings *within* the uses of one word, notably in the task of Word Sense Disambiguation or Word Sense Induction. Lexicological studies on the other hand, typically combine both perspectives: their scope is often defined on the type level as the different words of a lexical field or the set of near-synonyms referring to the same concept, but they then go on to do a fine-grained analysis on the token level of the uses of these words to find out how the semantic space is precisely structured. In our study, we will also take a concept-centered perspective and use as a starting point the 218 sets of Dutch near-synonymous nouns that Ruette et al. (2012) generated with their type-level SVS. For each synset, we then implement our own token-level SVS to model the individual occurrences of the nouns. The resulting token-by-token similarity matrix is then visualized to show how the occurrences of the different nouns are distributed over the semantic space that is defined by the synset's concept. Because Dutch has two national varieties (Belgium and the Netherlands) that show considerable lexical variation, and because this is typically of interest to lexicologists, we will also differentiate the Netherlandic and Belgian tokens in our SVS models and their visualization.

The rest of this paper is structured as follows. In the next section we present the corpus and the near-synonym sets we used for our study. Section 4 presents the token-level SVS implemented for modeling the occurrences of the nouns in the synsets. In section 5 we discuss the visualization of the SVS's token-by-token similarity matrices with Multi Dimensional Scaling and the Google Visualization API. Finally, section 6 wraps up with conclusions and prospects for future research.

3 Dutch corpus and synsets

The corpus for our study consists of Dutch newspaper materials from 1999 to 2005. For Netherlandic Dutch, we used the 500M words Twente Nieuws Corpus (Ordelman, 2002)[1], and for Belgian Dutch, the Leuven Nieuws Corpus (aka Mediargus corpus, 1.3 million words[2]). The corpora were automatically lemmatized, part-of-speech tagged and syntactically parsed with the Alpino parser (van Noord, 2006).

Ruette et al. (2012) used the same corpora for their semi-automatic generation of sets of Dutch near-synonymous nouns. They used a so-called dependency-based model (Padó and Lapata, 2007), which is a type-level SVS that models the semantics of a target word as the weighted co-occurrence frequencies with context words that apear in a set of pre-defined dependency relations with the target (a.o. adjectives that modify the target noun, and verbs that have the target noun as their subject). Ruette et al. (2012) submitted the output of their SVS to a clustering algorithm known as Clustering by Committee (Pantel and Lin, 2002). After some further manual cleaning, this resulted in 218 synsets containing 476 nouns in total. Table 1 gives some examples.

CONCEPT	nouns in synset
INFRINGEMENT	inbreuk, overtreding
GENOCIDE	volkerenmoord, genocide
POLL	peiling, opiniepeiling, rondvraag
MARIHUANA	cannabis, marihuana
COUP	staatsgreep, coup
MENINGITIS	hersenvliesontsteking, meningitis
DEMONSTRATOR	demonstrant, betoger
AIRPORT	vliegveld, luchthaven
VICTORY	zege, overwinning
HOMOSEXUAL	homo, homoseksueel, homofiel
RELIGION	religie, godsdienst
COMPUTER SCREEN	computerschem, beeldscherm, monitor

Table 1: Dutch synsets (sample)

[1]Publication years 1999 up to 2002 of *Algemeen Dagblad*, *NRC*, *Parool*, *Trouw* and *Volkskrant*

[2]Publication years 1999 up to 2005 of *De Morgen*, *De Tijd*, *De Standaard*, *Het Laatste Nieuws*, *Het Nieuwsblad* and *Het Belang van Limburg*

4 Token-level SVS

Next, we wanted the model the individual occurrences of the nouns. The token-level SVS we used is an adaptation the approach proposed by Schütze (1998). He models the semantics of a token as the frequency distribution over its so-called second order co-occurrences. These second-order co-occurrences are the type-level context features of the (first-order) context words co-occuring with the token. This way, a token's meaning is still modeled by the "context" it occurs in, but this context is now modeled itself by combining the type vectors of the words in the context. This higher order modeling is necessary to avoid data-sparseness: any token only occurs with a handful of other words and a first-order co-occurrence vector would thus be too sparse to do any meaningful vector comparison. Note that this approach first needs to construct a type-level SVS for the first-order context words that can then be used to create a second-order token-vector.

In our study, we therefore first constructed a type-level SVS for the 573,127 words in our corpus with a frequency higher than 2. Since the focus of this study is visualization rather than finding optimal SVS parameter settings, we chose settings that proved optimal in our previous studies (Peirsman et al., 2008; Heylen et al., 2008; Peirsman et al., 2010). For the context features of this SVS, we used a bag-of-words approach with a window of 4 to the left and right around the targets. The context feature set was restricted to the 5430 words, that were the among the 7000 most frequent words in the corpus, (minus a stoplist of 34 high-frequent function words) AND that occurred at least 50 times in both the Netherlandic and Belgian part of the corpus. The latter was done to make sure that Netherlandic and Belgian type vectors were not dissimilar just because of topical bias from proper names, place names or words relating to local events. Raw co-occurrence frequencies were weighted with Pointwise Mutual Information and negative PMI's were set to zero.

In a second step, we took a random sample of 100 Netherlandic and a 100 Belgian newspaper issues from the corpus and extracted all occurrences of each of the 476 nouns in the synsets described above. For each occurrence, we built a token-vector by averaging over the type-vectors of the words in a window of 5 words to the left and right of the token. We experimented with two averaging functions. In a first version, we followed Schütze (1998) and just summed the type vectors of a token's context words, normalizing by the number of context words for that token:

$$\vec{o_i^w} = \frac{\sum_{j \in C_i^w}^{n} \vec{c_j}}{n}$$

where $\vec{o_i^w}$ is the token vector for the ith occurrence of noun w and C_i^w is the set of n type vectors $\vec{c_j}$ for the context words in the window around that i^{th} occurrence of noun w. However, this summation means that each first order context word has an equal weight in determining the token vector. Yet, not all first-order context words are equally informative for the meaning of a token. In a sentence like "While walking to work, the teacher saw a dog barking and chasing a cat", *bark* and *cat* are much more indicative of the meaning of *dog* than say *teacher* or *work*. In a second, weighted version, we therefore increased the contribution of these informative context words by using the first-order context words' PMI values with the noun in the synset. PMI can be regarded as a measure for informativeness and target-noun/context-word PMI-values were available anyway from our large type-level SVS. The PMI of a noun w and a context word c_j can now be seen as a weight $pmi_{c_j}^w$. In constructing the token vector $\vec{o_i^w}$ for the ith occurrence of noun w, we now multiply the type vector $\vec{c_j}$ of each context word with the PMI weight $pmi_{c_j}^w$, and then normalize by the sum of the pmi-weights:

$$\vec{o_i^w} = \frac{\sum_{j \in C_i^w}^{n} pmi_{c_j}^w * \vec{c_j}}{\sum_j^n pmi_{c_j}^w}$$

The token vectors of all nouns from the same synset were then combined in a token by second-order-context-feature matrix. Note that this matrix has the same dimensionality as the underlying type-level SVS (5430). By calculating the cosine between all pairs of token-vectors in the matrix, we get the final token-by-token similarity matrix for each of the 218 synsets [3].

[3]string operations on corpus text files were done with Python 2.7. All matrix calculations were done in Matlab R2009a for Linux

5 Visualization

The token-by-token similarity matrices reflect how the different synonyms carve up the "semantic space" of the synset's concept among themselves. However, this information is hard to grasp from a large matrix of decimal figures. One popular way of visualizing a similarity matrix for interpretative purposes is Multidimensional Scaling (Cox and Cox, 2001). MDS tries to give an optimal 2 or 3 dimensional representation of the similarities (or distances) between objects in the matrix. We applied Kruskal's non-metric Multidimensional Scaling to the all the token-by-token similarity matrices using the `isoMDS` function in the `MASS` package of R. Our visualisation software package (see below) forced us to restrict ourselves to a 2 dimensional MDS solution for now, even tough stress levels were generally quite high (0.25 to 0.45). Future implementation may use 3D MDS solutions. Of course, other dimension reduction techniques than MDS exist: PCA is used in Latent Semantic Analysis (Landauer and Dumais, 1997) and has been applied by Sagi et al. (2009) for modeling token semantics. Alternatively, Latent Dirichlect Allocation (LDA) is at the heart of Topic Models (Griffiths et al., 2007) and was adapted by Brody and Lapata (2009) for modeling token semantics. However, these techniques all aim at bringing out a latent structure that abstracts away from the "raw" underlying SVS similarities. Our aim, on the other hand, is precisely to investigate how SVSs structure semantics based on contextual distribution properties BEFORE additional latent structuring is applied. We therefore want a 2D representation of the token similarity matrix that is as faithful as possible and that is what MDS delivers [4].

In a next step we wanted to intergrate the 2 dimensional MDS plots with different types of meta-data that might be of interest to the lexicologist. Furthermore, we wanted the plots to be interactive, so that a lexicologist can choose which information to visualize in the plot. We opted for the Motion Charts[5] provided by Google

[4]Stress is a measure for that faithfulness. No such indication is directly available for LSA or LDA. However, we do think LSA and LDA can be used to provide extra structure to our visualizations, see section 6.

[5]To avoid dependence on commercial software, we also made an implementation based on the plotting options of R and the Python Image Library(`https://perswww.`

Chart Tools[6], which allows to plot objects with 2D co-ordinates as color-codable and re-sizeable bubbles in an interactive chart. If a time-variable is present, the charts can be made dynamic to show the changing position of the objects in the plot over time[7]. We used the R-package `googleVis` (Gesmann and Castillo, 2011), an interface between R and the Google Visualisation API, to convert our R datamatrices into Google Motion Charts. The interactive charts, both those based on the weighted and unweighted token-level SVSs, can be explored on our website (`https://perswww.kuleuven.be/~u0038536/googleVis`).

To illustrate the information that is available through this visualization, we discuss the weighted chart for the concept COMPUTER SCREEN (Figure 1 shows a screen cap, but we strongly advise to look at the interactive version on the website). In Dutch, this concept can be refered to with (at least) three near-synonyms, which are color coded in the chart: *beeldscherm* (blue), *computerscherm* (green) and *monitor* (yellow). Each bubble in the chart is an occurrence (token) of one these nouns. As Figure 2 shows, roling over the bubbles makes the stretch of text visible in which the noun occurs (These contexts are also available in the lower right side bar). This usage-in-context allows the lexicologist to interpret the precise meaning of the occurrence of the noun. The plot itself is a 2D representation of the semantic distances between all tokens (as measured with a token-level SVS) and reflects how the synonyms are distributed over the "semantic space". As can be expected with synonyms, they partially populate the same area of the space (the right hand side of the plot). Hovering over the bubbles and looking at the contexts, we can see that they indeed all refer to the concept COMPUTER SCREEN (See example contexts 1 to 3 in Table 2). However, we also see that a considerable part on the left hand side of the plot shows no overlap and is only populated by tokens of *monitor*. Looking more closely at these occurrences, we see that they are instantiations of another meaning of *monitor*, viz. "supervisor of youth leisure activities" (See example context 4 in Table 2). Remember that our corpus is stratified for Belgian and Netherlandic Dutch. We can make this stratification visible by changing the color coding of the bubbles to COUNTRY in the top right-hand drop-down menu. Figure 3 shows that the left-hand side, i.e. *monitor*-only area of the plot, is also an all-Belgian area (hovering over the BE value in the legend makes the Belgian tokens in the plot flash). Changing the color coding to WORDBYCOUNTRY makes this even more clear. Indeed the youth leader meaning of *monitor* is only familiar to speakers of Belgian Dutch. Changing the color coding to the variable NEWSPAPER shows that the youth leader meaning is also typical for the popular, working class newspapers *Het Laatste Nieuws* (LN) and *Het Nieuwsblad* (NB) and is not prevelant in the Belgian high-brow newspapers. In order to provide more structure to the plot, we also experimented with including different K-means clustering solutions (from 2 up to 6 clusters) as color-codable features, but these seem not very informative yet (but see section 6).

nr	example context
1	De analisten houden met één oog de **computerschermen** in de gaten *The analists keep one eye on the computer screen*
2	Met een digitale camera... kan je je eigen foto op het **beeldscherm** krijgen *With a digital camera, you can get your own photo on the computer screen*
3	Met een paar aanpassingen wordt het beeld op de **monitoren** nog completer *With a few adjustments, the image on the screen becomes even more complete*
4	Voor augustus zijn de speelpleinen nog op zoek naar **monitoren** *For August, the playgrounds are still looking for supervisors*

Table 2: Contexts (shown in chart by mouse roll-over)

On the whole, the token-level SVS succeeds fairly well in giving an interpretable semantic structure to the tokens and the chart visualizes this. However, SVSs are fully automatic ways of modeling semantics and, not unexpectedly, some tokens are out of place. For example, in the lower left corner of the yellow cluster with *monitor* tokens referring to youth leader, there is also one blue Netherlandic token of *beeldscherm*. Thanks to the visualisation, such outliers can easily be

`kuleuven.be/~u0038536/committees`)

[6](`http://code.google.com/apis/chart/interactive/docs/gallery/motionchart.html`)

[7]Since we worked with synchronic data, we did not use this feature. However, Motion Charts have been used by Hilpert (`http://omnibus.uni-freiburg.de/~mh608/motion.html`) to visualize language change in MDS plots of hand coded diachronic linguistic data.

detected by the lexicologist who can then report them to the computational linguist. The latter can then try to come up with a model that gives a better fit.

Finally, let us briefly look at the chart of another concept, viz. COLLISION with its near-synonyms *aanrijding* and *botsing*. Here, we expect the literal collissions (between cars), for which both nouns can be used, to stand out form the figurative ones (differences in opinion between people), for which only *botsing* is apropriate in both varieties of Dutch. Figure 4 indeed shows that the right side of the chart is almost exclusively populated by *botsing* tokens. Looking at their contexts reveals that they indeed overwhelmingly instantiate the metaphorical meaning og collision. Yet also here, there are some "lost" *aanrijding* tokens with a literal meaning and the visualization shows that the current SVS implementation is not yet a fully adequate model for capturing the words' semantics.

6 General discussion

Although Vector Spaces have become the mainstay of modeling lexical semantics in current statistical NLP, they are mostly used in a black box way, and how exactly they capture word meaning is not very clear. By visualizing their output, we hope to have at least partially cracked open this black box. Our aim is not just to make SVS output easier to analyze for computer linguists. We also want to make SVSs accessible for lexicologists and lexicographers with an interest in quantitative, empirical data analysis. Such co-operation brings mutual benefits: Computer linguists get access to expert evaluation of their models. Lexicologists and lexicographers can use SVSs to identify preliminary semantic structure based on large quantities of corpus data, instead of heaving to sort through long lists of unstructured examples of a word's usage (the classical concordances). To our knowledge, this paper is one of the first attempts to visualize Semantic Vector Spaces and make them accessible to a non-technical audience.

Of course, this is still largely work in progress and a number of improvements and extensions are still possible. First of all, the call-outs for the bubbles in the Google Motion Charts were not designed to contain large stretches of text. Current corpus contexts are therefore to short to analyze the precise meaning of the tokens. One option would be to have pop-up windows with larger contexts appear by clicking on the call-outs.

Secondly, we didn't use the motion feature that gave the charts its name. However, if we have diachronic data, we could e.g. track the centroid of a word's tokens in the semantic space through time and at the same time show the dispersion of tokens around that centroid[8].

Thirdly, in the current implementation, one important aspect of the black-box quality of SVSs is not dealt with: it's not clear which context features cause tokens to be similar in the SVS output, and, consequently, the interpreation of the distances in the MDS plot remains quite obscure. One option would be to use the cluster solutions, that are already available as color codable variables, and indicate the highest scoring context features that the tokens in each cluster have in common. Another option for bringing out sense-distinguishing context words was proposed by Rohrdantz et al. (2011) who use Latent Dirichlet Allocation to structure tokens. The loadings on these latent topics could also be color-coded in the chart.

Fourthly, we already indicated that two dimensional MDS solutions have quite high stress values and a three dimensional solution would be better to represent the token-by-token similarities. This would require the 3D Charts, which are not currently offered by the Google Chart Tools. However both R and Matlab do have interactive 3D plotting functionality.

Finally, and most importantly, the plots currently do not allow any input from the user. If we want the plots to be the starting point of an in-depth semantic analysis, the lexicologist should be able to annotate the occurrences with variables of their own. For example, they might want to code whether the occurrence refers to a laptop screen, a desktop screen or cell phone screen, to find out whether their is a finer-grained division of labor among the synonyms. Additionally, an evaluation of the SVS's performance might include moving wrongly positioned tokens in the plot and thus re-group tokens, based on the lexicologist's insights. Tracking these corrective movements might then be valuable input for the computer linguists to improve their models. Of course, this

[8] This is basically the approach of Sagi et al. (2009) but after LSA and without interactive visualization

goes well beyond our rather opportunistic use of the Google Charts Tool.

References

Marco Baroni and Alessandro Lenci. 2011. How we BLESSed distributional semantic evaluation. In *Proceedings of the GEMS 2011 Workshop on GEometrical Models of Natural Language Semantics*, pages 1–10, Edinburgh, UK. Association for Computational Linguistics.

Samuel Brody and Mirella Lapata. 2009. Bayesian Word Sense Induction. In *Proceedings of the 12th Conference of the European Chapter of the ACL (EACL 2009)*, pages 103–111, Athens, Greece. Association for Computational Linguistics.

Paul Cook and Suzanne Stevenson. 2010. Automatically Identifying Changes in the Semantic Orientation of Words. In *Proceedings of the Seventh International Conference on Language Resources and Evaluation (LREC'10)*, pages 28–34, Valletta, Malta. ELRA.

Trevor Cox and Michael Cox. 2001. *Multidimensional Scaling*. Chapman & Hall, Boca Raton.

Dirk Geeraerts. 2010a. The doctor and the semantician. In Dylan Glynn and Kerstin Fischer, editors, *Quantitative Methods in Cognitive Semantics: Corpus-Driven Approaches*, pages 63–78. Mouton de Gruyter, Berlin.

Dirk Geeraerts. 2010b. *Theories of Lexical Semantics*. Oxford University Press, Oxford.

Markus Gesmann and Diego De Castillo. 2011. Using the Google Visualisation API with R: googleVis-0.2.4 Package Vignette.

Dylan Glynn and Kerstin Fischer. 2010. *Quantitative Methods in Cognitive Semantics: Corpus-driven Approaches*, volume 46. Mouton de Gruyter, Berlin.

Thomas L. Griffiths, Mark Steyvers, and Joshua Tenenbaum. 2007. Topics in Semantic Representation. *Psychological Review*, 114:211–244.

Kris Heylen, Yves Peirsman, Dirk Geeraerts, and Dirk Speelman. 2008. Modelling Word Similarity. An Evaluation of Automatic Synonymy Extraction Algorithms. In *Proceedings of the Language Resources and Evaluation Conference (LREC 2008)*, pages 3243–3249, Marrakech, Morocco. ELRA.

Thomas K Landauer and Susan T Dumais. 1997. A Solution to Plato's Problem: The Latent Semantic Analysis Theory of Acquisition, Induction and Representation of Knowledge. *Psychological Review*, 104(2):240–411.

Roeland J F Ordelman. 2002. Twente Nieuws Corpus (TwNC). Technical report, Parlevink Language Techonology Group. University of Twente.

Sebastian Padó and Mirella Lapata. 2007. Dependency-based construction of semantic space models. *Computational Linguistics*, 33(2):161–199.

Patrick Pantel and Dekang Lin. 2002. Document clustering with committees. In *Proceedings of the 25th annual international ACM SIGIR conference on Research and development in information retrieval*, SIGIR '02, pages 199–206, New York, NY, USA. ACM.

Yves Peirsman, Kris Heylen, and Dirk Geeraerts. 2008. Size matters: tight and loose context definitions in English word space models. In *Proceedings of the ESSLLI Workshop on Distributional Lexical Semantics*, pages 34–41, Hamburg, Germany. ESSLLI.

Yves Peirsman, Dirk Geeraerts, and Dirk Speelman. 2010. The automatic identification of lexical variation between language varieties. *Natural Language Engineering*, 16(4):469–490.

Christian Rohrdantz, Annette Hautli, Thomas Mayer, Miriam Butt, Daniel A Keim, and Frans Plank. 2011. Towards Tracking Semantic Change by Visual Analytics. In *Proceedings of the 49th Annual Meeting of the Association for Computational Linguistics: Human Language Technologies*, pages 305–310, Portland, Oregon, USA, June. Association for Computational Linguistics.

Tom Ruette, Dirk Geeraerts, Yves Peirsman, and Dirk Speelman. 2012. Semantic weighting mechanisms in scalable lexical sociolectometry. In Benedikt Szmrecsanyi and Bernhard Wälchli, editors, *Aggregating dialectology and typology: linguistic variation in text and speech, within and across languages*. Mouton de Gruyter, Berlin.

Eyal Sagi, Stefan Kaufmann, and Brady Clark. 2009. Semantic Density Analysis: Comparing Word Meaning across Time and Phonetic Space. In *Proceedings of the Workshop on Geometrical Models of Natural Language Semantics*, pages 104–111, Athens, Greece. Association for Computational Linguistics.

Hinrich Schütze. 1998. Automatic word sense discrimination. *Computational Linguistics*, 24(1):97–124.

Peter D. Turney and Patrick Pantel. 2010. From Frequency to Meaning: Vector Space Models of Semantics. *Journal of Artificial Intelligence Research*, 37(1):141–188.

Gertjan van Noord. 2006. At Last Parsing Is Now Operational. In *Verbum Ex Machina. Actes de la 13e conference sur le traitement automatique des langues naturelles (TALN06)*, pages 20–42, Leuven, Belgium. Presses universitaires de Louvain.

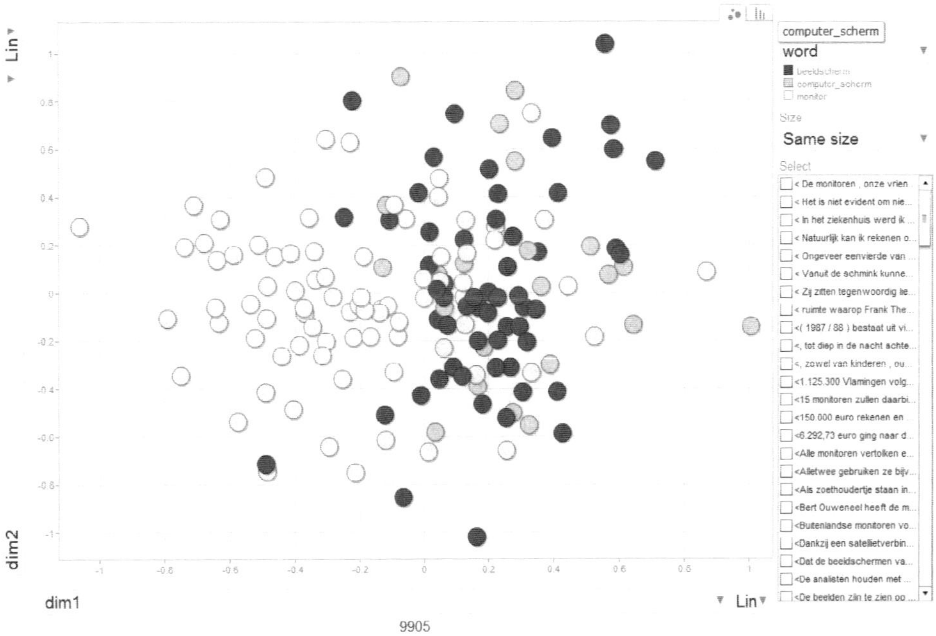

Figure 1: Screencap of Motion Chart for COMPUTER SCREEN

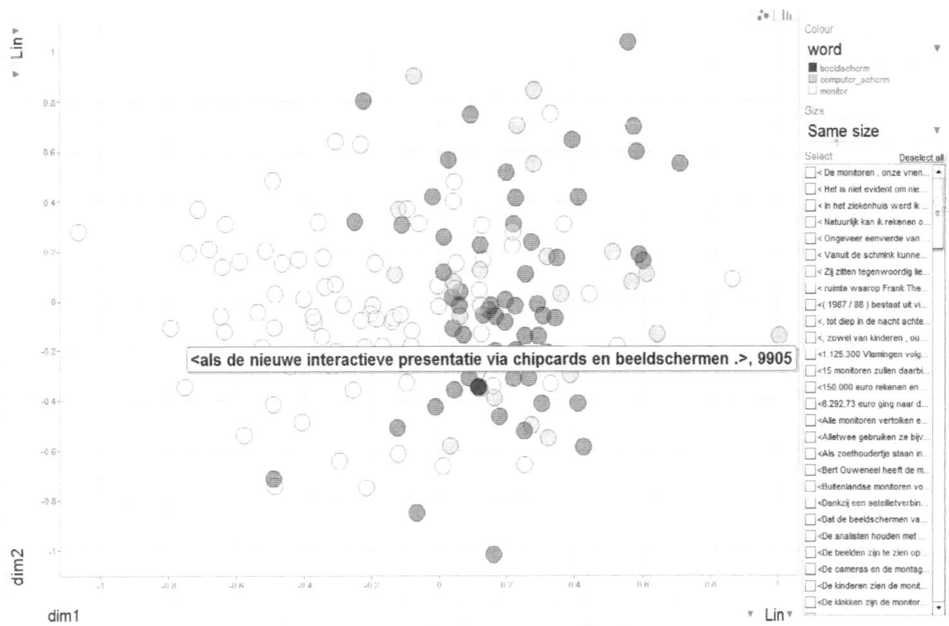

Figure 2: token of *beeldscherm* with context

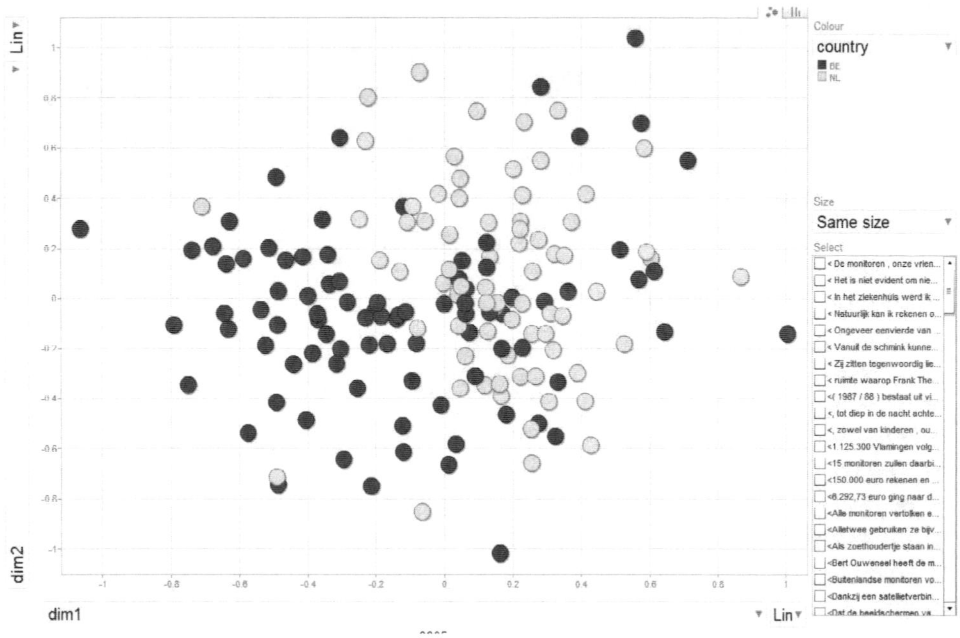

Figure 3: COMPUTER SCREEN tokens stratified by country

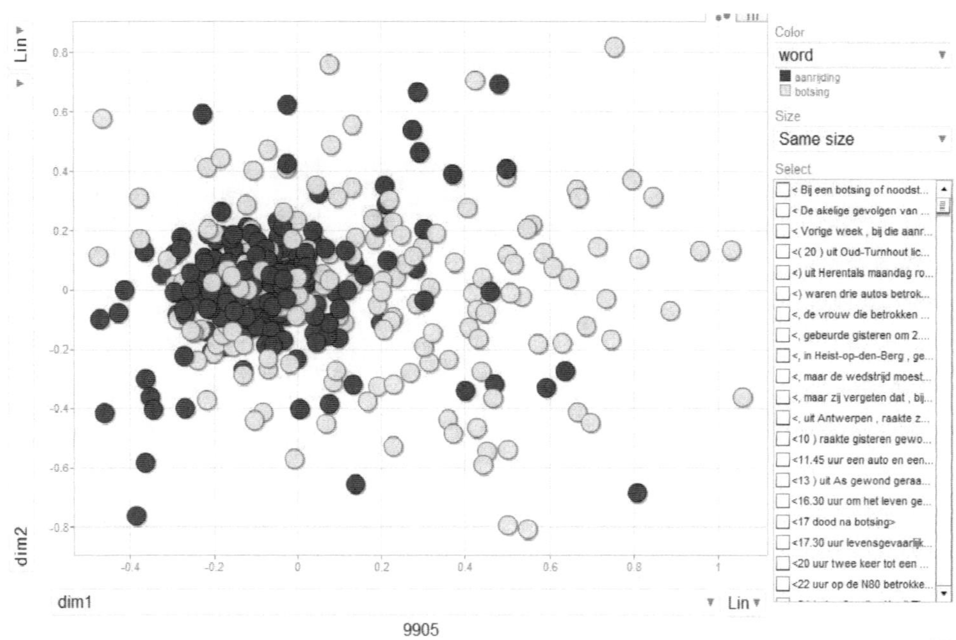

Figure 4: Screencap of Motion Chart for COLLISION

First steps in checking and comparing Princeton WordNet and Estonian Wordnet

Ahti Lohk
Tallinn University of Technology
Raja 15-117
Tallinn, ESTONIA
[ahti.lohk@ttu.ee]

Kadri Vare
University of Tartu
Liivi 2-308
Tartu, ESTONIA
[kadri.vare@ut.ee]

Leo Võhandu
Tallinn University of Technology
Raja 15-117
Tallinn, ESTONIA
[leov@staff.ttu.ee]

Abstract

Each expanding and developing system requires some feedback to evaluate the normal trends of the system and also the unsystematic steps. In this paper two lexical-semantic databases – Princeton WordNet (PrWN) and Estonian Wordnet (EstWN)- are being examined from the visualization point of view. The visualization method is described and the aim is to find and to point to possible problems of synsets and their semantic relations.

1 Introduction

Wordnets for different languages have been created for a quite a long time[1]; also these wordnets have been developed further and updated with new information. Typically there is a special software for editing wordnets, for example VisDic[2], WordnetLoom (Piasecki et al 2010), Polaris (Louw, 1998). These editing tools often present only one kind of view of the data which might not be enough for feedback or for detecting problematic synsets/semantic relations. The visualization method described here can be used separately from the editing tool; therefore it provides an additional view to data present in wordnet.

For initial data PrWN version 3.0[3] and EstWN version 63[4] have been taken. PRWN contains of 117 374 synsets and EstWn of 51 688 synsets. The creation of EstWN started in 1998 within the EuroWordNet project[5]. At present the main goal is to increase EstWN with new concepts and enrich EstWN with different kinds of semantic relations. But at the same time it is necessary to check and correct the concepts already present (Kerner, 2010).

The main idea and basic design of all wordnets in the project came from Princeton WordNet (more in Miller et al 1990). Each wordnet is structured along the same lines: synonyms (sharing the same meaning) are grouped into synonym sets (synsets). Synsets are connected to each other by semantic relations, like hyperonymy (is-a) and meronymy (is-part-of). As objects of analysis only noun synsets and hyperonymy-hyponymy relations are considered (of course, it is possible to extend the analysis over different word classes and different semantic relations). So, due to these constraints we have taken 82 115 synsets from PRWN (149 309 different words in synsets) and 41 938 synsets from EstWN (64 747 different words in synsets).

2 Method

We will explain our method's main idea with a small artificial example. Let us have a small separated subset presented as a matrix:

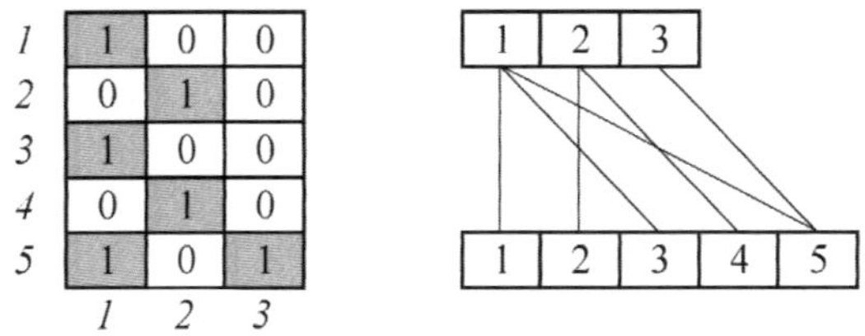

Figure 1. Relation-matrix and bipartite graph

In the rows of that table we have synsets and in columns hyperonyms. On the right side of

[1] http://www.globalwordnet.org/
[2] http://deb.fi.muni.cz/clients-debvisdic.php
[3] http://wordnet.princeton.edu/
[4] http://www.cl.ut.ee/ressursid/teksaurus/
[5] http://www.illc.uva.nl/EuroWordNet/

Proceedings of the EACL 2012 Joint Workshop of LINGVIS & UNCLH, pages 25–29,
Avignon, France, April 23 - 24 2012.

that figure we have presented the same data as a bipartite graph where all column numbers are positioned on the upper line and all rows on the lower line. Every connecting line on the right side has been drawn between every "1"-s column and row number. As we see a lot of line crossings there exist even in our very small example. It is possible to reorder the rows and columns of that table into optimal positions so that the number of line crossings would be minimal possible. If there is full order then there will be no crossings of lines.

Generally this crossing number minimization is a NP-complete task. We are using the idea of Stephan Niermann's (2005) evolutionary algorithm to minimize the number of line crossings.

In our example the optimal result will be:

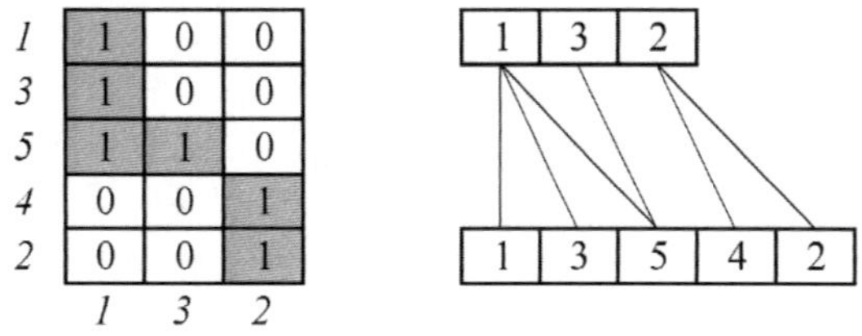

Figure 2. Reordered (arranged) relation-matrix and bipartite graph

As we can see there are no crossings and all connections are separated into two classes – let's call them closed sets. We have got a nice and natural ordering for rows and columns. With that kind of picture the relations between words (synsets) are easier to see and understand. We will present real cases from PrWN and EstWN later.

3 Practical application of the method

Next we will describe the steps that should be taken in order to obtain visual pictures for lexicographers.

- First the word class and a semantic relation of interest is chosen from wordnet. For nouns and verbs hyperonymy and hyponymy are probably the most informative relations, for adjectives and adverbs near_synonymy (but of course this method allows us to choose different semantic relations in combination with different word classes).
- In order to find closed sets we use the connected component separating algorithm for graphs given in D. Knuth (1968). For example using hyponym-hyperonym relation and word classes of nouns then there will be 7 907 closed sets for EstWN and 15 452 closed sets for PrWN. Every closed set is presented in a table as a row with different lengths. An arbitrary closed set is similar to the following picture in Figure 3.

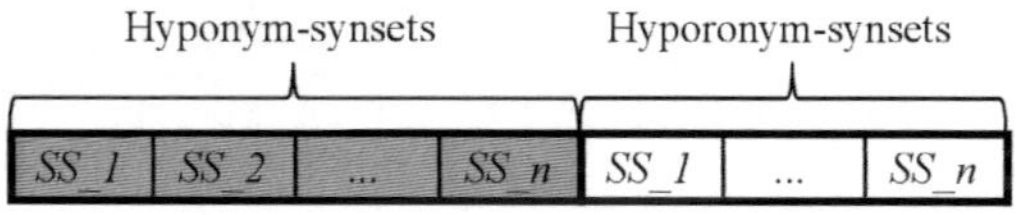

SS1 - synset 1, SS2 - synset 2, ...

Figure 3. Example of a closed set

- As a next step we use all connections for those two sets in a wordnet to get the relation matrix as it is shown in Figure 1 left part.
- Then the minimal crossing algorithm is used (result is seen on the right side of Figure 2).
- As the last step a lexicographer analyzes the figures.

It is still important to mention that our approach is not quite useful for analyzing the large closed sets. The reason is that in Nierman's evolutionary algorithm if the size of the matrix grows than the time increases with the speed $O(n^2)$. For example, to solve the 30x30 matrix, it takes 3 minutes and to solve 60x60 matrix, it takes 60 minutes. That is the reason why in this paper only closed sets that do not exceed the 30 hyponym sets are considered. The pictures from closed sets (Figure 4, 5, 6) were solved as follows: Figure 4 (3 x 5 matrix) 0,28sec, Figure 5 (4 x 11 matrix) 1,5sec, Figure 6 (4 x 12 matrix) 1,7sec.

For larger closed sets it is better to use the modified Power Iteration Clustering method by Lin and Cohen (2010) instead of Niermann's algorithm.

As a matter of fact, the largest closed set in EstWN has 4103 hyponyms-synsets x 405 hyperonym-synsets and the largest closed set in PrWN has 2371 hyponyms-synsets x 167 hyperonym-synsets (Figure 3). As for large closed sets, it could be sensible to use only the relation matrix (Figure 2, left side) to detect where possible problematic places occur.

4 Intermediate results

In this paper we focus on the synsets having two or more hyperonyms, which is the reason of closed sets, since it is more likely to find problematic places in these synsets.

For example in EstWN only one hyperonym for a synset should ideally exist (Vider, 2001). In EstWN there are currently 1 674 concepts with two hyperonyms, 145 concepts with three or more hyperonyms and the concept which has the most hyperonyms - 9 - is 'alkydcolour'.

In PrWN there are 1 442 concepts with two hyperonyms, 34 concepts with three or more hyperonyms and the concept with the most hyperonyms – 5 – is 'atropine'.

Of course in wordnets a synset can have multiple hyperonyms in many cases, in EstWN many of the onomatopoetic words, for example (typically they have hyperonyms which denote movement and sound). But also there are cases where one of the hyperonyms is in some ways more suitable than another. Even if a synset has multiple hyperonyms a cluster still often presents a homogeneous semantic field.

One of the purposes of the visual pictures is to help in detecting so called human errors, for example:

- in a situation where in the lexicographic (manual) work a new and more precise hyperonym is added during editing process but the old one is not deleted;
- lexicographer could not decide which hyperonym fits better;
- lexicographer has connected completely wrong senses (or words) with hyperonymy relation;
- lexicographer has not properly completed the domain-specific synsets etc.

The first three points can indicate the reason of why one synset has multiple hyperonym-synsets.

For example, in Figure 4 all the members of the cluster seem to form a typical set of allergic and hypersensitivity conditions and illnesses. In EstWN currently allergies and diseases caused by allergies do not form such a cluster, because they do not share hyperonyms. But also different clusters exist where some problems can appear.

For example, in Figure 5 where all the other characters (suicide bomber, terrorist, spy etc) except 'programmer' are bad or criminal by their nature. This leads to a thought that maybe 'programmer' as a hyperonym to 'hacker' and 'cracker' is not the best; it might be that 'programmer' is connected with some other semantic relation.

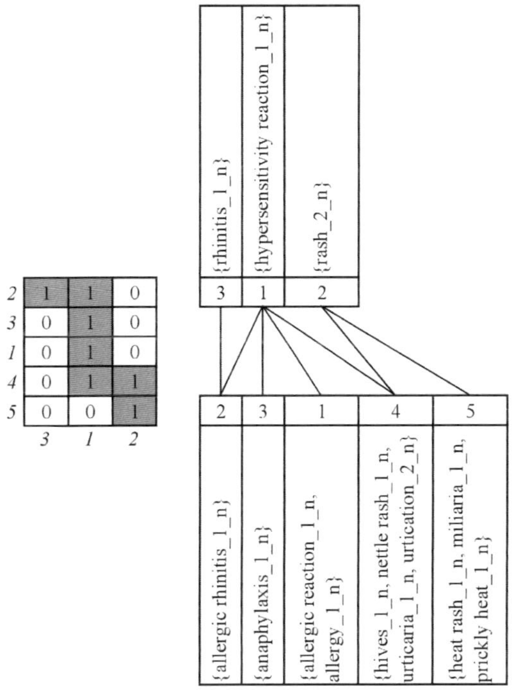

Figure 4. Rearranged bipartite graph, PrWN

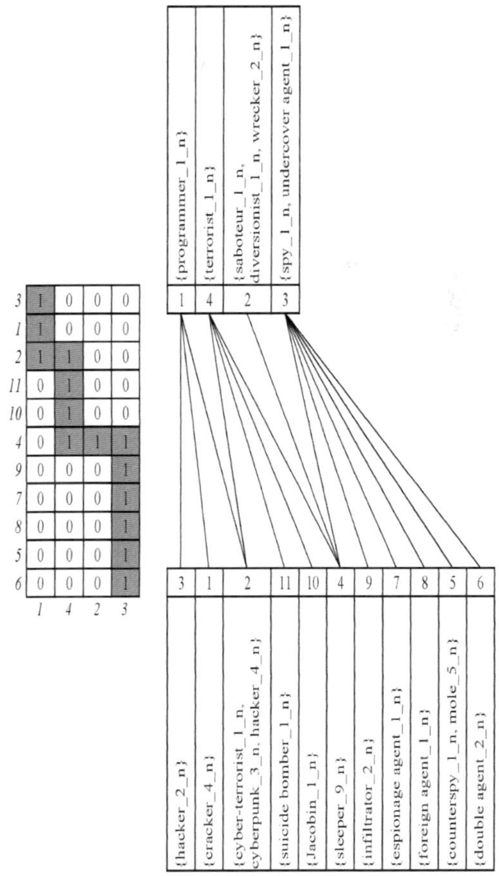

Figure 5. Rearranged bipartite graph, PrWN

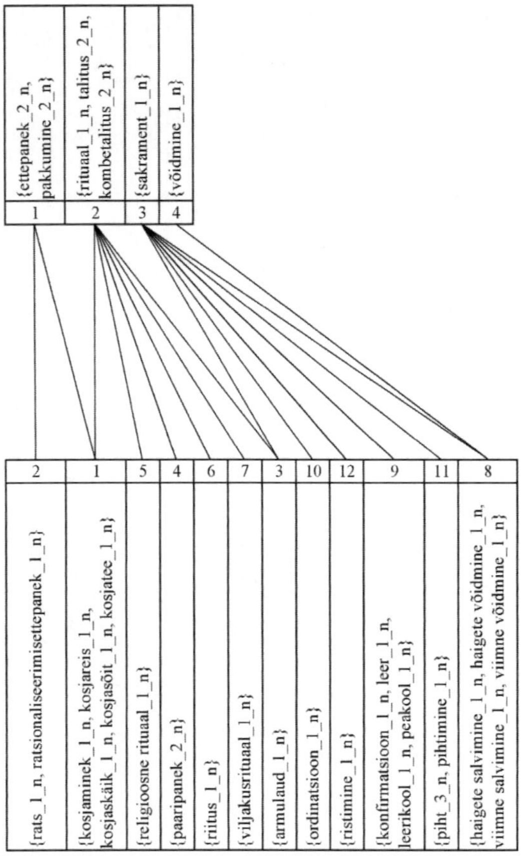

Figure 6. Rearranged bipartite graph, EstWN

Hyperonym-synsets:
1. ettepanek, pakkumine - proposal
2. rituaal, talitus, ... - rituaal
3. sakrament - sacrament
4. võidmine - unction, anoiting

Hyponym-synsets:
4. paaripanek - marriage ritual
6. riitus - rite
7. viljakusrituaal - fertility rite
3. armulaud - Holy Communion
10. ordinatsioon - ordination
12. ristimine - baptism
9. konformatsioon, ... - confirmation
11. piht, pihtimine - confession
8. haigete salvimine, ... - extreme unction
2. rats, ratsionaliseerimisettepanek - proposal for rationalization
1. kosjaminek, kosjareis, ... - a visit to bride's house to make a marriage proposal
5. religioosne rituaal - religious ritual

From EstWN many problematic synsets and/or semantic relations were discovered by using this method. In Figure 6, for example, from EstWN there is an example of a closed set for nouns. It can be seen that the word *ratsionaliseerimis-ettepanek* ('proposal to rationalization') does not belong to this semantic field (this semantic field can be named 'different kinds of rituals' for example). It is strange that words *ratsionaliseerimisettepanek* ('proposal to rationalization') and *kosjakäik* ('a visit to bride's house to make a marriage proposal') belong to the same closed set. Both these synsets share a hyperonym *ettepanek* ('proposal'), but *kosjakäik* should be connected to *ettepanek* ('proposal') by is_involved relation and the hyperonym to *kosjakäik* should be 'ritual' instead.

Also the relation of hyperonyms *võidmine* ('unction') and *sakrament* ('sacrament'). should be interesting. It can be seen that all the semantic relations of hyperonym *võidmine* ('unction') belong actually to *sakrament* ('sacrament'). So it is possible to state that sacrament should be hyperonym to unction. Another question arises with the word *armulaud* ('Holy Communion'). In principle, this word is correctly connected to both sacrament and ritual, but still – all of the hyponyms of sacrament are some sorts of services. These connections are probably missing from the system.

In addition, a minor detail – although *abielu* ('marriage') belongs to sacrament, it is in EstWN categorized only as a ritual and not even directly but implicitly by the word *paaripanek* ('marriage ritual')

5 Conclusion

In order to find mistakes from closed sets it is not necessary to use a bipartite graph. In some cases only the relation-matrix will be enough (Figure 1,2 left side). Clear created groupings can be considered as an advantage of bipartite graphs, which present the hyponym synsets connecting the hyperonym synsets. Often these connections can turn out as the problematic ones. Sometimes it is necessary to use the wordnet database in order to move a level up to understand the meaning of a synset.

Out of the 20 arbitrarily extracted closed sets 6 seemed to have some problems. And in PrWN there were 185 closed sets with hyperonym synsets having at least three hyperonyms. This seems to be a promising start towards using visual pictures. The situation is similar in EstWN, and since EstWN is far from "being completed" then this method has already proven useful for lexicographers in the revision work.

To conclude, the structured bipartite figures are informative in following ways:

- It is possible to use different kinds of semantic relations to create closed sets.
- It is possible to detect subgroups.
- It is possible to detect wrong and missing semantic relations.

Acknowledgments

In this paper Kadri Vare is supported by META-NORD project (CIP-ICT-PSP.2010-4 Theme 6: Multilingual Web: Machine translation for the multilingual web); Estonian Ministry of Education and Research (Target financed research theme SF0180078s08, "Development and implementation of formalisms and efficient algorithms of natural language processing for the Estonian language") and National Programme for Estonian Language Technology.

References

Ashok K. Chandra, Dexter C. Kozen, and Larry J.Stockmeyer. 1981. Alternation. Journal of the Association for Computing Machinery, 28(1):114-133.

Association for Computing Machinery. 1983. Computing Reviews, 24(11):503-512.

Dan Gusfield. 1997. Algorithms on Strings, Trees and Sequences. Cambridge University Press, Cambridge, UK.

Donald E. Knuth. 1968, *Fundamental Algorithms, vol. 1 of Art of Computer Programming* (Reading, MA, Addison-Wesley), §2.3.3.

Frank Lin and William W. Cohen. 2010. *Power Iteration Clustering* in ICML-2010.

George Miller, Richard Beckwith, Christiane Fellbaum, Derek Gross and Kathrine Miller. 1990. *Introduction to WordNet: An On-line Lexical database.* – International Journal of Lexicography 3, 235-312.

Kadri Kerner, Heili Orav and Sirli Parm. 2010. Growth and Revision of Estonian WordNet. *In: Principles, Construction and Application of Multilingual Wordnets.* Proceeding of the 5th Global Wordnet Conference: 5th Global Wordnet Conference; Mumbai, India. (Ed.) Bhattacha-ryya, P.; Fellbaum, Ch.; Vossen, P. Mumbai, India: Narosa Publishing House, pp 198-202.

Kadri Vider. 2001. Eesti keele tesaurus - teooria ja tegelikkus Leksikograafiaseminar *"Sõna tänapäeva maailmas" Leksikografinen seminaari "Sanat nykymaailmassa". Ettekannete kogumik.* Toim. M. Langemets. Eesti Keele Instituudi toimetised 9. Tallinn, lk 134-156.

Michael Louw. 1998. *Polaris User's Guide.* Technical report, Lernout & Hauspie . Antwerp, Belgium.

Maciej Piasecki, Michal Marcinczuk, Adam Musial, Radoslav Ramocki and Marek Maziarz. 2010. *WordnetLoom: a Graph-based Visual Wordnet Development Framework.* In Proceedings of IMCSIT, 469-476.

Stefan Niermann. 2005. Optimizing the Ordering of Tables With Evolutionary Computation. *The American Statistician*, 59(1):41-46.

Visualising Typological Relationships: Plotting WALS with Heat Maps

Richard Littauer
University of Saarland
Computational Linguistics
Saarbrücken, Germany
richard.littauer@gmail.com

Rory Turnbull
Ohio State University
Department of Linguistics
Columbus, Ohio
turnbull@ling.osu.edu

Alexis Palmer
University of Saarland
Computational Linguistics
Saarbrücken, Germany
apalmer@coli.uni-sb.de

Abstract

This paper presents a novel way of visualising relationships between languages. The key feature of the visualisation is that it brings geographic, phylogenetic, and linguistic data together into a single image, allowing a new visual perspective on linguistic typology. The data presented here is extracted from the World Atlas of Language Structures (WALS) (Dryer and Haspelmath, 2011). After pruning due to low coverage of WALS, we filter the typological data by geographical proximity in order to ascertain areal typological effects. The data are displayed in heat maps which reflect the strength of similarity between languages for different linguistic features. Finally, the heat maps are annotated for language family membership. The images so produced allow a multi-faceted perspective on the data which we hope will facilitate the interpretation of results and perhaps illuminate new areas of research in linguistic typology.

1 Introduction

This paper presents a novel way of visualising relationships between languages. Relationships between languages can be understood with respect to linguistic features of the languages, their geographical proximity, and their status with respect to historical development. The visualisations presented in this paper are part of a new attempt to bring together these three perspectives into a single image. One line of recent work brings computational methods to bear on the formation and use of large typological databases, often using sophisticated statistical techniques to discover relations between languages (Cysouw, 2011; Daumé III and Campbell, 2007; Daumé III, 2009, among others), and another line of work uses typological data in natural language processing (Georgi et al., 2010; Lewis and Xia, 2008, for example). The task of visually presenting the resulting data in this way has been only infrequently addressed. We are aware of some similar work (Mayer et al., 2010; Rohrdantz et al., 2010) in visualising differences in linguistic typology, phylogeny (Multitree, 2009), and geographical variation (Wieling et al., 2011). Here, we present our method for addressing the visualisation gap, bringing together phylogeny, typology, and geography by using data from the World Atlas of Language Structures (Dryer and Haspelmath, 2011) to develop heat maps that can visually show the interconnected relationships between languages and language families.

The main envisioned application of our visualisations is in the area of linguistic typology. Typology has been used to derive implications about possible languages, and about the ordering of the human mind. Different theorists have taken different views on the relationship between typology and the universality of languages. For example, Greenberg (1963), a foundational work, identified a number of cross-linguistic typological properties and implications and aimed to present them as truly universal – relevant for *all* languages. In a similar vein, typological universals have been employed as evidence in a generative story regarding language learning (Chomsky, 2000).

Taking a different perspective, Dunn et al. (2011) argued that a language's typology relies upon the previous generations' language more than on any biological, environmental or cognitive constraints, and that there are pathways which

Proceedings of the EACL 2012 Joint Workshop of LINGVIS & UNCLH, pages 30–34,
Avignon, France, April 23 - 24 2012.

are generally followed in language change based on the previous parent language. What these arguments have in common is a reliance on a view of linguistic typology that is potentially restricted in its scope, due to insufficient access to broad-scale empirical data, covering many features of many languages of the world.

The most comprehensive computational resource for linguistic typology currently available is the World Atlas of Language Structures (WALS).[1] WALS is a large database of details of structural properties of several thousand languages (Dryer and Haspelmath, 2011). The properties were collected from descriptive sources by the project's 55 authors.

However, of the 2,678 languages and 192 features in WALS, only 16% of the possible data points are actually specified—the data are *sparse*, and the sparsity of the data naturally makes it difficult to perform reliable statistical analysis. One way to work around this limitation is to seek meaningful visualisations of the data in WALS, instead of simply relying on raw numbers. This is our approach.

In this paper, we first discuss in more detail the source data and the types of information extracted, followed by a discussion of some difficulties presented by the available data and our approaches for addressing those difficulties. Finally, we present a sample of the resulting visualisations.

2 Aspects of the Visualisations

The visualisations described here bring together three types of information: linguistic features, geographical distance, and phylogenetic distance. For the current study, all three types of information are extracted from the WALS database. In future work, we would explore alternate sources such as Ethnologue (Lewis, 2009) or MultiTree (2009) for alternate phylogenetic hierarchies.

2.1 Linguistic features

At the time of writing, WALS contains information for 2,678 languages. The linguistic features covered in WALS range from phonetic and phonological features, over some lexical and morphological features, to syntactic structures, word order tendencies, and other structural phenomena. A total of 192 features are represented, grouped in 144 different chapters, with each chapter addressing a set of related features. Ignoring the fact that a language having certain features will cancel out the possibility (or diminish the probability) of others, only 15.8% of WALS is described fully. In other words, if we consider WALS to be a 2,678x192 grid, fewer than 16% of the grid's squares contain feature values.

The coverage of features/chapters varies dramatically across languages, with an average of 28 feature values per language. The most populated feature has data for 1,519 languages. Because of the extreme sparsity of the data, we restricted our treatment to only languages with values for 30% or more of the available features—372 languages, with a total of 36k feature values.

2.2 Phylogenetic distance

Languages are related phylogenetically either vertically, by lineage, or horizontally, by contact. In WALS, each language is placed in a tree hierarchy that specifies phylogenetic relations. In the WALS data files, this is specified by linking at three different levels: family, such as 'Sino-Tibetan', sub-family, such as 'Tibeto-Burman', and genus, such as 'Northern Naga'. The WALS phylogenetic hierarchies do not take into account language contact. For that, we used geographic coordinates, which are present in WALS, as a proxy for contact.

2.3 Geographic distance

Geographic distance is an important aspect of typological study because neighbouring languages often come to share linguistic features, even in the absence of genetic relationship between the languages. Each language in WALS is associated with a geographical coordinate representing a central point for the main population of speakers of that language. We use these data to determine geographic distance between any two languages, using the haversine formula for orthodromic distance.[2] A crucial aspect of our visualisations is that we produce them only for sets of languages within a reasonable geographic proximity

[1]As of 2008, WALS is browsable online (http://www.wals.info).

[2]This measure is inexact, especially over long distances, due to the imperfect topography and non-spherical shape of the earth, but it is computationally simple and is accurate enough for our present purposes.

and with sufficient feature coverage in WALS.

For this study, we used two approaches to clustering languages according to geographic distance. First, we chose an arbitrary radius in order to create a decision boundary for clustering neighbouring languages. For each language, that language's location is fixed as the centroid of the cluster and every language within the given radius is examined. We found that a radius of 500 kilometres provides a sufficient number of examples even after cleaning low-coverage languages from the WALS data.

The second approach selected an arbitrary lower bound for the number of languages in the geographic area under consideration. If a sufficient percentage (enough to graph) of the total number of languages in the area remained after cleaning the WALS data, we took this as a useful area and did mapping for that area. This number is clearly under-representative of the amount of contact languages, as only half of the world's languages are present in WALS with any degree of coverage. This proxy was not as good as the radius method at choosing specific, useful examples for the *n*-nearest neighbours, as the languages chosen were often quite distant from one another.

3 Heat Map Visualisations

We focused on producing visualisations only for features that are salient for the maximal number of selected languages. We choose two heat maps for display here, from the least sparse data available, to demonstrate the output of the visualisation method. The remaining visualisations, along with all code used to produce the visualisations, are available in a public repository.[3]

All data was downloaded freely from WALS, all coding was done in either Python or R. The code was not computationally expensive to run, and the programming languages and methods are quite accessible.

In a two-dimensional heat map, each cell of a matrix is filled with a colour representing that cell's value. In our case, the colour of the cell represents the normalised value of a linguistic feature according to WALS. Languages with the same colour in a given row have the same value for

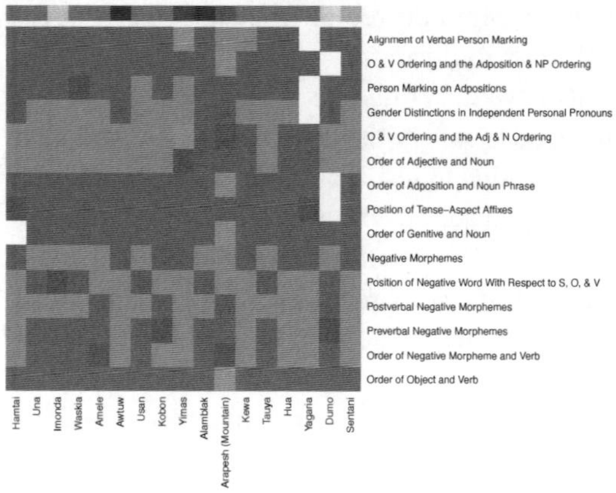

Figure 1: Geographically-focused heat map; see text for details. The bar at the top of the image represents the language family of the language in that column: Pink = Border; Red = Trans-New Guinea; Blue = Sepik; Brown = Lower Sepik-Ramu; Purple = Torricelli; Green = Skou; and Orange = Sentani.

that typological feature.[4] Below we discuss two types of heat maps, focusing first on geographic and then on phylogenetic features.

3.1 Geographically-focused heat maps

For the geographic distance maps, for each language present in the cleaned data, we identified all possible languages that lay within 500km, and sorted these languages until only the 16 closest neighbours were selected. Once the set of languages was determined, we selected for graphing only the most commonly-occurring features across that set of languages.

To present the visualisation, we first centred the source language in the map. This decision was made in order to reduce the effect of one of the primary issues with using distance on a two dimensional graph; distance between two non-source languages is not shown, meaning that one could be to the north and another to the south. This means that the languages on the extremes of the map may be far apart from each other, and should be viewed with caution.

Figure 1 shows a geographically-focused heat map with values for various morphological and word order features. The map is centred on Yimas, a language spoken in New Guinea. The features presented represent a particularly non-

[3] https://github.com/RichardLitt/visualizing-language

[4] Due to this reliance on colour, we strongly suggest viewing the heat maps presented here in colour.

sparse section of WALS for this language area. A number of insights can be gleaned here. Most prominently, these languages are quite homogenous with respect to the selected features. Given that most of the languages do indeed belong to the same language family (cf. top bar of the graph), this is unlikely to be a chance effect. In the 5th row ('O&V Ordering and the Adj&N Ordering'), we see via the cluster of red cells a partial grouping of languages close to Yimas, with less similarity at a greater distance. The nearly alternating pattern we see for 'Position of Negative Word With Respect to S,O,&V' may suggest areal groups that have been split by the data-centring function. Also, the checkerboard pattern for this feature and the one below ('Postverbal Negative Morphemes') suggests a possible negative correlation between these two linguistic features.

3.2 Phylogenetically-focused heat maps

To produce phylogenetically-focused visualisations, for each language we identified other languages coming from the same family, subfamily, or genus. Figure 2 shows a phylogenetically-focused heat map for Niger-Congo languages, arranged from west to east. A number of the western languages show red cells for features related to relative clauses; these can be compared to mostly blue cells in the eastern languages. We also see some apparent groupings for variable word order in negative clauses (red cells in western languages) and for NegSVO Order (purple cells in western languages). For some pairs of adjacent languages (most notably Bambara and Supyire), we see clusters of shared features. Especially give the importance of Bambara for syntactic argumentation (Culy, 1985), this graph is an excellent example of visualisation pointing out an intriguing area for closer analysis.

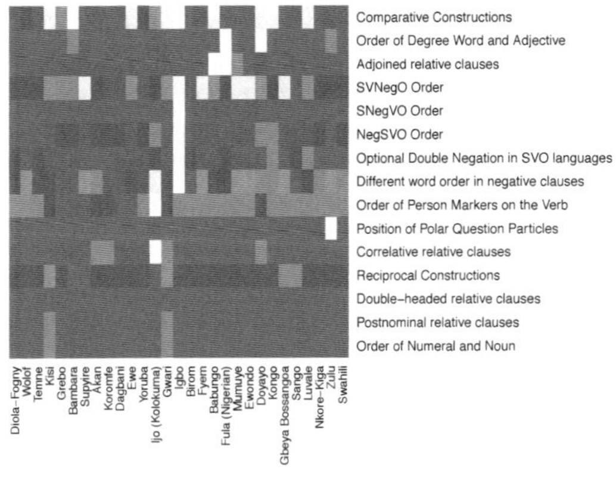

Figure 2: Phylogenetic heat-map of Niger-Congo languages, arranged from west to east.

4 Conclusion

In this paper we present a new approach to visualising relationships between languages, one which allows for the simultaneous viewing of linguistic features together with phylogenetic relationships and geographical location and proximity. These visualisations allow us to view language relationships in a multi-faceted way, seeking to work around the sparseness of available data and facilitate new insights into linguistic typology.

In this work we placed strong restrictions on both feature coverage and selection of salient features for representation, reducing the number of graphs produced to 6 with geographic focus and 8 with phylogenetic focus. One topic for future work is to explore other ways of working with and expanding the available data in order to access even more useful visualisations. In addition, it would be very interesting to apply this visualisation method to data from other sources, for example, data from multiple related dialects. In such cases, coverage is likely to be better, and the languages in question will have been selected already for their relatedness, thus avoiding some of the data-filtering issues that arise. Finally, we would like to investigate more principled approaches to selection, presentation, and ordering of linguistic features in the heat maps.

Acknowledgments

We are grateful to the three anonymous reviewers for helpful comments on the current paper as well as interesting suggestions for future work.

References

Noam Chomsky. 2000. *New Horizons in the Study of Language and Mind.* Cambridge University Press, Cambridge, UK.

Christopher Culy. 1985. The complexity of the vocabulary of Bambara. *Linguistics and Philosophy*, 8:345–351. 10.1007/BF00630918.

Michael Cysouw. 2011. Quantitative explorations of the world-wide distribution of rare characteristics, or: the exceptionality of northwestern european languages. In Horst Simon and Heike Wiese, editors, *Expecting the Unexpected*, pages 411–431. De Gruyter Mouton, Berlin, DE.

Hal Daumé III and Lyle Campbell. 2007. A Bayesian model for discovering typological implications. In *Conference of the Association for Computational Linguistics (ACL)*, Prague, Czech Republic.

Hal Daumé III. 2009. Non-parametric Bayesian model areal linguistics. In *North American Chapter of the Association for Computational Linguistics (NAACL)*, Boulder, CO.

Matthew Dryer and Martin Haspelmath, editors. 2011. *The World Atlas of Language Structures Online*. Max Planck Digital Library, Munich, 2011 edition.

Michael Dunn, Simon Greenhill, Stephen Levinson, and Russell Gray. 2011. Evolved structure of language shows lineage-specific trends in word-order universals. *Nature*, 473(7345):79–82.

Ryan Georgi, Fei Xia, and Will Lewis. 2010. Comparing language similarity across genetic and typologically-based groupings. In *Proceedings of COLING 2010*.

Joseph Greenberg. 1963. Some universals of grammar with particular reference to the order of meaningful elements. In Joseph Greenberg, editor, *Universals of Language*, pages 58–90. MIT Press, Cambridge, MA.

William Lewis and Fei Xia. 2008. Automatically identifying computationally relevant typological features. In *Proceedings of IJCNLP 2008*.

M. Paul Lewis, editor. 2009. *Ethnologue: Languages of the World*. SIL International, Dallas, TX, sixteenth edition.

Thomas Mayer, Christian Rohrdantz, Frans Plank, Peter Bak, Miriam Butt, and Daniel Keim. 2010. Consonant co-occurrence in stems across languages: automatic analysis and visualization of a phonotactic constraint. In *Proceedings of the 2010 Workshop on NLP and Linguistics: Finding the Common Ground*, NLPLING '10, pages 70–78, Stroudsburg, PA, USA. Association for Computational Linguistics.

Multitree. 2009. *Multitree: A digital library of language relationships*. Institute for Language Information and Techology (LINGUIST List), Eastern Michigan University, Ypsilanti, MI, 2009 edition.

Christian Rohrdantz, Thomas Mayer, Miriam Butt, Frans Plank, and Daniel Keim. 2010. Comparative visual analysis of cross-linguistic features. In *Proceedings of the International Symposium on Visual Analytics Science and Technology (EuroVAST 2010)*, pages 27–32. Poster paper; peer-reviewed (abstract).

Martijn Wieling, John Nerbonne, and R. Harald Baayen. 2011. Quantitative social dialectology: Explaining linguistic variation geographically and socially. *PLoS ONE*, 6(9):e23613, 09.

Automating Second Language Acquisition Research: Integrating Information Visualisation and Machine Learning

Helen Yannakoudakis
Computer Laboratory
University of Cambridge
United Kingdom
Helen.Yannakoudakis@cl.cam.ac.uk

Ted Briscoe
Computer Laboratory
University of Cambridge
United Kingdom
Ted.Briscoe@cl.cam.ac.uk

Theodora Alexopoulou
DTAL
University of Cambridge
United Kingdom
ta259@cam.ac.uk

Abstract

We demonstrate how data-driven approaches to learner corpora can support Second Language Acquisition research when integrated with visualisation tools. We present a visual user interface supporting the investigation of a set of linguistic features discriminating between pass and fail 'English as a Second or Other Language' exam scripts. The system displays directed graphs to model interactions between features and supports exploratory search over a set of learner scripts. We illustrate how the interface can support the investigation of the co-occurrence of many individual features, and discuss how such investigations can shed light on understanding the linguistic abilities that characterise different levels of attainment and, more generally, developmental aspects of learner grammars.

1 Introduction

The Common European Framework of Reference for Languages (CEFR)[1] is an international benchmark of language attainment at different stages of learning. The English Profile (EP)[2] research programme aims to enhance the learning, teaching and assessment of English as an additional language by creating detailed reference level descriptions of the language abilities expected at each level. As part of our research within that framework, we modify and combine techniques developed for information visualisation with methodologies from computational linguistics to support a novel and more empirical perspective on CEFR levels. In particular, we build a visual user interface (hereafter UI) which aids the development of hypotheses about learner grammars using graphs of linguistic features discriminating pass/fail exam scripts for intermediate English.

Briscoe et al. (2010) use supervised discriminative machine learning methods to automate the assessment of 'English as a Second or Other Language' (ESOL) exam scripts, and in particular, the First Certificate in English (FCE) exam, which assesses English at an upper-intermediate level (CEFR level B2). They use a binary discriminative classifier to learn a linear threshold function that best discriminates passing from failing FCE scripts, and predict whether a script can be classified as such. To facilitate learning of the classification function, the data should be represented appropriately with the most relevant set of (linguistic) features. They found a discriminative feature set includes, among other feature types, lexical and part-of-speech (POS) ngrams. We extract the discriminative instances of these two feature types and focus on their linguistic analysis[3]. Table 1 presents a small subset ordered by discriminative weight.

The investigation of discriminative features can offer insights into assessment and into the linguistic properties characterising the relevant CEFR level. However, the amount and variety of data potentially made available by the classifier is considerable, as it typically finds hundreds of thousands of discriminative feature instances. Even if investigation is restricted to the most discriminative ones, calculations of relationships be-

[1]http://www.coe.int/t/dg4/linguistic/cadre_en.asp
[2]http://www.englishprofile.org/

[3]Briscoe et al. (2010) POS tagged and parsed the data using the RASP toolkit (Briscoe et al., 2006). POS tags are based on the CLAWS tagset.

Proceedings of the EACL 2012 Joint Workshop of LINGVIS & UNCLH, pages 35–43,
Avignon, France, April 23 - 24 2012. ©2012 Association for Computational Linguistics

tween features can rapidly grow and become overwhelming. Discriminative features typically capture relatively low-level, specific and local properties of texts, so features need to be linked to the scripts they appear in to allow investigation of the contexts in which they occur. The scripts, in turn, need to be searched for further linguistic properties in order to formulate and evaluate higher-level, more general and comprehensible hypotheses which can inform reference level descriptions and understanding of learner grammars.

The appeal of information visualisation is to gain a deeper understanding of important phenomena that are represented in a database (Card et al., 1999) by making it possible to navigate large amounts of data for formulating and testing hypotheses faster, intuitively, and with relative ease. An important challenge is to identify and assess the usefulness of the enormous number of projections that can potentially be visualised. Exploration of (large) databases can lead quickly to numerous possible research directions; lack of good tools often slows down the process of identifying the most productive paths to pursue.

In our context, we require a tool that visualises features flexibly, supports interactive investigation of scripts instantiating them, and allows statistics about scripts, such as the co-occurrence of features or presence of other linguistic properties, to be derived quickly. One of the advantages of using visualisation techniques over command-line database search tools is that Second Language Acquisition (SLA) researchers and related users, such as assessors and teachers, can access scripts, associated features and annotation intuitively without the need to learn query language syntax.

We modify previously-developed visualisation techniques (Di Battista et al., 1999) and build a visual UI supporting hypothesis formation about learner grammars. Features are grouped in terms of their co-occurrence in the corpus and directed graphs are used in order to illustrate their relationships. Selection of different feature combinations automatically generates queries over the data and returns the relevant scripts as well as associations with meta-data and different types of errors committed by the learners[4]. In the next sections we describe in detail the visualiser, illustrate how it can support the investigation of individual features, and discuss how such investigations can shed light on the relationships between features and developmental aspects of learner grammars.

Feature	Example
VM_RR (POS bigram: +)	*could clearly*
,_because (word bigram: −)	*, because of*
necessary (word unigram: +)	*it is necessary that*
the_people (word bigram: −)	**the people are clever*
VV∅_VV∅ (POS bigram: −)	**we go see film*
NN2_VVG (POS bigram: +)	*children smiling*

Table 1: Subset of features ordered by discriminative weight; + and − show their association with either passing or failing scripts.

To the best of our knowledge, this is the first attempt to visually analyse as well as perform a linguistic interpretation of discriminative features that characterise learner English. We also apply our visualiser to a set of 1,244 publically-available FCE ESOL texts (Yannakoudakis et al., 2011) and make it available as a web service to other researchers[5].

2 Dataset

We use texts produced by candidates taking the FCE exam, which assesses English at an upper-intermediate level. The FCE texts, which are part of the Cambridge Learner Corpus[6], are produced by English language learners from around the world sitting Cambridge Assessment's ESOL examinations[7]. The texts are manually tagged with information about linguistic errors (Nicholls, 2003) and linked to meta-data about the learners (e.g., age and native language) and the exam (e.g., grade).

3 The English Profile visualiser

3.1 Basic structure and front-end

The English Profile (EP) visualiser is developed in Java and uses the Prefuse library (Heer et al., 2005) for the visual components. Figure 1 shows its front-end. Features are represented

[4]Our interface integrates a command-line Lucene search tool (Gospodnetic and Hatcher, 2004) developed by Gram and Buttery (2009).

[5]Available by request: http://ilexir.co.uk/applications/ep-visualiser/

[6]http://www.cup.cam.ac.uk/gb/elt/catalogue/subject/custom/item3646603/

[7]http://www.cambridgeesol.org/

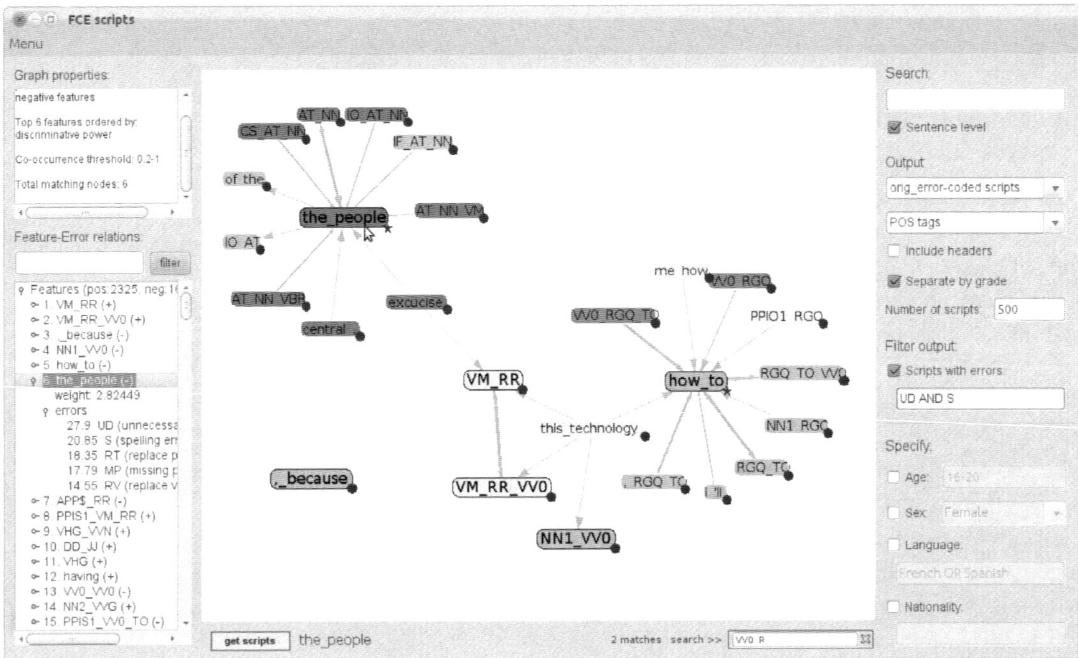

Figure 1: Front-end of the EP visualiser.

by a labelled node and displayed in the central panel; positive features (i.e., those associated with passing the exam) are shaded in a light green colour while negative ones are light red[8]. A field at the bottom right supports searching for features/nodes that start with specified characters and highlighting them in blue. An important aspect is the display of feature patterns, discussed in more detail in the next section (3.2).

3.2 Feature relations

Crucial to understanding discriminative features is finding the relationships that hold between them. We calculate co-occurrences of features at the sentence-level in order to extract 'meaningful' relations and possible patterns of use. Combinations of features that may be 'useful' are kept while the rest are discarded. 'Usefulness' is measured as follows:

Consider the set of all the sentences in the corpus $S = \{s_1, s_2, ..., s_N\}$ and the set of all the features $F = \{f_1, f_2, ..., f_M\}$. A feature $f_i \in F$ is associated with a feature $f_j \in F$, where $i \neq j$ and $1 \leq i, j \leq M$, if their relative co-occurrence score is within a predefined range:

$$\text{score}(f_j, f_i) = \frac{\sum_{k=1}^{N} \text{exists}(f_j, f_i, s_k)}{\sum_{k=1}^{N} \text{exists}(f_i, s_k)} \quad (1)$$

[8]Colours can be customised by the user.

where $s_k \in S$, $1 \leq k \leq N$, exists() is a binary function that returns 1 if the input features occur in s_k, and $0 \leq \text{score}(f_j, f_i) \leq 1$. We group features in terms of their relative co-occurrence within sentences in the corpus and display these co-occurrence relationships as directed graphs. Two nodes (features) are connected by an edge if their score, based on Equation (1), is within a user-defined range (see example below). Given f_i and f_j, the outgoing edges of f_i are modelled using $\text{score}(f_j, f_i)$ and the incoming edges using $\text{score}(f_i, f_j)$. Feature relations are shown via highlighting of features when the user hovers the cursor over them, while the strength of the relations is visually encoded in the edge width.

For example, one of the highest-weighted positive discriminative features is VM_RR (see Table 1), which captures sequences of a modal auxiliary followed by an adverb as in *will always (avoid)* or *could clearly (see)*. Investigating its relative co-occurrence with other features using a score range of 0.8–1 and regardless of directionality, we find that VM_RR is related to the following: (i) POS ngrams: RR_VB∅_AT1, VM_RR_VB∅, VM_RR_VH∅, PPH1_VM_RR, VM_RR_VV∅, PPIS1_VM_RR, PPIS2_VM_RR, RR_VB∅; (ii) word ngrams: will_also, can_only, can_also, can_just. These relations show us the syntactic environments of the feature (i) or its characteristic lexicalisations (ii).

3.3 Dynamic creation of graphs via selection criteria

Questions relating to a graph display may include information about the most connected nodes, separate components of the graph, types of interconnected features, etc. However, the functionality, usability and tractability of graphs is severely limited when the number of nodes and edges grows by more than a few dozen (Fry, 2007). In order to provide adequate information, but at the same time avoid overly complex graphs, we support dynamic creation and visualisation of graphs using a variety of selection criteria. The EP visualiser supports the flexible investigation of the top 4,000 discriminative features and their relations.

The *Menu* item on the top left of the UI in Figure 1 activates a panel that enables users to select the top N features to be displayed. The user can choose whether to display positive and/or negative features and set thresholds for, as well as rank by discriminative weight, connectivity with other features (i.e., the number of features it is connected to), and frequency. For instance, a user can choose to investigate features that have a connectivity between 500 and 900, rank them by frequency and display the top 100. Highly-connected features might tell us something about the learner grammar while infrequent features, although discriminative, might not lead to useful linguistic insights. Additionally, users can investigate feature relations and set different score ranges according to Equation (1), which controls the edges to be displayed.

Figure 2(a) presents the graph of the 5 most frequent negative features, using a score range of 0.8–1. The system displays only one edge, while the rest of the features are isolated. However, these features might be related to other features from the list of 4,000 (which are not displayed since they are not found in the top N list of features). Blue aggregation markers in the shape of a circle, located at the bottom right of each node, are used to visually display that information. When a node with an aggregation marker is selected, the system automatically expands the graph and displays the related features. The marker shape of an expanded node changes to a star, while a different border stroke pattern

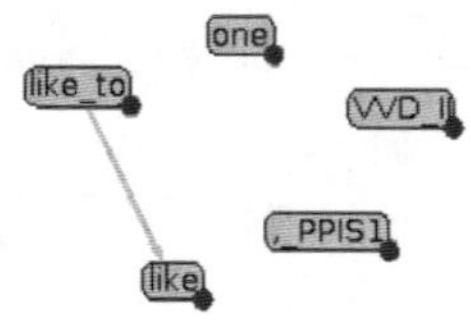

(a) Graph of the top 5 most frequent negative features using a score range of 0.8–1.

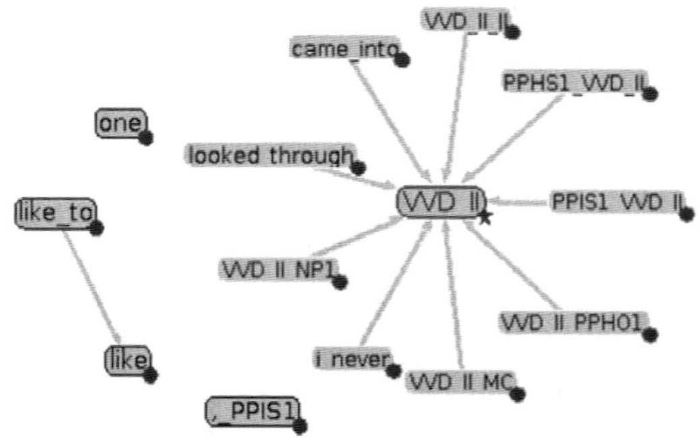

(b) Expanded graph when the aggregation marker for the feature VVD_II is selected.

Figure 2: Dynamic graph creation.

is used to visually distinguish the revealed nodes from the top N. Figure 2(b) presents the expanded graph when the aggregation marker for the feature VVD_II is selected. If the same aggregation marker is selected twice, the graph collapses and returns to its original form.

3.4 Feature–Error relations

The FCE texts have been manually error-coded (Nicholls, 2003) so it is possible to find associations between discriminative features and specific error types. The *Feature–Error relations* component on the left of Figure 1 displays a list of the features, ranked by their discriminative weight, together with statistics on their relations with errors. Feature–error relations are computed at the sentence level by calculating the proportion of sentences containing a feature that also contain a specific error (similar to Equation (1)). In the example in Figure 1, we see that 27% of the sentences that contain the feature bigram the_people also have an unnecessary determiner (UD) error, while 14% have a replace verb (RV) error[9].

[9] In the example image we only output the top 5 errors (can be customised by the user).

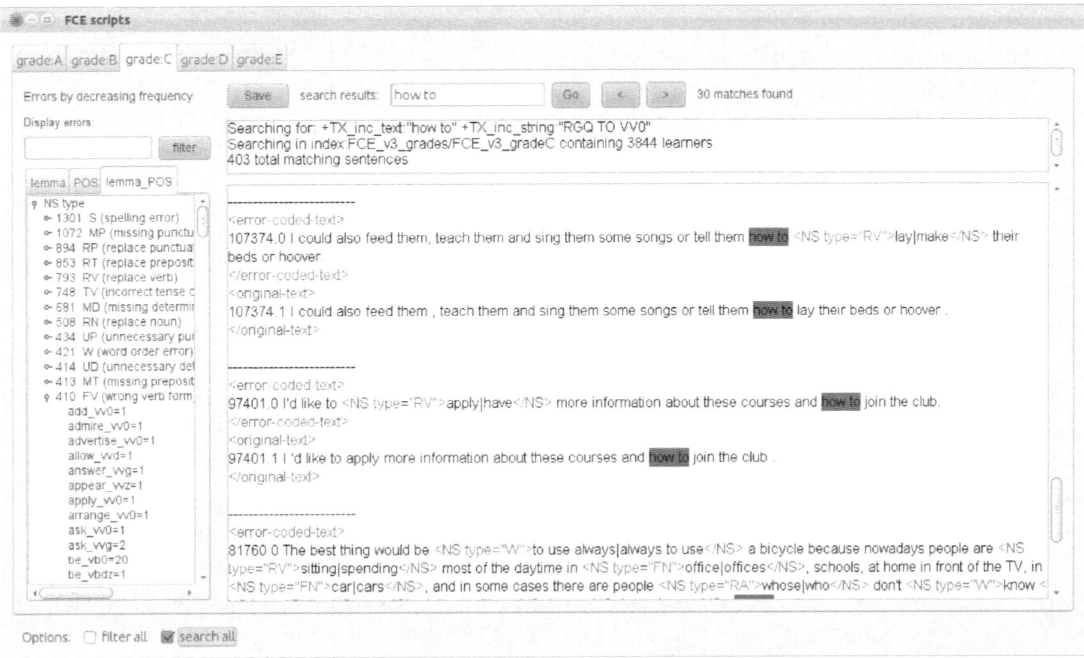

Figure 3: Sentences, split by grade, containing occurrences of how_to and RGQ_TO_VV∅. The list on the left gives error frequencies for the matching scripts, including the frequencies of lemmata and POSs inside an error.

3.5 Searching the data

In order to allow the user to explore how features are related to the data, the EP visualiser supports browsing operations. Selecting multiple features – highlighted in yellow – and clicking on the button *get scripts* returns relevant scripts. The right panel of the front-end in Figure 1 displays a number of search and output options. Users can choose to output the original/error-coded/POS-tagged text and/or the grammatical relations found by the RASP parser (Briscoe et al., 2006), while different colours are used in order to help readability. Data can be retrieved at the sentence or script level and separated according to grade. Additionally, Boolean queries can be executed in order to examine occurrences of (selected features and) specific errors only[10]. Also, users can investigate scripts based on meta-data information such as learner age.

Figure 3 shows the display of the system when the features how_to and RGQ_TO_VV∅ (*how to* followed by a verb in base form) are selected. The text area in the centre displays sentences instantiating them. A search box at the top supports navigation, highlighting search terms in red, while a small text area underneath displays the current search query, the size of the database and the number of matching scripts or sentences. The *Errors by decreasing frequency* pane on the left shows a list of the errors found in the matching scripts, ordered by decreasing frequency. Three different tabs (lemma, POS and lemma_POS) provide information about and allow extraction of counts of lemmata and POSs inside an error tag.

3.6 Learner native language

Research on SLA highlights the possible effect of a native language (L1) on the learning process. Using the *Menu* item on the top left corner of Figure 1, users can select the language of interest while the system displays a new window with an identical front-end and functionality. Feature–error statistics are now displayed per L1, while selecting multiple features returns scripts written by learners speaking the chosen L1.

4 Interpreting discriminative features: a case study

We now illustrate in greater depth how the EP visualiser can support interpretation of discriminative features: the POS trigram RG_JJ_NN1 (−) is

[10]For example, users can activate the *Scripts with errors:* option and type 'R OR W'. This will return sentences containing replace or word order errors.

the 18th most discriminative (negative) feature. It corresponds to a sequence of a degree adverb followed by an adjective and a singular noun as in *very good boy*. The question is why such a feature is negative since the string is not ungrammatical. Visualisation of this feature using the 'dynamic graph creation' component of the visualiser allows us to see the features it is related to. This offers an intuitive and manageable way of investigating the large number of underlying discriminative features.

We find that RG_JJ_NN1 is related to its discriminative lexicalisation, very_good (−), which is the 513th most discriminative feature. Also, it is related to JJ_NN1_II (−) (e.g., *difficult sport at*), ranked 2,700th, which suggests a particular context for RG_JJ_NN1 when the noun is followed by a preposition. Searching for this conjunction of features in scripts, we get production examples like *1a,b,c*. Perhaps more interestingly, RG_JJ_NN1 is related to VBZ_RG (−) (ranked 243rd): *is* followed by a degree adverb. This relation suggests a link with predicative structures since putting the two ngrams together yields strings VBZ_ RG_JJ_NN1 corresponding to examples like *1c,d*; if we also add _II we get examples like *1c*.

1a *It might seem to be* ***very difficult sport at*** *the beginning.*

1b *We know a lot about* ***very difficult situation in*** *your country.*

1c *I think it's* ***very good idea to*** *spending vacation together.*

1d *Unix* ***is very powerful system*** *but there is one thing against it.*

The associations between features already give an idea of the source of the problem. In the sequences including the verb *be* the indefinite article is omitted. So the next thing to investigate is if indeed RG_JJ_NN1 is associated with article omission, not only in predicative contexts, but more generally. The *Feature–Error relations* component of the UI reveals an association with MD (missing determiner) errors: 23% of sentences that contain RG_JJ_NN1 also have a MD error. The same holds for very_good, JJ_NN1_II and VBZ_RG with percentages 12%, 14% and

Language	f_1	f_2	f_3	f_4
all	0.26	0.40	0.02	0.03
Turkish	0.29	0.48	0.04	0.03
Japanese	0.17	0.39	0.02	0.02
Korean	0.30	0.58	0.06	0.03
Russian	0.35	0.52	0.03	0.03
Chinese	0.25	0.56	0.02	0.03
French	0.21	0.41	0.00	0.03
German	0.19	0.41	0.00	0.02
Spanish	0.27	0.32	0.00	0.03
Greek	0.30	0.35	0.02	0.02

Table 2: $f_{1/2/3/4}$:doc ratios for different L1s.

15% respectively. We then compared the number of MD errors per script across different types of scripts. Across all scripts the ratio MD:doc is 2.18, that is, approximately 2 MD errors per script; in RG_JJ_NN1 scripts this ratio goes up to 2.75, so that each script has roughly 3 MD errors. VBZ_RG follows with 2.68, JJ_NN1_II with 2.48, and very_good with 2.32. In scripts containing all features the ratio goes up to 4.02 (3.68 without very_good), and in scripts containing VBZ_RG_JJ the ratio goes up to 2.73. Also, in most of these scripts the error involves the indefinite article. The emerging picture then is that there is a link between these richer nominal structures that include more than one modifier and the omission of the article. Two questions arise: (i) why these richer nominals should associate with article omission and (ii) why only singular nouns are implicated in this feature.

Article omission errors are typical of learners coming from L1s lacking an article system (Robertson, 2000; Ionin and Montrul, 2010; Hawkins and Buttery, 2010). Trenkic (2008) proposes that such learners analyse articles as adjectival modifiers rather than as a separate category of determiners or articles. When no adjective is involved, learners may be aware that bare nominals are ungrammatical in English and provide the article. However, with complex adjectival phrases, learners may omit the article because of the presence of a degree adverb. In order to evaluate this hypothesis further we need to investigate if article omission is indeed more pronounced in our data with more complex adjectival phrases e.g., *very difficult situation* than with simpler ones e.g., *nice boy* and whether this is primarily the case for learners from L1s lacking articles.

Again, using the *Errors by decreasing frequency* pane we found that the MD:doc ratio in scripts containing the bigram JJ_NN1 is 2.20. Additionally, in scripts containing JJ_NN1 and not RG_JJ_NN1 it goes down to 2.04. These results are much lower compared to the MD:doc ratio in scripts containing RG_JJ_NN1 and/or the features with which it is related (see above), further supporting our hypothesis. We also found the ratio of RG_JJ_NN1 (f_1) occurrences per document across different L1s, as well as the ratio of VBZ_RG_JJ (f_2), VBZ_RG_JJ_NN1 (f_3) and RG_JJ_NN1_II (f_4). As shown in Table 2 there is no correlation between these features and the L1, with the exception of f_1 and f_2 which are more pronounced in Korean and Russian speakers, and of f_3 which seems completely absent from French, German and Spanish which all have articles. The exception is Greek which has articles but uses bare nominals in predicative structures.

However, a more systematic pattern is revealed when relations with MD errors are considered (using the *Feature–Error relations* and *Errors by decreasing frequency* components for different L1s). As shown in Table 3, there is a sharp contrast between L1s with articles (French, German, Spanish and Greek) and those without (Turkish, Japanese, Korean, Russian, Chinese), which further supports our hypothesis. A further question is why only the singular article is implicated in this feature. The association with predicative contexts may provide a clue. Such contexts select nominals which require the indefinite article only in the singular case; compare *Unix is (a) very powerful system* with *Macs are very elegant machines*.

In sum, navigating the UI, we formed some initial interpretations for why a particular feature is negatively discriminative. In particular, nominals with complex adjectival phrases appear particularly susceptible to article omission errors by learners of English with L1s lacking articles. The example illustrates not just the usefulness of visualisation techniques for navigating and interpreting large amounts of data, but, more generally the relevance of features weighted by discriminative classifiers. Despite being superficial in their structure, POS ngrams can pick up syntactic environments linked to particular phenomena. In this case, the features do not just identify a high rate of article omission errors, but, importantly, a particular syntactic environment triggering higher rates of such errors.

	sentences%		MD:doc	
Language	f_1	f_2	f_1	f_2
all	23.0	15.6	2.75	2.73
Turkish	45.2	29.0	5.81	5.82
Japanese	44.4	22.3	4.48	3.98
Korean	46.7	35.0	5.48	5.31
Russian	46.7	23.4	5.42	4.59
Chinese	23.4	13.5	3.58	3.25
French	6.9	6.7	1.32	1.49
German	2.1	3.0	0.91	0.92
Spanish	10.0	9.6	1.18	1.35
Greek	15.5	12.9	1.60	1.70

Table 3: $f_{1/2}$ relations with MD errors for different L1s, where sentences% shows the proportion of sentences containing $f_{1/2}$ that also contain a MD.

5 Previous work

To the best of our knowledge, this is the first attempt to visually analyse as well as perform a linguistic interpretation of discriminative features that characterise learner English.

Collins (2010) in his dissertation addresses visualisation for NLP research. The *Bubble Sets* visualisation draws secondary set relations around arbitrary collections of items, such as a linguistic parse tree. *VisLink* provides a general platform within which multiple visualisations of language (e.g., a force-directed graph and a radial graph) can be connected, cross-queried and compared. Moreover, he explores the space of content analysis. *DocuBurst* is an interactive visualisation of document content, which spatially organizes words using an expert-created ontology (e.g., WordNet). *Parallel Tag Clouds* combine keyword extraction and coordinated visualisations to provide comparative overviews across subsets of a faceted text corpus. Recently, Rohrdantz et al. (2011) proposed a new approach to detecting and investigating changes in word senses by visually modelling and plotting aggregated views about the diachronic development in word contexts.

Visualisation techniques have been successfully used in other areas including the humanities (e.g., Plaisant et al. (2006) and Don et al. (2007)), as well as genomics (e.g., Meyer et al. (2010a) and Meyer et al. (2010b)). For example, Meyer et al. (2010a) present a system that supports the inspection and curation of data sets showing gene expression over time, in conjunction with the spatial location of the cells where the genes are expressed.

Graph layouts have been effectively used in the analysis of domains such as social networks (e.g., terrorism network) to allow for a systematic exploration of a variety of Social Network Analysis measures (e.g., Gao et al. (2009) and Perer and Shneiderman (2006)). Heer and Boyd (2005) have implemented *Vizster*, a visualisation system for the exploration of on-line social networks (e.g., facebook) designed to facilitate the discovery of people, promote awareness of community structure etc. Van Ham et al. (2009) introduce *Phrase Net*, a system that analyses unstructured text by taking as input a predefined pattern and displaying a graph whose nodes are words and whose edges link the words that are found as matches.

We believe our integration of highly-weighted discriminative features identified by a supervised classifier into a graph-based visualiser to support linguistic SLA research is, however, novel.

6 Conclusions

We have demonstrated how a data-driven approach to learner corpora can support SLA research when guided by discriminative features and augmented with visualisation tools. We described a visual UI which supports exploratory search over a corpus of learner texts using directed graphs of features, and presented a case study of how the system allows SLA researchers to investigate the data and form hypotheses about intermediate level learners. Although the usefulness of the EP visualiser should be confirmed through more rigorous evaluation techniques, such as longitudinal case studies (Shneiderman and Plaisant, 2006; Munzner, 2009) with a broad field of experts, these initial explorations are encouraging. One of the main advantages of using visualisation techniques over command-line database search tools is that SLA researchers can start developing and testing hypotheses without the need to learn a query syntax first.

We would also like to point out that we adopted a user-driven development of the visualiser based on the needs of the third author, an SLA researcher who acted as a design partner during the development of the tool and was eager to use and test it. There were dozens of meetings over a period of seven months, and the feedback on early interfaces was incorporated in the version described here. After the prototype reached a satisfactory level of stability, the final version overall felt enjoyable and inviting, as well as allowed her to form hypotheses and draw on different types of evidence in order to substantiate it (Alexopoulou et al., 2012). Future work will include the development, testing and evaluation of the UI with a wider range of users, as well as be directed towards investigation and evaluation of different visualisation techniques of machine learned or extracted features that support hypothesis formation about learner grammars.

Acknowledgments

We are grateful to Cambridge ESOL for supporting this research. We would like to thank Marek Rei, Øistein Andersen, Paula Buttery and Angeliki Salamoura for fruitful discussions and feedback, Tim Parish for making the tool available on the web, as well as the anonymous reviewers for their valuable comments and suggestions.

References

Theodora Alexopoulou, Helen Yannakoudakis, and Angeliki Salamoura. 2012. Classifying intermediate Learner English: a data-driven approach to learner corpora. *to appear*.

Ted Briscoe, John Carroll, and Rebecca Watson. 2006. The second release of the RASP system. In *Proceedings of the COLING/ACL*, volume 6.

Ted Briscoe, Ben Medlock, and Øistein Andersen. 2010. *Automated Assessment of ESOL Free Text Examinations*. University of Cambridge, Computer Laboratory, TR-790.

Stuart K. Card, Jock D. Mackinlay, and Ben Shneiderman. 1999. *Readings in information visualization: using vision to think*. Morgan Kaufmann.

Christopher M. Collins. 2010. *Interactive Visualizations of natural language*. Ph.D. thesis, University of Toronto.

Giuseppe Di Battista, Peter Eades, Roberto Tamassia, and Ioannis G. Tollis. 1999. *Graph Drawing: Algorithms for the Visualization of Graphs*. Prentice Hall Press.

Anthony Don, Elena Zheleva, Machon Gregory, Sureyya Tarkan, Loretta Auvil, Tanya Clement, Ben Shneiderman, and Catherine Plaisant. 2007. Discovering interesting usage patterns in text collections: integrating text mining with visualization. In

Proceedings of the sixteenth ACM conference on information and knowledge management, pages 213–222. ACM.

Ben Fry. 2007. *Visualizing Data: Exploring and Explaining Data with the Processing Environment*. O'Reilly Media.

Jie Gao, Kazuo Misue, and Jiro Tanaka. 2009. A Multiple-Aspects Visualization Tool for Exploring Social Networks. *Human Interface and the Management of Information*, pages 277–286.

Otis Gospodnetic and Erik Hatcher. 2004. *Lucene in Action*. Manning Publications.

Lu Gram and Paula Buttery. 2009. A tutorial introduction to iLexIR Search. unpublished.

John Hawkins and Paula Buttery. 2010. Criterial features in Learner Corpora: theory and illustrations. *English Profile Journal*, 1(1):1–23.

Jeffrey Heer and Danah Boyd. 2005. Vizster: visualizing online social networks. *IEEE Symposium on Information Visualization (INFOVIS)*, pages 32–39.

Jeffrey Heer, Stuart K. Card, and James A. Landay. 2005. Prefuse: a toolkit for interactive information visualization. In *Proceedings of the SIGCHI conference on Human factors in computing systems*, pages 421–430, New York, USA. ACM.

Tania Ionin and Silvina Montrul. 2010. The role of l1 transfer in the interpretation of articles with definite plurals in l2 english. *Language Learning*, 60(4):877–925.

Miriah Meyer, Tamara Munzner, Angela DePace, and Hanspeter Pfister. 2010a. MulteeSum: a tool for comparative spatial and temporal gene expression data. *IEEE transactions on visualization and computer graphics*, 16(6):908–17.

Miriah Meyer, Bang Wong, Mark Styczynski, Tamara Munzner, and Hanspeter Pfister. 2010b. Pathline: A tool for comparative functional genomics. *Computer Graphics*, 29(3).

Tamara Munzner. 2009. A Nested Model for Visualization Design and Validation. *IEEE Transactions on Visualization and Computer Graphics*, 15(6).

Diane Nicholls. 2003. The Cambridge Learner Corpus-error coding and analysis for lexicography and ELT. In *Proceedings of the Corpus Linguistics 2003 conference*, pages 572–581.

Adam Perer and Ben Shneiderman. 2006. Balancing Systematic and Flexible Exploration of Social Networks. *IEEE Transactions on Visualization and Computer Graphics*, 12(5):693–700.

Catherine Plaisant, James Rose, Bei Yu, Loretta Auvil, Matthew G. Kirschenbaum, Martha N. Smith, Tanya Clement, and Greg Lord. 2006. Exploring erotics in Emily Dickinson's correspondence with text mining and visual interfaces. In *Proceedings of the 6th ACM/IEEE-CS joint conference on Digital libraries*, pages 141–150. ACM.

Daniel Robertson. 2000. Variability in the use of the English article system by Chinese learners of English. *Second Language Research*, 2:135–172.

Christian Rohrdantz, Annette Hautli, Thomas Mayer, and Miriam Butt. 2011. Towards tracking semantic change by visual analytics. *Proceedings of the 49th Meeting of the Association for Computational Linguistics*, pages 305–310.

Ben Shneiderman and Catherine Plaisant. 2006. Strategies for evaluating information visualization tools: multi-dimensional in-depth long-term case studies. In *Proceedings of the 2006 AVI workshop on BEyond time and errors: novel evaluation methods for information visualization*. ACM.

Danijela Trenkic. 2008. The representation of English articles in second language grammars: Determiners or adjectives? *Bilingualism: Language and Cognition*, 11(01):1–18.

Frank Van Ham, Martin Wattenberg, and Fernanda B. Viégas. 2009. Mapping text with phrase nets. *IEEE Transactions on Visualization and Computer Graphics*, 15(6):1169–76.

Helen Yannakoudakis, Ted Briscoe, and Ben Medlock. 2011. A New Dataset and Method for Automatically Grading ESOL Texts. In *Proceedings of the 49th Annual Meeting of the Association for Computational Linguistics: Human Language Technologies*.

Visualising Linguistic Evolution in Academic Discourse

Verena Lyding
European Academy of Bolzano-Bozen
verena.lyding@eurac.edu

Ekaterina Lapshinova-Koltunski
Saarland University
e.lapshinova@mx.uni-saarland.de

Stefania Degaetano-Ortlieb
Saarland University
s.degaetano@mx.uni-saarland.de

Henrik Dittmann
European Academy of Bolzano-Bozen
henrik.dittmann@eurac.edu

Christopher Culy
The University of Tübingen
christopher.culy@uni-tuebingen.de

Abstract

The present paper describes procedures to visualise diachronic language changes in academic discourse to support analysis. These changes are reflected in the distribution of different lexico-grammatical features according to register. Findings about register differences are relevant for both linguistic applications (e.g., discourse analysis and translation studies) and NLP tasks (notably automatic text classification).

1 Introduction

The present paper describes procedures to visualise diachronic language changes in academic discourse with the aim to facilitate analysis and interpretation of complex data. Diachronic changes are reflected by linguistic features of registers under analysis. Registers are patterns of language according to use in context, cf. (Halliday and Hasan, 1989).

To analyse register change, we extract lexico-grammatical features from a diachronic corpus of academic English, and visualise our extraction results with *Structured Parallel Coordinates* (SPC), a tool for the visualisation of structured multidimensional data, cf. (Culy *et al.*, 2011).

Our approach is based on the inspection and comparison of how different features change over time and registers. The major aim is to determine and describe tendencies of features, which might become rarer, more frequent or cluster in new ways. The amount and complexity of the interrelated data, which is obtained for nine disciplines in two time periods (see section 2) makes the analysis more difficult.

Structured Parallel Coordinates provide a tool for the compact visual presentation of complex data. The visualisation of statistical values for different linguistic features laid out over time and register supports data analysis as tendencies become apparent. Furthermore, interactive features allow for taking different views on the data and focussing on interesting aspects.

2 Data to Analyse

2.1 Features and theoretical background

When defining lexico-grammatical features, we refer to Systemic Functional Linguistics (SFL) and register theory, e.g., (Quirk, 1985), (Halliday and Hasan, 1989) and (Biber, 1995), which are concerned with linguistic variation according to contexts of use, typically distinguishing the three contextual variables of *field*, *tenor* and *mode* of discourse. Particular settings of these variables are associated with the co-occurrences of certain lexico-grammatical features, creating distinctive registers (e.g., the language of linguistics in academic discourse). We also consider investigations of recent language change, observed, e.g., by (Mair, 2006), who analyses changes in preferences of lexico-grammatical selection in English in the 1960s vs. the 1990s.

As a case study, we show an analysis of modal verbs (falling into the contextual variable of *tenor*), which we group according to (Biber, 1999) into three categories of meaning that represent three features: *obligation*, *permission* and *volition* (see Table 1).

2.2 Resources

The selected features are extracted from SciTex, cf. (Degaetano *et al.*, 2012) and (Teich and

Proceedings of the EACL 2012 Joint Workshop of LINGVIS & UNCLH, pages 44–48,
Avignon, France, April 23 - 24 2012.

categories of meanings (feature)	realisation
obligation/necessity (obligaton)	*can, could, may*, etc.
permission/possibility/ability (permission)	*must, should*, etc.
volition/prediction (volition)	*will, would, shall*, etc.

Table 1: Categories of modal meanings for feature extraction

Fankhauser, 2010), an English corpus which contains full English scientific journal articles from nine disciplines (see Figure 1). The corpus covers two time periods: the 1970/early 1980s (SaSciTex) and the early 2000s (DaSciTex), and includes ca. 34 million tokens. Our focus is especially on the subcorpora representing contact registers, i.e. registers emerged out of register contact, in our case with computer science: computational linguistics (B1), bioinformatics (B2), digital construction (B3), and microelectronics (B4).

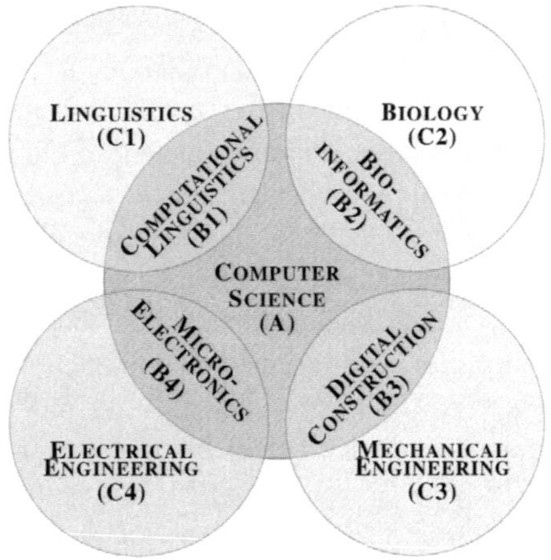

Figure 1: Scientific disciplines in the SciTex corpus

SciTex is annotated[1] with information on token, lemma, part-of-speech and sentence boundary, as well as further information on text boundary, register information, etc., and can be queried in form of regular expressions by the Corpus Query Processor (CQP), cf. (Evert, 2005).

2.3 Feature Extraction and Analysis

To extract the above described features for the two time slices (1970/80s and 2000s) and for all nine registers of SciTex, we elaborate queries, which include both lexical (based on token and lemma information) and grammatical (based on part-of-speech or sentence boundary information) constraints.

[1]Annotations were obtained by means of a dedicated processing pipeline (Kermes, 2011).

Annotations on the register information allow us to sort the extracted material according to specific subcorpora. This enables the analysis of features possibly involved in creating distinctive registers. Comparing differences and/or commonalities in the distribution of features for A-B-C triples of subcorpora (e.g., A-computer science, B1-computational linguistics, C1-linguistics, cf. Figure 1), we analyse whether the contact disciplines (B-subcorpora) are more similar to computer science (A-subcorpus), the discipline of origin (C-subcorpus) or distinct from both (A and C). The two time periods in SciTex (70/80s vs. 2000s) enable a diachronic analysis. A more fine-grained diachronic analysis is also possible with the information on the publication year annotated in the corpus.

3 Analysing language changes with SPC

3.1 SPC visualisation

Structured Parallel Coordinates (Culy *et al.*, 2011) are a specialisation of the *Parallel Coordinates* visualisation (cf. (d'Ocagne, 1885), (Inselberg, 1985), (Inselberg, 2009)) for representing multidimensional data using a two-dimensional display. *Parallel Coordinates* place data on vertical axes, with the axes lined up horizontally. Each axis represents a separate data dimension and can hold either categorical or numerical data. Data points on different axes are related which is indicated by colored lines connecting all data items belonging to one record.

Targeted to the application to language data, SPC additionally provide for ordered characteristics of data within and across data dimensions. In the *n-grams with frequencies/KWIC*[2] implementations of SPC, ordered axes represent the linear ordering of words in text.

In our analysis of language change based on linguistic features, we are interested in two directions of changes across data sets that can be represented by ordering: changes over time and

[2]www.eurac.edu/linfovis

changes across registers, e.g., from linguistics and computer science to computational linguistics.

3.2 Adjustments to SPC

For the analysis of linguistic features with SPC, we start off with the *n-grams with frequencies* implementation. In analyzing just two time dimensions the ordered aspect of SPC is not as crucial and a similar analysis could have been done with Parallel Coordinates. However, the setup of *n-grams with frequencies* conveniently provides us with the combination of categorical and numerical data dimensions in one display but separated visually. For our diachronic register analysis, we create a *subcorpus comparison* application where the feature under analysis as well as some of the corpus data are placed on the unordered categorical axes, and frequencies for the two time periods are placed on ordered axes with numerical scales. As shown in Figure 2 below, unordered dimensions are followed by ordered dimensions, the inverse situation to *n-grams with frequencies*. To visually support the categorical nature of data on the first three axes, SPC was adjusted to display the connecting lines in discrete colors instead of the default color scale shading from red to blue. To improve the comparability of values on numerical axes, a function for switching between comparable and individual scales was added that applies to all axes right of the separating red line. Figure 2 and 3 present numerical values as percentages on comparable scales scaled to 100.

3.3 Interactive features for analysis

SPC provide a number of interactive features that support data analysis. To highlight and accentuate selected parts of the data, an axis can be put into focus and parts of axes can be selected. Lines are colored according to the axis under focus, and filters apply to the selected portions of axes, with the other data rendered in gray. Users can switch between discrete colors and scaled coloring of connecting lines. The scales of numerical axes can be adjusted interactively, as described above. Hovering over a determined connecting line brings it out as a slightly wider line and gives a written summary of the values of that record.

4 Interpreting Visualisation Results

Visualised structures provided by SPC supply us with information on development tendencies, and thus, deliver valuable material for further interpretation of language variation across registers and time.

To analyse the frequencies of modal meanings (see Table 1) for A-B-C triples of subcorpora, we use the *subcorpus comparison* option of SPC. The interactive functionality of SPC allows us to focus on different aspects and provides us with dynamically updated versions of the visualisation.

First, by setting focus on the axis of modal meanings, the visualisation in Figure 2 shows diachronic changes of the modal meanings from the 1970/80s to the early 2000s. In both time periods the *permission* (blue) meaning is most prominent and has considerably increased over time. The *volition* (green) and *obligation* (orange) meanings are less prominent and we can observe a decrease of *volition* and a very slight decrease of *obligation*.

Second, by setting the axis of the registers into focus and selecting the disciplines one by one, we can explore whether there are changes in the use of modal meanings between the A register, the contact registers (B), and the respective C registers. In Figure 3, for example, computer science and biology have been selected (gray shaded) on the 'disciplines' axis. For this selection, the structures starting from the 'registers' axis represent (1) computer science (blue) being the A register, (2) biology (green) from the C registers, and (3) bioinformatics (orange) from the B registers as the corresponding contact register. In terms of register changes, Figure 3 shows that bioinformatics differs in the development tendencies (a) of *permission* from biology and computer science (less increase than the former, more increase than the latter) and (b) of *obligation* from biology (decrease for biology, whereas nearly stable for bioinformatics and computer science).

5 Conclusion and Future Work

The results described above show that *Structured Parallel Coordinates* provides us with a means for the interactive inspection of complex data sets facilitating our diachronic register analysis. The visualisation allows to gain an overview and detect tendencies by accomodating a complex set of data in one display (nine registers over two time periods for three meanings).

The interactive features of SPC give the possibility to put different aspects of the data into fo-

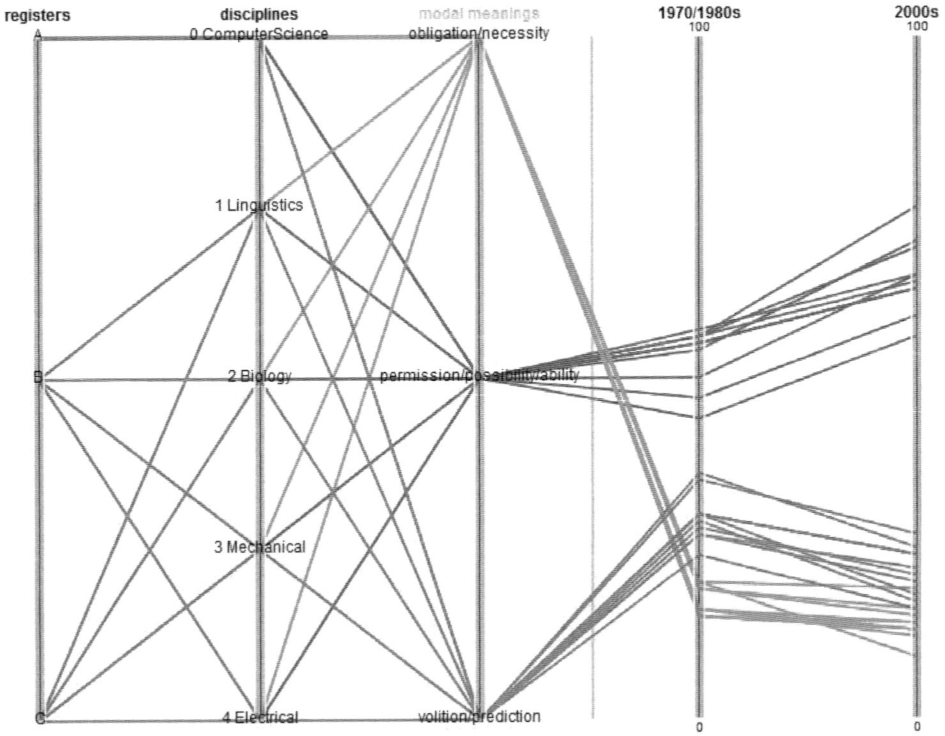

Figure 2: Modal meanings in SciTex in the 1970/80s and 2000s

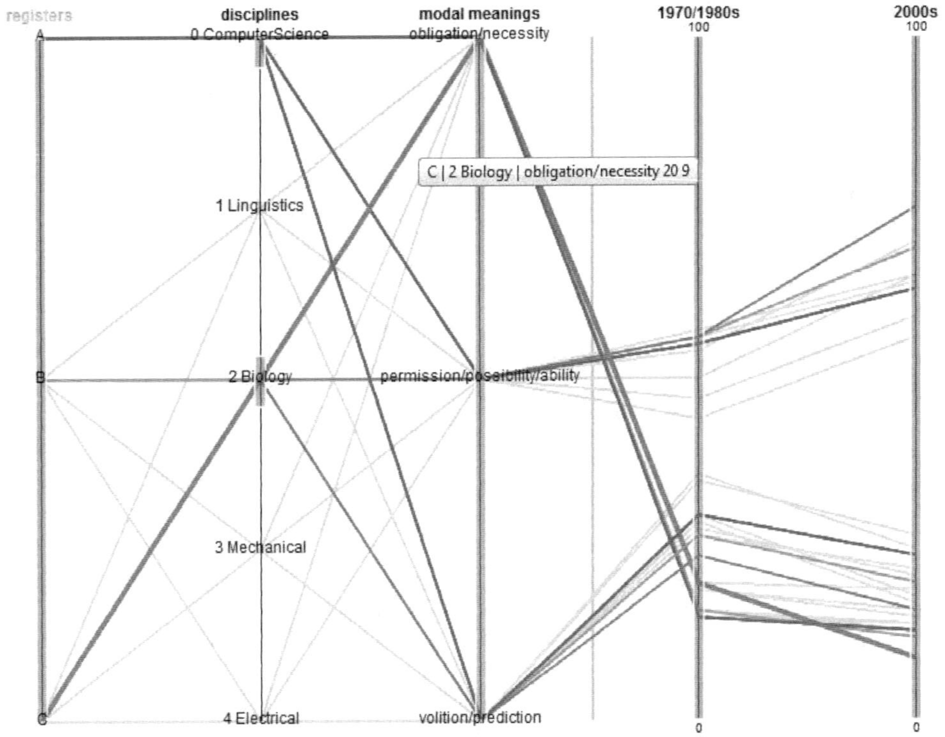

Figure 3: Modal meanings in computer science (A-subcorpus; blue), bioinformatics (from B-subcorpus; orange) and biology (from C-subcorpus; green)

cus, and thus to successively zoom into specific subsets of the data for detailed analyses. In this way, we can determine general tendencies (e.g., increase of *permission* over time) or provide detailed analyses for certain linguistic features and registers by selecting subparts of the data and by highlighting different data dimensions (e.g., comparing changes between different registers).

Future work comprises to use the data obtained from the corpus to feed several different SPC visualisations. For example, the data presented in Figure 2 can also be layed out to place values for registers instead of values for time periods on the numerical axes.

Future analyses will focus on inspecting further tendencies in the feature development for the three contextual variables mentioned in 2.1, e.g., verb valency patterns for *field* or conjunctive relations expressing cohesion for *mode*. We also aim at analysing several linguistic features at the same time to possibly detect feature sets involved in register variation of contact registers. Additionally, a more fine-grained diachronic analysis according to the publication years, which are annotated in the corpus, might also prove to be useful.

From a technical point of view, the issue with fully overlapping lines being displayed in one color only will be tackled by experimenting with semi-transparent or stacked lines. Furthermore, SPC should in the future be expanded by a function for restructuring the underlying data to create different layouts. This could also include the merging of axes with categorical values (e.g., axes *registers* and *disciplines* in Figure 2 above). Furthermore on each data dimension a 'summary' category could be introduced that would represent the sum of all individual values, and would provide an extra point of reference for the analysis. For interactive data analysis, support could be provided to select data items based on crossings or declination of their connecting lines.

References

Douglas Biber. 1995. *Dimensions of Register Variation. A Cross-linguistic Comparison.* Cambridge: Cambridge University Press.

Douglas Biber. 1999. *Longman Grammar of Spoken and Written English.* Harlow: Pearson ESL.

Chris Culy, Verena Lyding, and Henrik Dittmann. 2011. Structured Parallel Coordinates: a visualization for analyzing structured language data. In *Proceedings of the 3rd International Conference on Corpus Linguistics, CILC-11*, April 6-9, 2011, Valencia, Spain, 485–493.

Stefania Degaetano-Ortlieb, Hannah Kermes, Ekaterina Lapshinova-Koltunski and Elke Teich. 2012. SciTex – A Diachronic Corpus for Analyzing the Development of Scientific Registers. In: Paul Bennett, Martin Durrell, Silke Scheible & Richard J. Whitt (eds.), *New Methods in Historical Corpus Linguistics*. CLIP, Vol. 2, Narr: Tübingen.

Stefan Evert. 2005. The CQP Query Language Tutorial. IMS, Universität Stuttgart.

M.A.K. Halliday and Ruqaiya Hasan. 1989. Language, context and text: Aspects of language in a social semiotic perspective. OUP.

Alfred Inselberg. 2009. *Parallel Coordinates: VISUAL Multidimensional Geometry and its Applications.* New York: Springer.

Alfred Inselberg. 1985. The plane with parallel coordinates. *The Visual Computer* 1(2), pp. 69–91.

Hannah Kermes. 2011. Automatic corpus creation. Manual. Institute of Applied Linguistics, Translation and Interpreting, Universität des Saarlandes, Saarbrücken.

Christian Mair. 2006. *Twentieth-Century English: History, Variation and Standardization.* Cambridge: Cambridge University Press.

Maurice d'Ocagne. 1885. *Coordonnées Parallèles et Axiales: Méthode de transformation géométrique et procédé nouveau de calcul graphique déduits de la considération des coordonnées parallèlles.* Paris: Gauthier-Villars.

Randolph Quirk, Sidney Greenbaum, Geoffrey Leech and Jan Svartvik. 1985. *A comprehensive grammar of the English language.* Harlow: Longman

Elke Teich and Peter Fankhauser. 2010. Exploring a corpus of scientific texts using data mining. In: Gries S., S. Wulff and M. Davies (eds), *Corpus-linguistic applications - Current studies, new directions.* Rodopi, Amsterdam and New York, pp. 233–247.

Similarity Patterns in Words

Grzegorz Kondrak
Department of Computing Science
University of Alberta
Edmonton, Alberta, Canada, T6G 2E8
gkondrak@ualberta.ca

Abstract

Words are important both in historical linguistics and natural language processing. They are not indivisible abstract atoms; much can be gained by considering smaller units such as morphemes, phonemes, syllables, and letters. In this presentation, I attempt to sketch the similarity patterns among a number of diverse research projects in which I participated.

1 Introduction

Languages are made up of words, which continuously change their form and meaning. Languages that are related contain cognates — reflexes of proto-words that survive in some form in the daughter languages. Sets of cognates regularly exhibit recurrent sound correspondences. Together, cognates and recurrent sound correspondences provide evidence of a common origin of languages.

Although I consider myself more a computer scientist than a linguist, I am deeply interested in words. Even though many NLP algorithms treat words as indivisible abstract atoms, I think that much can be gained by considering smaller units: morphemes, phonemes, syllables, and letters. Words that are similar at the sub-word level often exhibit similarities on the syntactic and semantic level as well. Even more important, as we move beyond written text towards speech and pronunciation, the make-up of words cannot be ignored anymore.

I commenced my NLP research by investigating ways of developing computer programs for various stages of the language reconstruction process (Kondrak, 2002a). From the very start, I aimed at proposing language-independent solutions grounded in the current advances in NLP, bioinformatics, and computer science in general. The algorithms were evaluated on authentic linguistic data and compared quantitatively to previous proposals. The projects directly related to language histories still form an important part of my research. In Section 2, I refer to several of my publications on the subject, while in Section 3, I focus on other NLP applications contributions that originate from my research on diachronic linguistics.

2 Diachronic NLP

The comparative method is the technique applied by linguists for reconstructing proto-languages. It consists of several stages, which include the identification of cognates by semantic and phonetic similarity, the alignment of cognates, the determination of recurrent sound correspondences, and finally the reconstruction of the proto-forms. The results of later steps are used to refine the judgments made in earlier ones. The comparative method is not an algorithm, but rather a collection of heuristics, which involve intuitive criteria and broad domain knowledge. As such, it is a very time-consuming process that has yet to be accomplished for many language families.

Since the comparative method involves detection of regularities in large amounts of data, it is natural to investigate whether it can be performed by a computer program. In this section, I discuss methods for implementing several steps of the comparative method that are outlined above. The ordering of projects is roughly chronological. For an article-length summary see (Kondrak, 2009).

Proceedings of the EACL 2012 Joint Workshop of LINGVIS & UNCLH, pages 49–53,
Avignon, France, April 23 - 24 2012.

2.1 Alignment

Identification of the corresponding segments in sequences of phonemes is a necessary step in many applications in both diachronic and synchronic phonology. ALINE (Kondrak, 2000) was originally developed for aligning corresponding phonemes in cognate pairs. It combines a dynamic programming alignment algorithm with a scoring scheme based on multi-valued phonetic features. ALINE has been shown to generate more accurate alignments than comparable algorithms (Kondrak, 2003b).

Bhargava and Kondrak (2009) propose a different method of alignment, which is an adaptation of Profile Hidden Markov Models developed for biological sequence analysis. They find that Profile HMMs work well on the tasks of multiple cognate alignment and cognate set matching.

2.2 Phonetic Similarity

In many applications, it is necessary to algorithmically quantify the similarity exhibited by two strings composed of symbols from a finite alphabet. Probably the most well-known measure of string similarity is the edit distance, which is the number of insertions, deletions and substitutions required to transform one string into another. Other measures include the length of the longest common subsequence, and the bigram Dice coefficient. Kondrak (2005b) introduces a notion of n-gram similarity and distance, and shows that edit distance and the length of the longest common subsequence are special cases of n-gram distance and similarity, respectively.

Another class of similarity measures are specifically for phonetic comparison. The ALINE algorithm chooses the optimal alignment on the basis of a similarity score, and therefore can also be used for computing phonetic similarity of words. Kondrak (2001) shows that it performs well on the task of cognate identification.

The above algorithms have the important advantage of not requiring training data, but they cannot adapt to a specific task or language. Researchers have therefore investigated adaptive measures that are learned from a set of training pairs. Mackay and Kondrak (2005) propose a system for computing string similarity based on Pair HMMs. The parameters of the model are automatically learned from training data that consists of pairs of strings that are known to be similar.

Kondrak and Sherif (2006) test representatives of the two principal approaches to computing phonetic similarity on the task of identifying cognates among Indoeuropean languages, both in the supervised and unsupervised context. Their results suggest that given a sufficiently large training set of positive examples, the learning algorithms achieve higher accuracy than manually-designed metrics.

Techniques such as Pair HMMs improve on the baseline approaches by using a set of similar words to re-weight the costs of edit operations or the score of sequence matches. A more flexible approach is to learn from both positive and negative examples of word pairs. Bergsma and Kondrak (2007a) propose such a discriminative algorithm, which achieves exceptional performance on the task of cognate identification.

2.3 Recurrent Sound Correspondences

An important phenomenon that allows us to distinguish between cognates and borrowings or chance resemblances is the regularity of sound change. The regularity principle states that a change in pronunciation applies to sounds in a given phonological context across all words in the language. Regular sound changes tend to produce recurrent sound correspondences of phonemes in corresponding cognates.

Although it may not be immediately apparent, there is a strong similarity between the task of matching phonetic segments in a pair of cognate words, and the task of matching words in two sentences that are mutual translations. The consistency with which a word in one language is translated into a word in another language is mirrored by the consistency of sound correspondences. Kondrak (2002b) proposes to adapt an algorithm for inducing word alignment between words in bitexts (bilingual corpora) to the task of identifying recurrent sound correspondences in word lists. The method is able to determine correspondences with high accuracy in bilingual word lists in which less than a third the word pairs are cognates.

Kondrak (2003a) extends the approach to the identification of complex correspondences that involve groups of phonemes by employing an algorithm designed for extracting non-compositional compounds from bitexts. In experimental evaluation against a set of correspondences manually identified by linguists, it achieves approximately 90% F-score on raw dictionary data.

2.4 Semantic Similarity

Only a fraction of all cognates can be detected by analyzing Swadesh-type word lists, which are usually limited to at most 200 basic meanings. A more challenging task is identifying cognates directly in bilingual dictionaries, which define the meanings of words in the form of glosses. The main problem is how to quantify semantic similarity of two words on the basis of their respective glosses.

Kondrak (2001) proposes to compute similarity of glosses by augmenting simple string-matching with a syntactically-informed keyword extraction. In addition, the concepts mentioned in glosses are mapped to WordNet synsets in an attempt to account for various types of diachronic semantic change, such as generalization, specialization, and synechdoche.

Kondrak (2004) presents a method of combining distinct types of cognation evidence, including the phonetic and semantic similarity, as well as simple and complex recurrent sound correspondences. The method requires no manual parameter tuning, and performs well when tested on cognate identification in the Indoeuropean word lists and Algonquian dictionaries.

2.5 Cognate Sets

When data from several related languages is available, it is preferable to identify cognate sets simultaneously across all languages rather than perform pairwise analysis. Kondrak et al. (2007) apply several of the algorithms described above to a set of diverse dictionaries of languages belonging to the Totonac-Tepehua family in Mexico. They show that by combining expert linguistic knowledge with computational analysis, it is possible to quickly identify a large number of cognate sets within the family, resulting in a basic comparative dictionary. The dictionary subsequently served as a starting point for generating lists of putative cognates between the Totonacan and Mixe-Zoquean families. The project eventually culminated in a proposal for establishing a super-family dubbed Totozoquean (Brown et al., 2011).

Bergsma and Kondrak (2007b) present a method for identifying sets of cognates across groups of languages using the global inference framework of Integer Linear Programming. They show improvements over simple clustering techniques that do not inherently consider the transitivity of cognate relations.

Hauer and Kondrak (2011) present a machine-learning approach that automatically clusters words in multilingual word lists into cognate sets. The method incorporates a number of diverse word similarity measures and features that encode the degree of affinity between pairs of languages.

2.6 Phylogenetic Trees

Phylogenetic methods are used to build evolutionary trees of languages given data that may include lexical, phonological, and morphological information. Such data rarely admits a perfect phylogeny. Enright and Kondrak (2011) explore the use of the more permissive conservative Dollo phylogeny as an alternative approach that produces an output tree minimizing the number of borrowing events directly from the data. The approach which is significantly faster than the more commonly known perfect phylogeny, is shown to produce plausible phylogenetic trees on three different datasets.

3 NLP Applications

In this section, I mention several NLP projects which directly benefitted from insights gained in my research on diachronic linguistics.

Statistical machine translation in its original formulation disregarded the actual forms of words, focusing instead exclusively on their co-occurrence patterns. In contrast, Kondrak et al. (2003) show that automatically identifying orthographically similar words in bitexts can improve the quality of word alignment, which is an important step in statistical machine translation. The improved alignment leads to better translation models, and, consequently, translations of higher quality.

Kondrak (2005a) further investigates **word alignment** in bitexts, focusing on on identifying cognates on the basis of their orthographic similarity. He concludes that word alignment links can be used as a substitute for cognates for the purpose of evaluating word similarity measures.

Many hundreds of drugs have names that either look or sound so much alike that doctors, nurses and pharmacists sometimes get them confused, dispensing the wrong one in errors that may injure or even kill patients. Kondrak and Dorr (2004) apply anumber of similarity measures to the task of identifying **confusable drug names**. They find that a combination of several measures outperforms all individual measures.

Cognate lists can also assist in **second-language learning**, especially in vocabulary expansion and reading comprehension. On the other hand, the learner needs to pay attention to *false friends*, which are pairs of similar-looking words that have different meanings. Inkpen et al. (2005) propose a method to automatically classify pairs of words as cognates or false friends, with focus on French and English. The results show that it is possible to achieve very good accuracy even without any training data by employing orthographic measures of word similarity.

Transliteration is the task of converting words from one writing script to another. Transliteration mining aims at automatically constructing bilingual lists of names for the purpose of training transliteration programs. The task of detecting phonetically-similar words across different writing scripts is quite similar to that of identifying cognates, Sherif and Kondrak (2007) applies several methods, including ALINE, to the task of extracting transliterations from an English-Arabic bitext, and show that it performs better than edit distance, but not as well as a bootstrapping approach to training a memoriless stochastic transducer. Jiampojamarn et al. (2009) employ ALINE for aligning transliterations from distinct scripts by mapping every character to a phoneme that is the most likely to be produced by that character. They observe that even such an imprecise mapping is sufficient for ALINE to produce high quality alignments.

Dwyer and Kondrak (2009) apply the ALINE algorithm to the task of **grapheme-to-phoneme conversion**, which is the process of producing the correct phoneme sequence for a word given its orthographic form. They find ALINE to be an excellent substitute for the expectation-maximization (EM) algorithm when the quantity of the training data is small.

Jiampojamarn and Kondrak (2010) confirm that ALINE is highly accurate on the task of **letter-phoneme alignment**. When evaluated on a manually aligned lexicon, its precision was very close to the theoretical upper bound, with the number of incorrect links less than one in a thousand.

Lastly, ALINE has also been used for the **mapping of annotations**, including syllable breaks and stress marks, from the phonetic to orthographic forms (Bartlett et al., 2008; Dou et al., 2009).

4 Conclusion

The problems involved in language reconstruction are easy to state but surprisingly hard to solve. As such, they lead to the development of new methods and insights that are not restricted in application to historical linguistics. Although the goal of developing a program that performs a fully automatic reconstruction of a proto-language has yet to been attained, the research conducted towards this goal has been, and is likely to continue to influence other areas of NLP.

Acknowledgments

This paper refers to research projects that were conducted jointly with the following colleagues: Susan Bartlett, David Beck, Shane Bergsma, Aditya Bhargava, Cecil Brown, Colin Cherry, Philip Dilts, Bonnie Dorr, Qing Dou, Elan Dresher, Ken Dwyer, Jessica Enright, Oana Frunza, Bradley Hauer, Graeme Hirst, Diana Inkpen, Sittichai Jiampojamarn, Kevin Knight, Wesley Mackay, Daniel Marcu, and Tarek Sherif.

References

Susan Bartlett, Grzegorz Kondrak, and Colin Cherry. 2008. Automatic syllabification with structured SVMs for letter-to-phoneme conversion. In *Proceedings of ACL-08: HLT*, pages 568–576.

Shane Bergsma and Grzegorz Kondrak. 2007a. Alignment-based discriminative string similarity. In *Proceedings of ACL*, pages 656–663.

Shane Bergsma and Grzegorz Kondrak. 2007b. Multilingual cognate identification using integer linear programming. In *Proceedings of the RANLP Workshop on Acquisition and Management of Multilingual Lexicons*, pages 11–18.

Aditya Bhargava and Grzegorz Kondrak. 2009. Multiple word alignment with Profile Hidden Markov Models. In *Proceedings of the Student Research Workshop at NAACL-HLT*, pages 43–48.

Cecil H. Brown, David Beck, Grzegorz Kondrak, James K. Watters, and Søren Wichmann. 2011. Totozoquean. *International Journal of American Linguistics*, 77(3):323–372, July.

Qing Dou, Shane Bergsma, Sittichai Jiampojamarn, and Grzegorz Kondrak. 2009. A ranking approach to stress prediction for letter-to-phoneme conversion. In *Proceedings of ACL-IJCNLP*, pages 118–126.

Kenneth Dwyer and Grzegorz Kondrak. 2009. Reducing the annotation effort for letter-to-phoneme conversion. In *Proceedings of ACL-IJCNLP*, pages 127–135.

Jessica Enright and Grzegorz Kondrak. 2011. The application of chordal graphs to inferring phylogenetic trees of languages. In *Proceedings of IJCNLP 2011: 5th International Joint Conference on Natural Language Processing*, pages 545–552.

Bradley Hauer and Grzegorz Kondrak. 2011. Clustering semantically equivalent words into cognate sets in multilingual lists. In *Proceedings of IJCNLP 2011: 5th International Joint Conference on Natural Language Processing*, pages 865–873.

Diana Inkpen, Oana Frunza, and Grzegorz Kondrak. 2005. Identification of cognates and false friends in french and english. In *Proceedings of the International Conference on Recent Advances in Natural Language Processing (RANLP 2005)*, pages 251–257.

Sittichai Jiampojamarn and Grzegorz Kondrak. 2010. Letter-phoneme alignment: An exploration. In *Proceedings of ACL*, pages 780–788.

Sittichai Jiampojamarn, Aditya Bhargava, Qing Dou, Kenneth Dwyer, and Grzegorz Kondrak. 2009. DirecTL: a language-independent approach to transliteration. In *Named Entities Workshop: Shared Task on Transliteration*, pages 28–31.

Grzegorz Kondrak and Bonnie Dorr. 2004. Identification of confusable drug names: A new approach and evaluation methodology. In *Proceedings of COLING 2004: 20th International Conference on Computational Linguistics*, pages 952–958.

Grzegorz Kondrak and Tarek Sherif. 2006. Evaluation of several phonetic similarity algorithms on the task of cognate identification. In *Proceedings of the COLING-ACL Workshop on Linguistic Distances*, pages 43–50.

Grzegorz Kondrak, Daniel Marcu, and Kevin Knight. 2003. Cognates can improve statistical translation models. In *Proceedings of HLT-NAACL*, pages 46–48. Companion volume.

Grzegorz Kondrak, David Beck, and Philip Dilts. 2007. Creating a comparative dictionary of Totonac-Tepehua. In *Proceedings of the ACL Workshop on Computing and Historical Phonology (9th Meeting of SIGMORPHON)*, pages 134–141.

Grzegorz Kondrak. 2000. A new algorithm for the alignment of phonetic sequences. In *Proceedings of NAACL 2000: 1st Meeting of the North American Chapter of the Association for Computational Linguistics*, pages 288–295.

Grzegorz Kondrak. 2001. Identifying cognates by phonetic and semantic similarity. In *Proceedings of NAACL 2001: 2nd Meeting of the North American Chapter of the Association for Computational Linguistics*, pages 103–110.

Grzegorz Kondrak. 2002a. *Algorithms for Language Reconstruction*. Ph.D. thesis, University of Toronto.

Grzegorz Kondrak. 2002b. Determining recurrent sound correspondences by inducing translation models. In *Proceedings of COLING 2002: 19th International Conference on Computational Linguistics*, pages 488–494.

Grzegorz Kondrak. 2003a. Identifying complex sound correspondences in bilingual wordlists. In *Proceedings of CICLing 2003: 4th International Conference on Computational Linguistics and Intelligent Text Processing*, pages 432–443.

Grzegorz Kondrak. 2003b. Phonetic alignment and similarity. *Computers and the Humanities*, 37(3):273–291.

Grzegorz Kondrak. 2004. Combining evidence in cognate identification. In *Proceedings of Canadian AI 2004: 17th Conference of the Canadian Society for Computational Studies of Intelligence*, pages 44–59.

Grzegorz Kondrak. 2005a. Cognates and word alignment in bitexts. In *Proceedings of MT Summit X: the Tenth Machine Translation Summit*, pages 305–312.

Grzegorz Kondrak. 2005b. N-gram similarity and distance. In *Proceedings of SPIRE: the 12th International Conference on String Processing and Information Retrieval*, pages 115–126.

Grzegorz Kondrak. 2009. Identification of cognates and recurrent sound correspondences in word lists. *Traitement automatique des langues et langues anciennes*, 50(2):201–235, October.

Wesley Mackay and Grzegorz Kondrak. 2005. Computing word similarity and identifying cognates with Pair Hidden Markov Models. In *Proceedings of CoNLL-2005: 9th Conference on Computational Natural Language Learning*, pages 40–47.

Tarek Sherif and Grzegorz Kondrak. 2007. Bootstrapping a stochastic transducer for arabic-english transliteration extraction. In *Proceedings of ACL 2007: 45th Annual Meeting of the Association for Computational Linguistics*, pages 864–871.

Language comparison through sparse multilingual word alignment

Thomas Mayer
Research Unit
Quantitative Language Comparison
LMU Munich
thommy.mayer@googlemail.com

Michael Cysouw
Research Center
Deutscher Sprachatlas
Philipp University of Marburg
cysouw@uni-marburg.de

Abstract

In this paper, we propose a novel approach to compare languages on the basis of parallel texts. Instead of using word lists or abstract grammatical characteristics to infer (phylogenetic) relationships, we use multilingual alignments of words in sentences to establish measures of language similarity. To this end, we introduce a new method to quickly infer a multilingual alignment of words, using the co-occurrence of words in a massively parallel text (MPT) to simultaneously align a large number of languages. The idea is that a simultaneous multilingual alignment yields a more adequate clustering of words across different languages than the successive analysis of bilingual alignments. Since the method is computationally demanding for a larger number of languages, we reformulate the problem using sparse matrix calculations. The usefulness of the approach is tested on an MPT that has been extracted from pamphlets of the Jehova's Witnesses. Our preliminary experiments show that this approach can supplement both the historical and the typological comparison of languages.

1 Introduction

The application of quantitative methods in historical linguistics has attracted a lot of attention in recent years (cf. Steiner et al. (2011) for a survey). Many ideas have been adapted from evolutionary biology and bioinformatics, where similar problems occur with respect to the genealogical grouping of species and the multiple alignment of strings/sequences. One of the main differences between those areas and attempts to uncover language history is the limited amount of suitable data that can serve as the basis for language comparison. A widely used resource are Swadesh lists or similar collections of translational equivalents in the form of word lists. Likewise, phylogenetic methods have been applied using structural characteristics (e.g., Dunn et al. (2005)). In this paper, we propose yet another data source, namely parallel texts.

Many analogies have been drawn between the evolution of species and languages (see, for instance, Pagel (2009) for such a comparison). One of the central problems is to establish what is the equivalent of the gene in the reproduction of languages. Like in evolutionary biology, where gene sequences in organisms are compared to infer phylogenetic trees, a comparison of the "genes" of language would be most appropriate for a quantitative analysis of languages. Yet, Swadesh-like wordlists or structural characteristics do not neatly fit into this scheme as they are most likely not the basis on which languages are replicated. After all, language is passed on as the expression of propositions, i.e. sentences, which usually consists of more than single words. Hence, following Croft (2000), we assume that the basic unit of replication is a linguistic structure embodied in a concrete utterance.

According to this view, strings of DNA in biological evolution correspond to utterances in language evolution. Accordingly, genes (i.e., the functional elements of a string of DNA) correspond to linguistic structures occurring in those utterances. Linguistic replicators (the "genes" of language) are thus structures in the context of an utterance. Such replicators are not only the words as parts of the sentence but also constructions to express a complex semantic structure, or phonetic

Proceedings of the EACL 2012 Joint Workshop of LINGVIS & UNCLH, pages 54–62,
Avignon, France, April 23 - 24 2012.

realizations of a phoneme, to give just a few examples.

In this paper, we want to propose an approach that we consider to be a first step in the direction of using the structure of utterances as the basic unit for the comparison of languages. For this purpose, a multilingual alignment of words in parallel sentences (as the equivalent of utterances in parallel texts) is computed, similar to multi-species alignments of DNA sequences.[1] These alignments are clusters of words from different languages in the parallel translations of the same sentence.[2]

The remainder of the paper is organized as follows. First, we quickly review the position of our approach in relation to the large body of work on parallel text analysis (Section 2). Then we describe the method for the multilingual alignment of words (Section 3). Since the number of languages and sentences that have to be analyzed require a lot of computationally expensive calculations of co-occurrence counts, the whole analysis is reformulated into manipulations of sparse matrices. The various steps are presented in detail to give a better overview of the calculations that are needed to infer the similarities. Subsequently, we give a short description of the material that we used in order to test our method (Section 4). In Section 5 we report on some of the experiments that we carried out, followed by a discussion of the results and their implications. Finally, we conclude with directions for future work in this area.

2 Word Alignment

Alignment of words using parallel texts has been widely applied in the field of statistical machine translation (cf. Koehn (2010)). Alignment methods have largely been employed for bitexts, i.e., parallel texts of two languages (Tiedemann, 2011). In a multilingual context, the same methods could in principle be used for each pair of languages in the sample. One of the goals of this paper, however, is to investigate what can be gained when including additional languages in the alignment process at the same time and not iteratively looking for correspondences in pairs of languages (see Simard (1999), Simard (2000) for a similar approach).

There are basically two approaches to computing word alignments as discussed in the literature (cf. Och and Ney (2003)): (i) statistical alignment models and (ii) heuristic models. The former have traditionally been used for the training of parameters in statistical machine translation and are characterized by their high complexity, which makes them difficult to implement and tune. The latter are considerably simpler and thus easier to implement as they only require a function for the association of words, which is computed from their co-occurrence counts. A wide variety of co-occurrence measures have been employed in the literature. We decided to use a heuristic method for the first steps reported on here, but plan to integrate statistical alignment models for future work.

Using a global co-occurrence measure, we pursue an approach in which the words are compared for each sentence individually, but for all languages at the same time. That is, a co-occurrence matrix is created for each sentence, containing all the words of all languages that occur in the corresponding translational equivalents for that sentence. This matrix then serves as the input for a partitioning algorithm whose results are interpreted as a partial alignment of the sentence. In most cases, the resulting alignments do not include words from all languages. Only those words that are close translational equivalents occur in alignments. This behavior, while not optimal for machine translation, is highly useful for language comparison because differences between languages are implicitly marked as such by splitting different structures into separate alignments.

The languages are then compared on the basis of having words in the same clusters with other languages. The more word forms they share in the same clusters, the more similar the languages are considered to be.[3] The form of the words themselves is thereby of no importance. What counts

[1] The choice of translational equivalents in the form of sentences rather than words accounts for the fact that some words cannot be translated accurately between some languages whereas most sentences can.

[2] In practice, we simply use wordforms as separated by spaces or punctuation instead of any more linguistically sensible notion of 'word'. For better performance, more detailed language-specific analysis is necessary, like morpheme separation, or the recognition of multi-word expressions and phrase structures.

[3] A related approach is discussed in Wälchli (2011). The biggest difference to the present approach is that Wälchli only compares languages pairwise. In addition, he makes use of a global glossing method and not an alignment of words within the same parallel sentence.

is their frequency of co-occurrence in alignments across languages. This is in stark contrast to methods which focus on the form of words with similar meanings (e.g., using Swadesh lists) in order to compute some kind of language similarity. One major disadvantage of the present approach for a comparison of languages from a historical perspective is the fact that such similarities also could be a consequence of language contact. This is a side effect that is shared by the word list approach, in which loanwords have a similar effect on the results. It has to be seen how strongly this influences the final results in order to assess whether our current approach is useful for the quantitative analysis of genealogical relatedness.

3 Method

We start from a massively parallel text, which we consider as an $n \times m$ matrix consisting of n different parallel sentences $S = \{S_1, S_2, S_3, ..., S_n\}$ in m different languages $L = \{L_1, L_2, L_3, ..., L_m\}$. This data-matrix is called $\mathbf{SL}$ ('sentences $\times$ languages'). We assume here that the parallel sentences are short enough so that most words occur only once per sentence. Because of this assumption we can ignore the problem of decoding the correct alignment of multiple occurring words, a problem we leave to be tackled in future research. We also ignore the complications of language-specific chunking and simply take spaces and punctuation marks to provide a word-based separation of the sentences into parts. In future research we are planning to include the (language-specific) recognition of bound morphemes, multi-word expressions and phrase structures to allow for more precise cross-language alignment.

Based on these assumptions, we decompose the $\mathbf{SL}$ matrix into two sparse matrices $\mathbf{WS}$ ('words $\times$ sentences') and $\mathbf{WL}$ ('words $\times$ languages') based on all words w that occur across all languages in the parallel texts. We define them as follows. First, $\mathbf{WS}_{ij} = 1$ when word w_i occurs in sentence S_j, and is 0 elsewhere. Second, $\mathbf{WL}_{ij} = 1$ when word w_i is a word of language L_j, and is 0 elsewhere. The product $\mathbf{WS^T} \cdot \mathbf{WL}$ then results in a matrix of the same size as $\mathbf{SL}$, listing in each cell the number of different words in each sentence. Instead of the current approach of using $\mathbf{WS}$ only for marking the occurrence of a word in a sentence (i.e., a 'bag of words' approach), it is also possible to include the order of words in the sentences by defining $\mathbf{WS}_{ij} = k$ when word w_i occurs in position k in sentence S_j. We will not use this extension in this paper.

The matrix $\mathbf{WS}$ will be used to compute co-occurrence statistics of all pairs of words, both within and across languages. Basically, we define $\mathbf{O}$ ('observed co-occurrences') and $\mathbf{E}$ ('expected co-occurrences') as:

$$\mathbf{O} = \mathbf{WS} \cdot \mathbf{WS^T}$$

$$\mathbf{E} = \mathbf{WS} \cdot \frac{\mathbf{1_{SS}}}{n} \cdot \mathbf{WS^T}$$

$\mathbf{E}_{ij}$ thereby gives the expected number of sentences where w_i and w_j occur in the corresponding translational equivalents, on the assumption that words from different languages are statistically independent of each other and occur at random in the translational equivalents. Note that the symbol '$\mathbf{1_{ab}}$' in our matrix multiplications refers to a matrix of size $a \times b$ consisting of only 1's. Widespread co-occurrence measures are pointwise mutual information, which under these definitions simply is $\log \mathbf{E} - \log \mathbf{O}$, or the cosine similarity, which would be $\frac{\mathbf{O}}{\sqrt{\mathbf{n \cdot E}}}$. However, we assume that the co-occurrence of words follow a poisson process (Quasthoff and Wolff, 2002), which leads us to define the co-occurrence matrix $\mathbf{WW}$ ('words $\times$ words') using a poisson distribution as:

$$\mathbf{WW} = -\log[\frac{\mathbf{E^O} \exp(-\mathbf{E})}{\mathbf{O}!}]$$

$$= \mathbf{E} + \log \mathbf{O}! - \mathbf{O} \log \mathbf{E}$$

This $\mathbf{WW}$ matrix represents a similarity matrix of words based on their co-occurrence in translational equivalents for the respective language pair. Using the alignment clustering that is based on the $\mathbf{WW}$ matrices for each sentence, we then decompose the words-by-sentences matrix $\mathbf{WS}$ into two sparse matrices $\mathbf{WA}$ ('words $\times$ alignments') and $\mathbf{AS}$ ('alignments $\times$ sentences') such that $\mathbf{WS} = \mathbf{WA} \cdot \mathbf{AS}$. This decomposition is the basic innovation of the current paper.

The idea is to compute concrete alignments from the statistical alignments in $\mathbf{WW}$ for each sentence separately, but for all languages at the same time. For each sentence S_i we take the subset of the similarity matrix $\mathbf{WW}$ only including those words that occur in the column $\mathbf{WS_i}$, i.e., only those words that occur in sentence S_i. We then perform a partitioning on this subset of the similarity matrix $\mathbf{WW}$. In this paper we use the affinity propagation clustering approach from Frey and Dueck (2007) to identify the clusters, but this is mainly a practical choice and other methods could be used here as well. The reason for this choice is that this clustering does not require a pre-defined number of clusters, but establishes the optimal number of clusters together with the clustering itself.[4] In addition, it yields an exemplar for each cluster, which is the most typical member of the cluster. This enables an inspection of intermediate results of what the clusters actually contain. The resulting clustering for each sentence identifies groups of words that are similar to each other, which represent words that are to be aligned across languages. Note that we do not force such clusters to include words from all languages, nor do we force any restrictions on the number of words per language in each cluster.[5] In practice, most alignments only include words from a small number of the languages included.

To give a concrete example for the clustering results, consider the English sentence given below (no. 93 in our corpus, see next section) together with its translational equivalents in German, Bulgarian, Spanish, Maltese and Ewe (without punctuation and capitalization).

i. who will rule with jesus (English, en)
ii. wer wird mit jesus regieren (German, de)
iii. кой ще управлява с исус (Bulgarian, bl)
iv. quiénes gobernarán con jesús (Spanish, es)
v. min se jaħkem ma ġesù (Maltese, mt)
vi. amekawoe aɖu fia kple yesu (Ewe, ew)

These six languages are only a subset of the 50 languages that served as input for the matrix $\mathbf{WW}$ where all words that occur in the respective sentence for all 50 languages are listed together with their co-occurrence significance. When restricting the output of the clustering to those words that occur in the six languages given above, however, the following clustering result is obtained:

1. исус$_{\text{bl}}$ jesus$_{\text{en}}$ fia$_{\text{ew}}$ yesu$_{\text{ew}}$ ġesù$_{\text{mt}}$ jesús$_{\text{es}}$ jesus$_{\text{de}}$
2. кой$_{\text{bl}}$ who$_{\text{en}}$ min$_{\text{mt}}$ wer$_{\text{de}}$
3. regieren$_{\text{de}}$
4. управлява$_{\text{bl}}$ aɖu$_{\text{ew}}$ jaħkem$_{\text{mt}}$ gobernarán$_{\text{es}}$
5. amekawoe$_{\text{ew}}$ quiénes$_{\text{es}}$
6. ще$_{\text{bl}}$ will$_{\text{en}}$ se$_{\text{mt}}$wird$_{\text{de}}$
7. с$_{\text{bl}}$ with$_{\text{en}}$ con$_{\text{es}}$ mit$_{\text{de}}$
8. kple$_{\text{ew}}$
9. ma$_{\text{mt}}$
10. rule$_{\text{en}}$

First note that the algorithm does not require all languages to be given in the same script. Bulgarian исус is grouped together with its translational equivalents in cluster 1 even though it does not share any grapheme with them. Rather, words from different languages end up in the same cluster if they behave similarly across languages in terms of their co-occurrence frequency. Further, note that the "question word" clusters 2 and 5 differ in their behavior as will be discussed in more detail in Section 5.2. Also note that the English "rule" and German "regieren" are not included in the cluster 4 with similar translations in the other languages. This turns out to be a side effect of the very low frequency of these words in the current corpus.

In the following, we will refer to these clusters of words as alignments (many-to-many mappings between words) within the same sentence across languages. For instance, sentences i., iii. and v. above would have the following alignment, where indices mark those words that are aligned by the alignment clusters (1.-10.) above:

who$_2$ will$_6$ rule$_{10}$ with$_7$ jesus$_1$
min$_2$ se$_6$ jaħkem$_4$ ma$_7$ ġesù$_1$
кой$_2$ ще$_6$ управлява$_4$ с$_7$ исус$_1$

All alignment-clusters from all sentences are summarized as columns in the sparse matrix $\mathbf{WA}$, defined as $\mathbf{WA}_{ij} = 1$ when word w_i is part of alignment A_j, and is 0 elsewhere.[6] We also establish the 'book-keeping' matrix $\mathbf{AS}$ to keep track

[4] Instead of a prespecified number of clusters, affinity propagation in fact takes a real number as input for each data point where data points with larger values are more likely to be chosen as exemplars. If no input preference is given for each data point, as we did in our experiments, exemplar preferences are initialized as the median of non infinity values in the input matrix.

[5] Again, this takes into account that some words cannot be translated accurately between some languages.

[6] For instance, the alignment in 2. above contains the four words {кой, who, min, wer}, which are thus marked with 1 whereas all other words have 0 in this column of the $\mathbf{WA}$ matrix.

of which alignment belongs to which sentence, defined as $\mathbf{AS}_{ij} = 1$ when the alignment A_i occurs in sentence S_j, and as 0 elsewhere. The alignment matrix $\mathbf{WA}$ is the basic information to be used for language comparison. For example, the product $\mathbf{WA} \cdot \mathbf{WA}^{\mathbf{T}}$ represents a sparse version of the words $\times$ words similarity matrix $\mathbf{WW}$.

A more interesting usage of $\mathbf{WA}$ is to derive a similarity between the alignments $\mathbf{AA}$. We define both a sparse version of $\mathbf{AA}$, based on the number of words that co-occur in a pair of alignments, and a statistical version of $\mathbf{AA}$, based on the average similarity between the words in the two alignments:

$$\mathbf{AA}_{sparse} = \mathbf{WA}^{\mathbf{T}} \cdot \mathbf{WA}$$

$$\mathbf{AA}_{statistical} = \frac{\mathbf{WA}^{\mathbf{T}} \cdot \mathbf{WW} \cdot \mathbf{WA}}{\mathbf{WA}^{\mathbf{T}} \cdot \mathbf{1}_{\mathbf{WW}} \cdot \mathbf{WA}}$$

The $\mathbf{AA}$ matrices will be used to select suitable alignments from the parallel texts to be used for language comparison. Basically, the statistical $\mathbf{AA}$ will be used to identify similar alignments within a single sentence and the sparse $\mathbf{AA}$ will be used to identify similar alignments across different sentences. Using a suitable selection of alignments (we here use the notation $\mathbf{A}'$ for a selection of alignments[7]), a similarity between languages $\mathbf{LL}$ can be defined as:

$$\mathbf{LL} = \mathbf{LA}' \cdot \mathbf{LA}'^{\mathbf{T}}$$

by defining $\mathbf{LA}'$ ('languages $\times$ alignments') as the number of words per language that occur in each selected alignment:

$$\mathbf{LA}' = \mathbf{WL}^{\mathbf{T}} \cdot \mathbf{WA}'$$

The similarity between two languages $\mathbf{LL}$ is then basically defined as the number of times words are attested in the selected alignments for both languages. It thus gives an overview of how structurally similar two languages are, where languages are considered to have a more similar structure the more words they share in the alignment clusters.

[7]Note that the prime in this case does not stand for the transpose of a matrix, as it is sometimes used.

4 Data

Parallel corpora have received a lot of attention since the advent of statistical machine translation (Brown et al., 1988) where they serve as training material for the underlying alignment models. For this reason, the last two decades have seen an increasing interest in the collection of parallel corpora for a number of language pairs (Hansard[8]), also including text corpora which contain texts in three or more languages (OPUS[9], Europarl[10], Multext-East[11]). Yet there are only few resources which comprise texts for which translations are available into many different languages. Such texts are here referred to as 'massively parallel texts' (MPT; cf. Cysouw and Wälchli (2007)). The most well-known MPT is the Bible, which has a long tradition in being used as the basis for language comparison. Apart from that, other religious texts are also available online and can be used as MPTs. One of them is a collection of pamphlets of the Jehova's Witnesses, some of which are available for over 250 languages.

In order to test our methods on a variety of languages, we collected a number of pamphlets from the Watchtower website `http://www.watchtower.org`) together with their translational equivalents for 146 languages in total. The texts needed some preprocessing to remove HTML markup, and they were aligned with respect to the paragraphs according to the HTML markup. We extracted all paragraphs which consisted of only one sentence in the English version and contained exactly one English question word (*how, who, where, what, why, whom, whose, when, which*) and a question mark at the end. From these we manually excluded all sentences where the "question word" is used with a different function (e.g., where *who* is a relative pronoun rather than a question word). In the end we were left with 252 questions in the English version and the corresponding sentences in the 145 other languages. Note that an English interrogative sentence is not necessarily translated as a question in each other language (e.g., the English question *what is the truth about God?* is simply translated into German as *die Wahrheit über Gott* 'the truth

[8]`http://www.isi.edu/natural-language/download/hansard/`

[9]`http://opus.lingfil.uu.se`

[10]`http://www.statmt.org/europarl/`

[11]`http://nl.ijs.si/ME/`

about God'). However, such translations appear to be exceptions.

5 Experiments

5.1 Global comparison of Indo-European

As a first step to show that our method yields promising results we ran the method for the 27 Indo-European languages in our sample in order to see what kind of global language similarity arises when using the present approach. In our procedure, each sentence is separated into various multilingual alignments. Because the structures of languages are different, not each alignment will span across all languages. Most alignments will be 'sparse', i.e., they will only include words from a subset of all languages included. In total, we obtained $6,660$ alignments (i.e., 26.4 alignments per sentence on average), with each alignment including on average 9.36 words. The number of alignments per sentence turns out to be linearly related to the average number of words per sentence, as shown in Fig. 1. A linear interpolation results in a slope of 2.85, i.e., there are about three times as many alignments per sentence as the average number of words. We expect that this slope depends on the number of languages that are included in the analysis: the more languages, the steeper the slope.

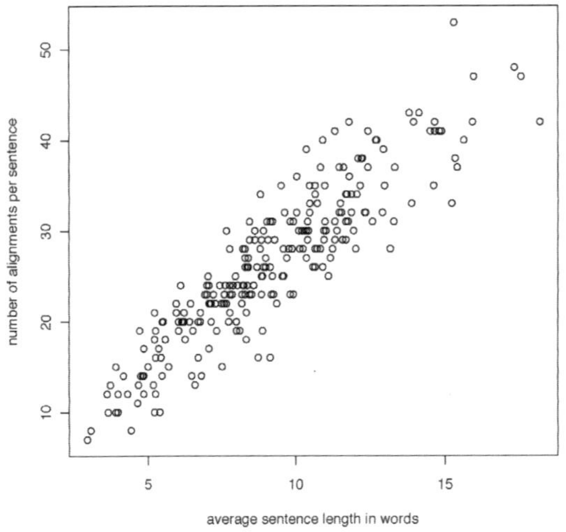

Figure 1: Linear relation between the average number of words per sentence and number of alignments per sentence

We use the **LL** matrix as the similarity matrix for languages including all $6,660$ alignments. For each language pair this matrix contains the number of times words from both languages are attested in the same alignment. This similarity matrix is converted into a distance matrix by subtracting the similarity value from the highest value that occurs in the matrix:

$$\mathbf{LL}_{dist} = max(\mathbf{LL}) - \mathbf{LL}$$

This distance matrix $\mathbf{LL_{dist}}$ is transformed into a NeighborNet visualization for an inspection of the structures that are latent in the distance matrix. The NeighborNet in Fig. 2 reveals an approximate grouping of languages according to the major language families, the Germanic family on the right, the Romance family on the top and the Slavic family at the bottom. Note that the sole Celtic language in our sample, Welsh, is included inside the Germanic languages, closest to English. This might be caused by horizontal influence from English on Welsh. Further, the only Baltic language in our sample, Lithuanian, is grouped with the Slavic languages (which is phylogenetically expected behavior in line with Gray and Atkinson (2003)), though note that it is grouped particularly close to Russian and Polish, which suggests more recent horizontal transfer. Interestingly, the separate languages Albanian and Greek roughly group together with two languages from the other families: Romanian (Romance) and Bulgarian (Slavic). This result is not in line with their phylogenetic relatedness but rather reflects a contact situation in which all four languages are part of the Balkan Sprachbund.

Although the NeighborNet visualization exhibits certain outcomes that do not correspond to the attested genealogical relationship of the languages, the method still fares pretty well based on a visual inspection of the resulting NeighborNet. In the divergent cases, the groupings can be explained by the fact that the languages are influenced by the surrounding languages (as is most clear for the Balkan languages) through direct language contact. As mentioned before, a similar problem also exists when using word lists to infer phylogenetic trees when loanwords introduce noise into the calculations and thus lead to a closer relationship of languages than is genealogically tenable. However, in the case of our alignments

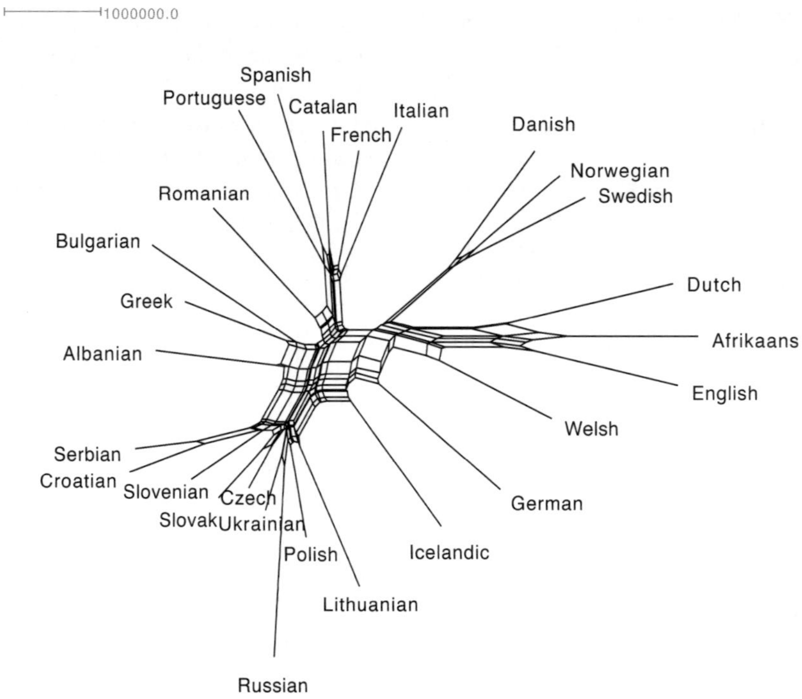

Figure 2: NeighborNet (created with SplitsTree, Huson and Bryant (2006)) of all Indo-European languages in the sample

the influence of language contact is not related to loanwords but to the borrowing of similar constructions or structural features. In the Balkan case, linguists have noted over one hundred such shared structural features, among them the loss of the infinitive, syncretism of dative and genitive case and postposed articles (cf. Joseph (1992) and references therein). These features are particularly prone to lead to a higher similarity in our approach where the alignment of words within sentences is sensitive to the fact that certain word forms are identical or different even though the exact form of the word is not relevant.

5.2 Typology of PERSON interrogatives

A second experiment we conducted involved a closer study of just a few questions in the data at hand to obtain a better impression of the results of the alignment procedure. For this experiment, we took the same 252 questions for a worldwide sample of 50 languages. After running the whole procedure, we selected just the six sentences in the sample that were formulated in English with a *who* interrogative, i.e., questions as to the person who did something. The English sentences are the following:

I Who will be resurrected?
II Who will rule with Jesus?
III Who created all living things?
IV Who are god's true worshipers on earth today?
V Who is Jesus Christ?
VI Who is Michael the Archangel?

We expected to be able to find all translations of English *who* in the alignments. Interestingly, this is not what happened. The six alignments that comprised the English *who* only included words in 23 to 30 other languages in the sample, so we are clearly not finding all translations of *who*. By using a clustering on $\mathbf{AA}_{statistical}$ we were able to find seven more alignments that appear to be highly similar to the six alignments including English *who*. Together, these 13 alignments included words for almost all languages in the six sentences (on average 47.7 words for each sentence). We computed a language similarity $\mathbf{LL}$ only on the basis of these 13 alignments, which represents a typology of the structure of PERSON interrogatives. This typology clearly separates into two clusters of languages, two 'types' so to speak, as can be seen in Fig. 3.

Investigating the reason for these two types, it turns out that the languages in the right cluster of Fig. 3 consistently separate the six sentences into two groups. The first, second, and fourth sentence are differently marked than the third, fifth and sixth sentence. For example, Finnish uses *ketkä* vs. *kuka* and Spanish *quiénes* vs. *quién*. These are both oppositions in number, suggesting that all languages in the right cluster of Fig. 3 distinguish between a singular and a plural form of *who*. Interpreting the meaning of the English sentences quoted above, this distinction makes complete sense. The Ewe form *amekawoe* in example *vi.* (see Section 3) contains the plural marker *-wo*, which distinguishes it from the singular form and indeed correctly clusters together with *quiénes* in the alignment cluster 5.

This example shows that it is possible to use parallel texts to derive a typology of languages for a highly specific characteristic.

6 Conclusion and Future Work

One major problem with using our approach for phylogentic reconstruction is the influence of language contact. Traits of the languages which are not inherited from a common proto-language but are transmitted through contact situations lead to noise in the similarity matrix which does not reflect a genealogical signal. However, other methods also suffer from the shortcoming that language contact cannot be automatically subtracted from the comparison of languages without manual input (such as manually created cognate lists). With translational equivalents, a further problem for the present approach is the influence of translationese on the results. If one version in a language is a direct translation of another language, the structural similarity might get a higher score due to the fact that constructions will be literally translated which otherwise would be expressed differently in that language.

The experiments that have been presented in this paper are only a first step. However, we firmly believe that a multilingual alignment of words is more appropriate for a large-scale comparison of languages than an iterative bilingual alignment. Yet so far we do not have the appropriate evaluation method to prove this. We therefore plan to include a validation scheme in order to test how much can be gained from the simultaneous analysis of more than two languages. Apart from this, we intend to improve the alignment method itself by integrating techniques from statistical alignment models, like adding morpheme separation or phrase structures into the analysis.

Another central problem for the further development of this method is the selection of alignments for the language comparison. As our second experiment showed, just starting from a selection of English words will not automatically generate the corresponding words in the other languages. It is possible to use the **AA** matrices to search for further similar alignments, but this procedure is not yet formalized enough to automatically produce language classification for selected linguistic domains (like for the PERSON interrogatives in our experiment). When this step is better understood, we will be able to automatically generate typological parameters for a large number of the world's languages, and thus easily produce more data on which to base future language comparison.

Acknowledgements

This work has been funded by the DFG project "Algorithmic corpus-based approaches to typological comparison". We are grateful to four anonymous reviewers for their valuable comments and suggestions.

References

Peter F. Brown, John Cocke, Stephen A. Della-Pietra, Vincent J. Della-Pietra, Frederick Jelinek, Robert L. Mercer, and Paul S. Roossin. 1988. A statistical approach to language translation. In *Proceedings of the 12th International Conference on Computational Linguistics (COLING-88)*, pages 71–76.

William Croft. 2000. *Explaining Language Change: An Evolutionary Approach*. Harlow: Longman.

Michael Cysouw and Bernhard Wälchli. 2007. Parallel texts: using translational equivalents in linguistic typology. *Sprachtypologie und Universalienforschung STUF*, 60(2):95–99.

Michael Dunn, Angela Terrill, Ger Reesink, R. A. Foley, and Steve C. Levinson. 2005. Structural phylogenetics and the reconstruction of ancient language history. *Science*, 309(5743):2072–5, 9.

Brendan J. Frey and Delbert Dueck. 2007. Clustering by passing messages between data points. *Science*, 315:972–976.

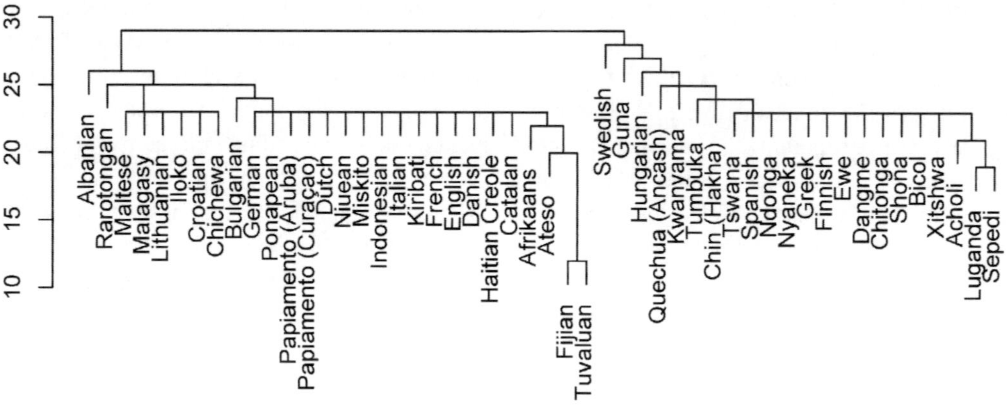

Figure 3: Hierarchical cluster using Ward's minimum variance method (created with R, R Development Core Team (2010)) depicting a typology of languages according to the structure of their PERSON interrogatives

Russell D. Gray and Quentin D. Atkinson. 2003. Language-tree divergence times support the Anatolian theory of Indo-European origin. *Nature*, 426:435–439.

Daniel H. Huson and David Bryant. 2006. Application of phylogenetic networks in evolutionary studies. *Molecular Biology and Evolution*, 23(2):254–267.

Brian D. Joseph. 1992. The Balkan languages. In William Bright, editor, *International Encyclopedia of Linguistics*, pages 153–155. Oxford: Oxford University Press.

Philipp Koehn. 2010. *Statistical Machine Translation*. Cambridge University Press.

Franz Josef Och and Hermann Ney. 2003. A systematic comparison of various statistical alignment models. *Computational Linguistics*, 29(1):19–51.

Mark Pagel. 2009. Human language as a culturally transmitted replicator. *Nature Reviews Genetics*, 10:405–415.

Uwe Quasthoff and Christian Wolff. 2002. The poisson collocation measure and its applications. In *Proceedings of the 2nd International Workshop on Computational Approaches to Collocations*, Vienna, Austria.

R Development Core Team, 2010. *R: A language and environment for statistical computing*. Wien: R Foundation for Statistical Computing.

Michel Simard. 1999. Text-translation alignment: Three languages are better than two. In *Proceedings of EMNLP/VLC-99*, pages 2–11.

Michel Simard. 2000. Text-translation alignment: Aligning three or more versions of a text. In Jean Véronis, editor, *Parallel Text Processing: Alignment and Use of Translation Corpora*, pages 49–67. Dordrecht: Kluwer Academic Publishers.

Lydia Steiner, Peter F. Stadler, and Michael Cysouw. 2011. A pipeline for computational historical linguistics. *Language Dynamics and Change*, 1(1):89–127.

Jörg Tiedemann. 2011. *Bitext Alignment*. Morgan & Claypool Publishers.

Bernhard Wälchli. 2011. Quantifying inner form: A study in morphosemantics. Arbeitspapiere. Bern: Institut für Sprachwissenschaft.

Recovering dialect geography from an unaligned comparable corpus

Yves Scherrer
LATL
Université de Genève
Geneva, Switzerland
yves.scherrer@unige.ch

Abstract

This paper proposes a simple metric of dialect distance, based on the ratio between identical word pairs and cognate word pairs occurring in two texts. Different variations of this metric are tested on a corpus containing comparable texts from different Swiss German dialects and evaluated on the basis of spatial autocorrelation measures. The visualization of the results as cluster dendrograms shows that closely related dialects are reliably clustered together, while multidimensional scaling produces graphs that show high agreement with the geographic localization of the original texts.

1 Introduction

In the last few decades, dialectometry has emerged as a field of linguistics that investigates the application of statistical and mathematical methods in dialect research. Also called quantitative dialectology, one of its purposes is to discover the regional distribution of dialect similarities from aggregated data, such as those collected in dialectological surveys.

The work presented here aims to apply dialectometric analysis and visualization techniques to a different type of raw data. We argue that classical dialectological survey data are word-aligned by design, whereas our data set, a comparable multidialectal corpus, has to be word-aligned by automatic algorithms.

We proceed in two steps. First, we present a cognate identification algorithm that allows us to extract cognate word pairs from the corpus. Then, we measure how many of these cognate word pairs are identical. This ratio gives us a measure of dialectal distance between two texts that is then shown to correlate well with geographic distance. The visualization of the resulting data allows us to recover certain characteristics of the Swiss German dialect landscape.

The paper is structured as follows. In Section 2, the multidialectal corpus is presented. We then discuss how this corpus differs from classical dialectological data, and how we can use techniques from machine translation to extract the relevant data (Section 3). In Section 4, we define dialect distance as a function of the number of cognate word pairs and identical word pairs. Both types of word pairs are in turn defined by different thresholds of normalized Levenshtein distance. Section 5 deals with the evaluation and visualization of the resulting data, the latter in terms of clustering and multi-dimensional scaling. We discuss the results and conclude in Section 6.

2 Data: the Archimob corpus

The Archimob corpus used in our experiments is a corpus of transcribed speech, containing texts from multiple Swiss German dialects.

The Archimob project was started in 1998 as an oral history project with the aim of gathering and archiving the people's memory of the Second World War period in Switzerland.[1] 555 surviving witnesses were interviewed in all Swiss language regions. The interviews of the German-speaking witnesses were conducted in their local dialect.

With the goal of obtaining spontaneous dialect data to complement ongoing work on dialect syntax (Bucheli and Glaser, 2002; Friedli, 2006; Steiner, 2006), researchers at the Univer-

[1] Archimob stands for "Archives de la mobilisation"; see www.archimob.ch.

Proceedings of the EACL 2012 Joint Workshop of LINGVIS & UNCLH, pages 63–71,
Avignon, France, April 23 - 24 2012.

BE1142:	*de vatter ìsch lokomitiiffüerer gsìì / de ìsch dispensiert gsìì vom dienscht nattürlech / und / zwo schwöschtere / hani ghaa / wobii ei gsch / eini gschtoorben ìsch u di ander ìsch ìsch ime autersheim / u soo bini ufgwachse ir lenggass / mit em / pruefsleer / mit wiiterbiudig nächheer / (?)*
Translation:	the father has been a train driver / he has been dispensed from military service of course / and / two sisters / I have had / where one / one has died and the other is is in a home for the elderly / this is how I have grown up in the Lenggass / with a / apprenticeship / with further education afterwards / (?)

ZH1270:	*min vatter isch / eh eeh / schlosser hät er gleert / und und isch aber dän schofföör woorde dur en verwante wo bim S. z züri / gschafft hät und dè hät gsait / chum tue doch umsattle bim S. vediensch mee / und dän hät dèè schofföör gleert und das isch doozmaal ja na eener en sältene pruef gsii / dän hät dè das gleert und ich bin schtolz gsii das min / vatter en / pruef ghaa hät wo französischsch töönt hät oder schofföör / ich han gfunde das seig en waansinige pruef*
Translation:	my father has / eh eeh / been a locksmith apprentice / and and has then become a driver through a relative who has worked at S. in Zurich and he said / come and switch jobs, at S. you earn more / and then he was a driver apprentice and this was rather a rare job at that time / so he learned that and I was proud that my / father / had a job which sounded French, you know, *chauffeur* / I found that this was an extraordinary job

Figure 1: Excerpts of two informants' turns in the Archimob corpus. The excerpts contain identical cognate pairs like ⟨*vatter, vatter*⟩, and non-identical cognate pairs like ⟨*ìsch, isch*⟩.

sity of Zurich selected a subset of the Swiss German Archimob interviews and transcribed them.[2] The selection process ensured that only interviews from non-mobile speakers (speakers that have not spent long periods of their life outside of their native town) were retained, and that the most important dialect areas of German-speaking Switzerland were represented.

As a result, 16 interviews were selected for transcription, amounting to 26 hours of speech. All texts were anonymized. In order to ensure consistency, all texts were transcribed by the same person.

The interviews were transcribed using the spelling system of Dieth (1986). This is an orthographic transcription system which intends to be as phonetically transparent as possible, while remaining readable for readers accustomed to Standard German orthography (see Figure 1 for two examples). For instance, the Dieth guidelines distinguish *ì* (IPA [ɪ]) from *i* (IPA [i]), while Standard German spelling only uses *i*.

In our experiments, we discarded the interviewer's questions and only used the witnesses' turns. The whole corpus contains 183 000 words, with individual interviews ranging from 6 500 to 16 700 words. Excerpts of two interviews are shown in Figure 1. The place of residence of the witness was given in the corpus metadata.

It should be stressed that our data set is very small in comparison with other studies in the field: it contains 16 data points (texts) from 15 different locations. Moreover, some dialect areas are not represented in the sample (e.g. Graubünden in the South-East and Fribourg in the West).[3] Therefore, the goal of the present study cannot be to induce a precise dialect landscape of German-speaking Switzerland. Rather, we aim to find out if geographically close texts can be shown to be linguistically close, and if the most important dialectal divisions of German-speaking Switzerland are reflected in the classification of the texts.

3 Corpora and word alignment

3.1 Comparable corpora

The machine translation community generally distinguishes between parallel and comparable corpora (McEnery and Xiao, 2008). A *parallel corpus* consists of a source text and its translations into other languages. Hence, the different language versions share the same content and the same order of paragraphs and sentences. On the other hand, such corpora have been criticized for containing "translationese", i.e., wording which

[2]The corpus is not yet publicly available, awaiting the completion of further annotation layers.

[3]For an overview of the geographic distribution of the texts, see Figure 3.

is influenced by the grammatical and informational structure of the source text and which is not necessarily representative of the target language. In contrast, a *comparable corpus* is a collection of original texts of different languages that share similar form and content (typically, same genre, same domain and same time period).

The Archimob corpus can be qualified as comparable: all texts deal with the same subject and the same time period (life in Switzerland at the outbreak of the Second World War), and they are collected in the same way, in the form of oral interviews guided by an interviewer.

3.2 Word alignment in dialectology

Dialectological analyses rely on word-aligned data. Traditionally, dialectological data are collected in surveys with the help of questionnaires. A typical question usually intends to elicit the local words or pronunciations of a given concept. The mere fact that two responses are linked to the same question number of the questionnaire suffices to guarantee that they refer to the same concept. This property leads us to consider dialectological survey data as *word-aligned by design*.

In contrast, the Archimob corpus is not aligned. Again, algorithms for aligning words in parallel and comparable corpora have been proposed in the field of machine translation. For large parallel corpora, distributional alignment methods based solely on cooccurrence statistics are sufficient (Och and Ney, 2003; Koehn et al., 2007). For comparable corpora, the order and frequency of occurrence of the words cannot be used as alignment cues. Instead, the phonetic and orthographic structures are used to match similar word pairs (Simard et al., 1992; Koehn and Knight, 2002; Kondrak and Sherif, 2006). Obviously, this approach only works for cognate word pairs – word pairs with a common etymology and similar surface forms. This task is known as *cognate identification*.

In the next section, we detail how cognate identification is used to compute the distance between different dialect versions of a comparable corpus.

4 Computing the linguistic similarity of two comparable texts

The hypothesis put forward in this paper is that the linguistic similarity of two comparable texts can be approximated by the degree of similarity of the cognate word pairs occurring in the texts. Computing the similarity of two texts amounts to the following two tasks:

1. Given two texts, extract the set of word pairs that are considered cognates. This corresponds to the *cognate identification* task presented above.

2. Given a set of cognate word pairs, determine the proportion of word pairs that are considered identical.

The underlying intuition is that identically pronounced cognate words account for evidence that the two dialects are closely related, whereas differently pronounced cognate words are evidence that the two dialects are distant. Word pairs that are not cognates are not relevant for our similarity measure.

Let us illustrate the idea with an example:

(1) *es schtòòt nìd*

(2) *wil si nìd schtoot*

Intuitively, two cognate word pairs can be found in the texts (1) and (2): ⟨*schtòòt*, *schtoot*⟩ and ⟨*nìd*, *nìd*⟩.[4] The words *es*, *wil*, *si* do not have cognate equivalents in the other text. As a result, the two texts have a similarity of $\frac{1}{2}$, one of the two cognate pairs consisting of identical words.

In the example above, we have assumed informal meanings of *cognate word pair* and *identical word pair*. In the following sections, we define these concepts more precisely.

4.1 Identifying cognate word pairs

Most recently proposed cognate identification algorithms are based on variants of Levenshtein distance, or string edit distance (Levenshtein, 1966; Heeringa et al., 2006; Kondrak and Sherif, 2006). Levenshtein distance is defined as the smallest number of insertion, deletion and substitution operations required to transform one string into another.

(3)

b	i	i	s	c	h	p	i	i	u
b	i		s	c	h	p	i		l
0	0	1	0	0	0	0	0	1	1

[4]Accented and unaccented characters are considered as different. See footnote 5.

Example (3) shows two words and the associated operation costs. There are two deletion operations and one substitution operation, hence Levenshtein distance between *biischpiiu* and *bischpil* is 3.[5]

Among other proposals, Heeringa et al. (2006) suggest normalizing Levenshtein distance by the length of the alignment. The underlying idea is that a Levenshtein distance of 2 for two long words does not mean the same as a Levenshtein distance of 2 for two very short words. In example (3), the length of the alignment is 10 (in this case, it is equal to the length of the longer word). Normalized Levenshtein distance is $\frac{3}{10} = 0.3$.

A cognate identification algorithm based on normalized Levenshtein distance requires a threshold such that only those word pairs whose distance is below the threshold are considered cognates. In order to identify sensible values for this threshold, we classified all word pairs of the corpus according to their distance. We evaluated nine thresholds between 0.05 and 0.4 to see if they effectively discriminate cognate pairs from non-cognate pairs. The evaluation was done on the basis of 100 randomly selected word pairs with a normalized Levenshtein distance lower or equal than the respective threshold.

In this evaluation, we distinguish between *form cognates* – words that represent the same inflected forms of the same lemma –, and *lemma cognates* – words that represent different inflected forms of the same lemma. Example (4) is a form cognate pair: it shows two dialectally different realizations of the singular form of the Standard German lemma *Gemeinde* 'municipality'. Example (5) is only a lemma cognate pair: one of the word contains the plural ending *-e*, while the other word is a singular form.

(4) gmeind — gmaind

(5) gmeind — gmainde

Table 1 shows the results of this evaluation. As the distance threshold increases, the proportion of cognates drops while the proportion of non-cognates rises. With thresholds higher than 0.25, the number of non-cognates surpasses the number of cognates. We therefore expect the cognate detection algorithm to work best below this threshold.

Let us conclude this section by some additional remarks about the evaluation:

- The distinction between form cognates and lemma cognates cannot be easily operationalized with an automatic approach. For instance, the correspondance *u* – *ü* may be a phonological one and distinguish two identical forms of different dialects. But it may also be a morphological correspondence that distinguishes singular from plural forms independently of the dialect. In the following experiments, we treat both types of cognate pairs in the same way.

- In practice, the reported figures are measures of precision. Recall may be estimated by the number of cognates situated above a given threshold. While we have not evaluated the entire distance interval, the given figures suggest that many true cognates are indeed found at high distance levels. This issue may be addressed by improving the string distance metric.

- Ambiguous words were not disambiguated according to the syntactic context and the dialect. As a result, all identical word pairs (threshold 0.00) are considered form cognates, although some of them may be false friends.

4.2 Identifying identical words

In common understanding, an *identical word pair* is a pair of words whose Levenshtein distance is 0. In some of the following experiments, we adopt this assumption.

However, we found it useful to relax this definition in order to avoid minor inconsistencies in the transcription and to neglect the smallest dialect differences. Therefore, we also carried out experiments where identical word pairs were defined as having a normalized Levenshtein distance of 0.10 or lower.

4.3 Experiments

Recall that we propose to measure the linguistic similarity of two texts by the ratio of identical word pairs among the cognate word pairs.

[5]Note that we treat all characters in the same way: replacing *o* by *k* yields the same cost as replacing it by *u* or by *ò*. This simple approach may not be the optimal solution when dealing with similar dialects. This issue will be addressed in future work.

Distance threshold	Word pairs	Form cognates	Lemma cognates	All cognates	Non-cognates	Non-words
0.00	5230	100%	0%	100%	0%	0%
0.05	5244	98%	0%	98%	0%	2%
0.10	6611	94%	4%	98%	1%	1%
0.15	10674	79%	16%	95%	4%	1%
0.20	18582	55%	16%	71%	29%	0%
0.25	27383	48%	13%	61%	38%	1%
0.30	36002	40%	12%	52%	47%	1%
0.35	49011	29%	10%	39%	61%	0%
0.40	65955	20%	13%	33%	67%	0%

Table 1: Manual evaluation of the cognate identification task. Percentages are based on a random sample of 100 word pairs with a normalized Levenshtein distance below or equal to the given threshold. Form cognate and lemma cognate counts are summed up in the 'All cognates' column. The interviewees sometimes made false starts and stopped in the middle of the word; these incomplete words, together with obvious typing errors in the transcription, are counted in the last column.

Cognate pairs as well as identical word pairs are characterized by different thresholds of normalized Levenshtein distance. We experiment with thresholds of 0.20, 0.25, 0.30, 0.35 and 0.40 for cognate word pairs, and with thresholds of 0 and 0.10 for identical word pairs.

4.4 Normalization by text length

A major issue of using comparable corpora is the large variation in text length and vocabulary use. This has to be accounted for in our experiments. First, all counts refer to types of word pairs, not tokens. We argue that the frequency of a word in a given text depends too much on the content of the text and is not truly representative of its dialect. Second, if few identical words are found, this does not necessarily mean that the two texts are dialectally distant, but may also be because one text is much shorter than the other. Hence, the proportion of identical words is normalized by the number of cognate words contained in the shorter of the two texts.

5 Evaluation and visualisation

By computing the linguistic distance for all pairs of texts in our corpus, we obtain a two-dimensional distance matrix. Recent dialectometric tradition provides several techniques to evaluate and visualize the data encoded in this matrix.

First, one can measure how well the linguistic distances correlate with geographic distances (Section 5.1). Second, one can group the texts into maximally homogeneous clusters (Section 5.2). Third, one can plot the texts as data points on a two-dimensional graph and visually compare this graph with the geographical locations of the texts (Section 5.3).

5.1 Numerical measures of spatial autocorrelation

A general postulate of spatial analysis is that "on average, values at points close together in space are more likely to be similar than points further apart" (Burrough and McDonnell, 1998, 100). This idea that the distance of attribute values correlates with their geographical distance is known as *spatial autocorrelation*. The same idea has been coined the *fundamental dialectological postulate* by Nerbonne and Kleiweg (2005, 10): "Geographically proximate varieties tend to be more similar than distant ones."

Here, we use this postulate to evaluate the different threshold combinations of our dialect similarity measure: the higher a threshold combination correlates with geographic distance (i.e., places of residence of the interviewees), the better it is able to discriminate the dialects. Here, the results obtained with two correlation measures are reported.

Local incoherence has been proposed by Nerbonne and Kleiweg (2005). The idea of this measure is that the correlation between linguistic and geographic distances is local and does not need to hold over larger geographical distances. In practice, for every data point, the 8 linguistically most similar points[6] are inspected according to their linguistic distance value. Then, the geographic distance of these pairs of points is measured and summed up. This means that high incoherence values represent poor measurements, while lower values stand for better results.

The **Mantel-Test** (Sokal and Rohlf, 1995, 813-819) is a general statistical test which applies to data expressed as dissimilarities. It is often used in evolutionary biology and ecology, for example, to correlate genetic distances of animal populations with the geographic distances of their range. The Mantel coefficient Z is computed by computing the Hadamard product of the two matrices. The statistical significance of this coefficient is obtained by a randomization test. A sample of permutations is created, whereby the elements of one matrix are randomly rearranged. The correlation level depends on the proportion of samples whose Z-value is higher than the Z-value of the reference matrix. All experiments were carried out with a sample size of 999 permutations, which corresponds to a simulated p-value of 0.001.

Table 2 shows the results of both correlation measures for all experiments. These results are in line with the manual evaluation of Table 1. At first, increasing the cognate pair threshold leads to more data, and in consequence, to better results. Above 0.35 however, the added data is essentially noise (i.e., non-cognate pairs), and the results drop again.

According to local incoherence, the best threshold combination is $\langle 0.10, 0.35\rangle$. In terms of Mantel test correlation, the $\langle 0.10, 0.25\rangle$ threshold performs slightly better. Adopting an identical pair threshold of 0.00 results in slightly inferior correlations.

5.2 Clustering

The distance matrix can also be used as input to a clustering algorithm. Clustering has become one of the major data analysis techniques in dialectometry (Mucha and Haimerl, 2005), but has also been used with plain text data in order to improve information retrieval (Yoo and Hu, 2006).

Hierarchical clustering results in a *dendrogram* which represents the distances between every two data points as a tree. However, clustering is known to be unreliable: small changes in the distance matrix may result in completely different dendrograms. To counter this issue, *noisy clustering* has been proposed (Nerbonne et al., 2008): clustering is repeated 100 times, and at each run, random amounts of noise are added to the different cells of the distance matrix. This gives an indication of the reliability of the resulting clusters. Figure 2 shows a dendrogram obtained with noisy clustering. We used both group average and weighted average clustering algorithms, and a noise level of 0.2.[7] Figure 3 localizes the data points on a geographical map. All clusters show a reliability score of 92% or above.

Distance thresholds		Local	Mantel Test	
Identical	Cognate	inc.	r	p
0.00	0.20	0.59	0.56	0.001
	0.25	0.47	0.68	0.001
	0.30	0.49	0.66	0.001
	0.35	**0.41**	**0.70**	0.001
	0.40	0.46	0.65	0.001
0.10	0.20	0.55	0.65	0.001
	0.25	0.41	**0.73**	0.001
	0.30	0.43	0.70	0.001
	0.35	**0.37**	0.72	0.001
	0.40	0.43	0.67	0.001

Table 2: Correlation values for the different experiments. The first and second columns define each experiment in terms of two Levenshtein distance thresholds. For local incoherence, lower values are better. For the Mantel test figures, we report the correlation coefficient r as well as the significance level p.

Clustering allows us to recover certain characteristics of the Swiss German dialect landscape. First, texts from the same canton (whose IDs contain the same two-letter abreviation) are grouped together with high reliability. Second, the dendrogram shows – albeit with lower reliability scores – a three-fold East-West stratification with blue regions in the West (BE), green regions in Central Switzerland (AG, LU) and yellow areas in the East (ZH, SZ, GL). The border between Western and Central dialects roughly corresponds to the so-called Brünig-Napf line. The border between Central and Eastern varieties is also confirmed by former dialectological research (Haas, 1982; Hotzenköcherle, 1984). Third, three dialects are

[6]The restriction to 8 points is the key of the local component of this measure. The exact value of this parameter has been determined empirically by the authors of the measure.

[7]These are the default settings of the Gabmap program (Nerbonne et al., 2011).

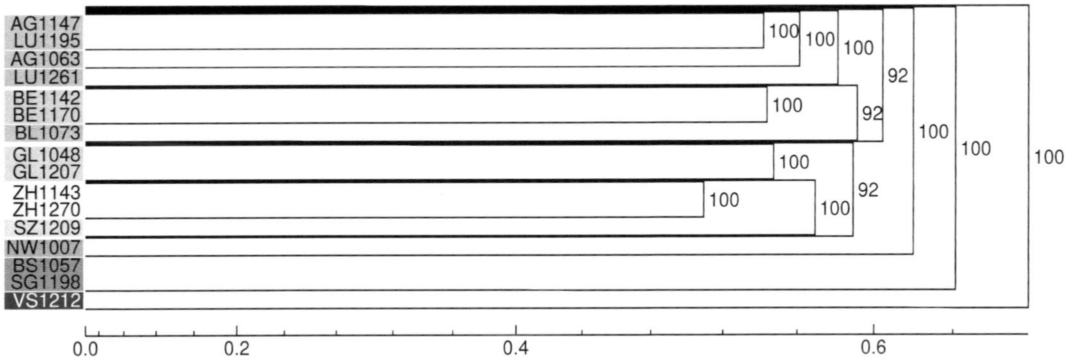

Figure 2: Dendrogram obtained with a threshold setting of $\langle 0.10, 0.35 \rangle$. The scale at the bottom of the graphics represents the distance of the clusters, while the numbers on the vertical lines represent the reliability of the clusters (i.e. in how many of the 100 runs a cluster has been found).

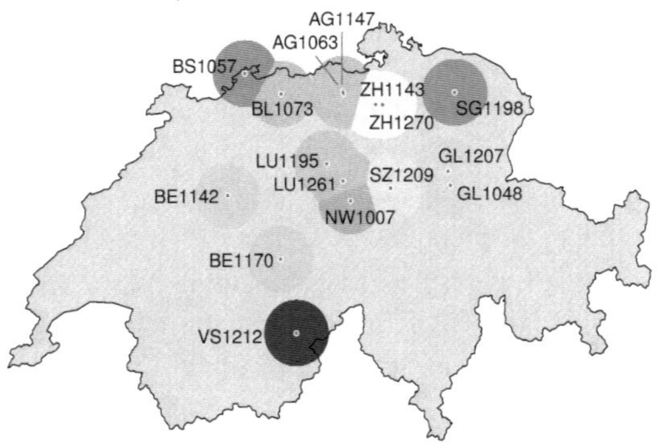

Figure 3: Geographic localization of the Archimob texts, according to the place of residence of the interviewed persons. The colors represent the linguistic distance between texts; they correspond to the colors used in the dendrogram of Figure 2.

clearly considered as outliers: the Northwestern dialect of Basel (BS1057), the Northeastern dialect of St. Gallen (SG1198), and most of all the Southwestern Wallis dialect (VS1212). Again, these observations are in line with common dialectological knowledge.

5.3 Multidimensional scaling

The Swiss German dialect landscape has been known to feature major East-West divisions (see above) as well as several levels of stratification on the North-South axis. Our hypothesis is that the linguistic distances represented in the distance matrix should be able to recover this mainly two-dimensional organization of Swiss German dialects. Since the distance matrix defines a multidimensional space in which all data points (texts) are placed, this space has to be reduced to two dimensions. For this purpose, we use multidimensional scaling. If the linguistic distances are correctly defined and the multidimensional scaling algorithm truly extracts the two main dimensions of variation, the resulting two-dimensional graph should be comparable with a geographic map.

Figure 4 shows the resulting graph for one experiment. Figures 5 and 6 show the values of each data point in grey levels for the two first dimensions obtained by multi-dimensional scaling.

One observes that the localization of data points in Figure 4 closely corresponds to their geographic location (as illustrated in Figure 3): the major North-South divisions as well as some East-West divisions are clearly recovered.

More surprisingly, the two main dimensions of multidimensional scaling correspond to diagonals in geographic terms. The first dimension (Figure 5) allows to distinguish Northwestern from Southeastern variants, while the second dimension (Figure 6) distinguishes Northeastern from Southwestern variants. Instead of +-shaped dialect divisions put forward by traditional dialectology, our approach rather finds X-shaped dialect divisions.

6 Discussion and future work

We have proposed a simple measure that approximates the linguistic distance between two texts according to the ratio of identical words among the cognate word pairs. The definitions of *identical word pair* and *cognate word pair* are operationalized with fixed thresholds of normalized

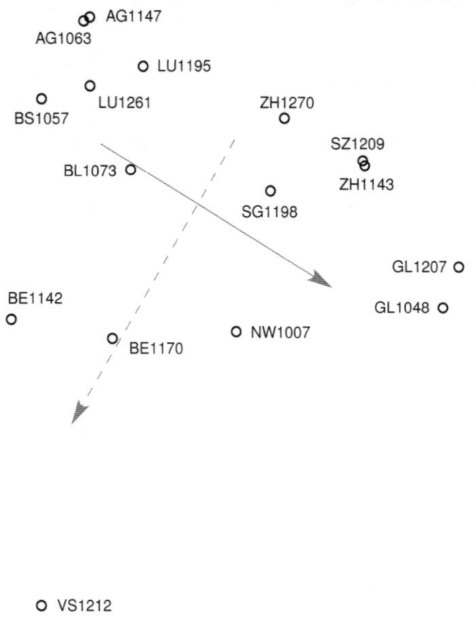

Figure 4: Plot representing the first two dimensions of multi-dimensional scaling applied to the experiment with $\langle 0.10, 0.35 \rangle$ thresholds.

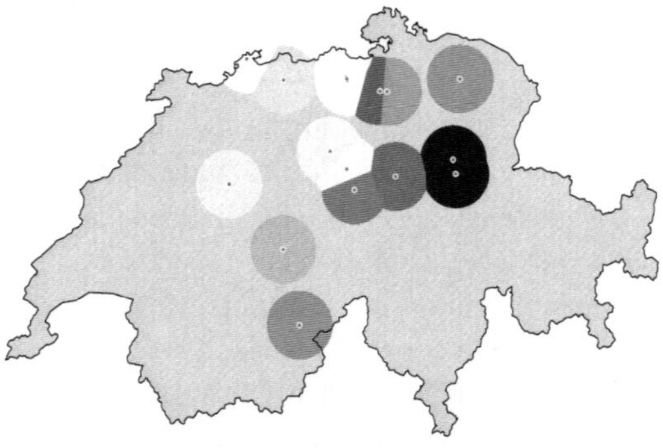

Figure 5: Map representing the first dimension of multi-dimensional scaling (same experiment as Fig. 4).

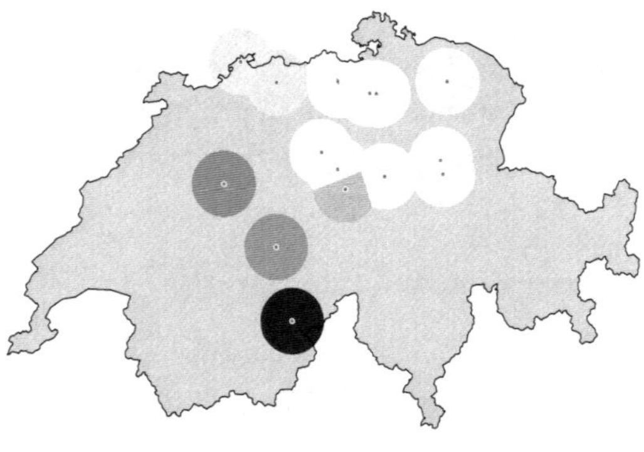

Figure 6: Map representing the second dimension of multi-dimensional scaling (same experiment as Fig. 4).

Levenshtein distance. The resulting distance matrix has been analyzed with correlation measures, and visualized with clustering and multidimensional scaling techniques. The visualizations represent the main characteristics of the Swiss German dialect landscape in a surprisingly faithful way.

The close relation obtained among texts from the same canton may suggest that the distance measure is biased towards proper nouns. For example, two Zurich German texts are more likely to use toponyms from the Zurich region than a Bernese German text. If there are many of these (likely identically pronounced) toponyms, the similarity value will increase. However, manual inspection of the relevant texts did not show such an effect. Region-specific toponyms are rare.

The results suggest that a more fine-grained variant of Levenshtein distance might be useful. In the following paragraphs, we present several improvements for future work.

The results suggest that a more fine-grained variant of Levenshtein distance might improve the precision and recall of the cognate detection algorithm. Notably, it has been found that vowels change more readily than consonant in closely related language varieties. In consequence, changing one vowel by another should be penalized less than changing a vowel by a consonant (Mann and Yarowsky, 2001). The same holds for accented vs. non-accented characters. Complex graphemes representing a single phoneme appear rather frequently in the Dieth transcription system (e.g. for long vowels) and should also be treated separately.

We should also mention that the proposed method likely faces a problem of scale. Indeed, each word of each text has to be compared with each word of each text. This is only manageable with a small corpus like ours.

We conclude by pointing out a limitation of this approach: the automatic alignment process based on the concept of cognate pairs obviously only works for phonetically related word pairs. This contrasts with other dialectometric approaches based on lexical differences, in whose data sets different lemmas have been aligned. Future work on the Archimob corpus shall add normalization and lemmatization layers. This information could be useful to improve word alignment beyond cognate pairs.

Acknowledgments

The author wishes to thank Prof. Elvira Glaser, Alexandra Bünzli, Anne Göhring and Agnes Kolmer (University of Zurich) for granting access to the Archimob corpus and giving detailed information about its constitution. Furthermore, the anonymous reviewers are thanked for most helpful remarks.

References

Claudia Bucheli and Elvira Glaser. 2002. The syntactic atlas of Swiss German dialects: empirical and methodological problems. In Sjef Barbiers, Leonie Cornips, and Susanne van der Kleij, editors, *Syntactic Microvariation*, volume II. Meertens Institute Electronic Publications in Linguistics, Amsterdam.

Peter A. Burrough and Rachael A. McDonnell. 1998. *Principles of Geographical Information Systems*. Oxford University Press, Oxford.

Eugen Dieth. 1986. *Schwyzertütschi Dialäktschrift*. Sauerländer, Aarau, 2nd edition.

Matthias Friedli. 2006. Der Komparativanschluss im Schweizerdeutschen – ein raumbildendes Phänomen. In Hubert Klausmann, editor, *Raumstrukturen im Alemannischen*, pages 103–108. Neugebauer, Graz/Feldkirch.

Walter Haas, 1982. *Die deutschsprachige Schweiz*, pages 71–160. Benziger, Zürich.

Wilbert Heeringa, Peter Kleiweg, Charlotte Gooskens, and John Nerbonne. 2006. Evaluation of string distance algorithms for dialectology. In *Proceedings of the ACL 2006 Workshop on Linguistic Distances*, pages 51–62, Sydney, Australia.

Rudolf Hotzenköcherle. 1984. *Die Sprachlandschaften der deutschen Schweiz*. Sauerländer, Aarau.

Philipp Koehn and Kevin Knight. 2002. Learning a translation lexicon from monolingual corpora. In *Proceedings of the ACL 2002 Workshop on Unsupervised Lexical Acquisition (SIGLEX 2002)*, pages 9–16, Philadelphia, PA.

Philipp Koehn, Hieu Hoang, Alexandra Birch, Chris Callison-Burch, Marcello Federico, Nicola Bertoldi, Brooke Cowan, Wade Shen, Christine Moran, Richard Zens, Chris Dyer, Ondrej Bojar, Alexandra Constantin, and Evan Herbst. 2007. Moses: Open source toolkit for statistical machine translation. In *Proceedings of the ACL 2007 demonstration session*, Prague, Czech Republic.

Grzegorz Kondrak and Tarek Sherif. 2006. Evaluation of several phonetic similarity algorithms on the task of cognate identification. In *Proceedings of the ACL 2006 Workshop on Linguistic Distances*, pages 43–50, Sydney, Australia.

Vladimir I. Levenshtein. 1966. Binary codes capable of correcting deletions, insertions, and reversals. *Soviet Physics Doklady*, 10(8):707–710.

Gideon S. Mann and David Yarowsky. 2001. Multipath translation lexicon induction via bridge languages. In *Proceedings of NAACL 2001*, Pittsburgh, PA, USA.

Tony McEnery and Richard Xiao. 2008. Parallel and comparable corpora: What is happening? In Gunilla Anderman and Margaret Rogers, editors, *Incorporating Corpora: The Linguist and the Translator*, chapter 2, pages 18–31. Multilingual Matters, Clevedon.

Hans-Joachim Mucha and Edgar Haimerl. 2005. Automatic validation of hierarchical cluster analysis with application in dialectometry. In C. Weihs and W. Gaul, editors, *Classification – the Ubiquitous Challenge*, pages 513–520. Springer, Berlin.

John Nerbonne and Peter Kleiweg. 2005. Toward a dialectological yardstick. *Journal of Quantitative Linguistics*, 5.

John Nerbonne, Peter Kleiweg, Wilbert Heeringa, and Franz Manni. 2008. Projecting dialect differences to geography: Bootstrap clustering vs. noisy clustering. In Christine Preisach, Lars Schmidt-Thieme, Hans Burkhardt, and Reinhold Decker, editors, *Data Analysis, Machine Learning, and Applications. Proceedings of the 31st Annual Meeting of the German Classification Society*, pages 647–654. Springer, Berlin.

John Nerbonne, Rinke Colen, Charlotte Gooskens, Peter Kleiweg, and Therese Leinonen. 2011. Gabmap – a web application for dialectology. *Dialectologia, Special Issue*, II:65–89.

Franz Josef Och and Hermann Ney. 2003. A systematic comparison of various statistical alignment models. *Computational Linguistics*, 29(1):19–51.

Michel Simard, George F. Foster, and Pierre Isabelle. 1992. Using cognates to align sentences in bilingual corpora. In *Proceedings of the Fourth International Conference on Theoretical and Methodological Issues in Machine Translation (TMI 1992)*, pages 67–81, Montréal, Canada.

Robert R. Sokal and F. James Rohlf. 1995. *Biometry: the principles and practice of statistics in biological research*. W.H. Freeman, New York, 3rd edition.

Janine Steiner. 2006. Syntaktische Variation in der Nominalphrase – ein Fall für die Dialektgeographin oder den Soziolinguisten? In Hubert Klausmann, editor, *Raumstrukturen im Alemannischen*, pages 109–115. Neugebauer, Graz/Feldkirch.

Illhoi Yoo and Xiaohua Hu. 2006. A comprehensive comparison study of document clustering for a biomedical digital library MEDLINE. In *Proceedings of the 6th ACM/IEEE-CS joint conference on Digital libraries*, JCDL '06, pages 220–229, Chapel Hill, NC, USA.

Detecting Shibboleths

Jelena Prokić
Ludwig-Maximilians-Universität
j.prokic@lmu.de

Çağrı Çöltekin
University of Groningen
c.coltekin@rug.nl

John Nerbonne
University of Groningen
j.nerbonne@rug.nl

Abstract

A SHIBBOLETH is a pronunciation, or, more generally, a variant of speech that betrays where a speaker is from (*Judges* 12:6). We propose a generalization of the well-known precision and recall scores to deal with the case of detecting distinctive, characteristic variants when the analysis is based on numerical difference scores. We also compare our proposal to Fisher's linear discriminant, and we demonstrate its effectiveness on Dutch and German dialect data. It is a general method that can be applied both in synchronic and diachronic linguistics that involve automatic classification of linguistic entities.

1 Introduction and Background

The background of this contribution is the line of work known as DIALECTOMETRY (Séguy, 1973; Goebl, 1982), which has made computational work popular in dialectology. The basic idea of dialectometry is simple: one acquires large samples of corresponding material (e.g., a list of lexical choices, such as the word for carbonated soft drink, which might be 'soda', 'pop', 'tonic' etc.) from different sites within a language area, and then, for each pair of samples, one counts (or more generally measures) the difference at each point of correspondence. The differences are summed, and, given representative and sufficiently large samples, the results characterizes the degree to which one site differs from another.

Earlier work in dialectology mapped the distributions of individual items, recording lines of division on maps, so-called ISOGLOSSES, and then sought bundles of these as tell-tale indicators of important divisions between DIALECT AREAS. But as Chambers & Trudgill (1998) note, the earlier methodology is fraught with problems, many of which stem from the freedom of choice with respect to isoglosses, and their (normal) failure to 'bundle' neatly. Nerbonne (2009) notes that dialectometry improves on the traditional techniques in many ways, most of which stem from the fact that it shifts focus to AGGREGATE LEVEL of differences. Dialectometry uses large amounts of material; it reduces the subjectivity inherent in choosing isoglosses; it frequently analyzes material in ways unintended by those who designed dialect data collection efforts, including more sources of differences; and finally it replaces search for categorical overlap by a statistical analysis of differences.

Dialectometry does not enjoy overwhelming popularity in dialectology, however, and one of the reasons is simply that dialectologists, but also laymen, are interested not only in the aggregate relations among sites, or even the determination of dialect areas (or the structure of other geographic influence on language variation, such as dialect continua), but are quite enamored of the details involved. Dialectology scholars, but also laymen, wish to now where 'coffee' is ordered (in English) with a labialized /k/ sound ([k^{w}ɔfi]) or where in Germany one is likely to hear [p] and where [p͡f] in words such as *Pfad* 'path' or *Pfund* 'pound'.

Such characteristic features are known as SHIBBOLETHS, following a famous story in the old testament where people were killed because of where they were from, which was betrayed by their inability to pronounce the initial [ʃ] in the word 'shibboleth' (*Judges* 12:6). We propose a generalization of the well-known precision and

Proceedings of the EACL 2012 Joint Workshop of LINGVIS & UNCLH, pages 72–80,
Avignon, France, April 23 - 24 2012. ©2012 Association for Computational Linguistics

recall scores, appropriate when dealing with distances, and which are designed to detect distinctive, characteristic variants when the analysis is based on numerical difference scores. We also compare our proposal to Fisher's linear discriminant, and we demonstrate its effectiveness on Dutch and German dialect data. Finally we evaluate the success of the proposal by visually examining an MDS plot showing the distances one obtains when the analysis is restricted to the features determined to be characteristic.

The paper proceeds from a dialectometric perspective, but the technique proposed does not assume an aggregate analysis, only that a group of sites has been identified somehow or another. The task is then to identify characteristic features of (candidate) dialect areas.

1.1 Related Work

Wieling and Nerbonne (2011) introduced two measures seeking to identify elements characteristic of a given group, REPRESENTATIVENESS and DISTINCTIVENESS. The intuition behind representativeness is simply that a feature increases in representativeness to the degree that it is found at each site in the group. We simplify their definition slightly as they focus on sound correspondences, i.e. categorical variables, while we shall formulate ideas about features in general.

$$\text{Representativeness}(f, g) = \frac{|g^f|}{|g|}$$

where f is a feature (in their case sound correspondence) in question, g is the set of sites in a given cluster, and g^f denotes the set of sites where feature f is observed.

As Wieling (2012) notes, if one construes the sites in the given group as 'relevant documents' and features as 'queries', then this definition is equivalent to RECALL in information retrieval (IR).

The intuition behind distinctiveness is similar to that behind IR's PRECISION, which measures the fraction of positive query responses that identify relevant documents. In our case this would be the fraction of those sites instantiating a feature that are indeed in the group we seek to characterize. In the case of groups of sites in dialectological analysis, however, we are dealing with groups that may make up significant fractions of the entire set of sites. Wieling and Nerbonne therefore introduced a correction for 'chance instantiation'. This is derived from the relative size of the group in question:

$$\begin{aligned}
\text{RelSize}(g) &= \frac{|g|}{|G|} \\
\text{RelOcc}(f, g) &= \frac{|g^f|}{|G^f|} \\
\text{Distinct}(f, g) &= \frac{\text{RelOcc}(f,g) - \text{RelSize}(g)}{1 - \text{RelSize}(g)}
\end{aligned}$$

where, G is the set of sites in the larger area of interest.

As a consequence, smaller clusters are given larger scores than clusters that contain many objects. Distinctiveness may even fall below zero, but these will be very uninteresting cases — those which occur relatively more frequently outside the group under consideration than within it.

Critique

There are two major problems with the earlier formulation which we seek to solve in this paper. First, the formulation, if taken strictly, applies only to individual values of categorical features, not to the features themselves. Second, many dialectological analyses are based on numerical measures of feature differences, e.g., the edit distance between two pronunciation transcriptions or the distance in formant space between two vowel pronunciations (Leinonen, 2010).

We seek a more general manner of detecting characteristic features below, i.e. one that applies to features, and not just to their (categorical) values and, in particular, one that can work hand in hand with numerical measures of feature differences.

2 Characteristic Features

Since dialectometry is built on measuring differences, we assume this in our formulation, and we seek those features which differ little within the group in question and a great deal outside that group. We focus on the setting where we examine one candidate group at a time, seeking features which characterize it best in distinction to elements outside the group.

We assume therefore, as earlier, a group g that we are examining consisting of $|g|$ sites among a larger area of interest G with $|G|$ sites including the sites s both within and outside g. We further explicitly assume a measure of difference d between sites, always with respect to a given feature

f. Then we calculate a mean difference with respect to f within the group in question:

$$\bar{d^g_f} = \frac{2}{|g|^2 - |g|} \sum_{s,s' \in g} d_f(s, s')$$

and a mean difference with respect f involving elements from outside the group:

$$\bar{d^{\not g}_f} = \frac{1}{|g|(|G| - |g|)} \sum_{s \in g, s' \notin g} d_f(s, s')$$

We then propose to identify characteristic features as those with relatively large differences between $\bar{d^{\not g}_f}$ and $\bar{d^g_f}$. However, we note that scale of these calculations are sensitive to a number of factors, including the size of the group and the number of individual differences calculated (which may vary due to missing values). To remedy the difficulties of comparing different features, and possibly very different distributions, we standardize both $\bar{d^{\not g}_f}$ and $\bar{d^g_f}$ and calculate the difference between the *z-scores*, where mean and standard deviation of the difference values are estimated from all distance values calculated with respect to feature f. As a result, we use the measure

$$\frac{\bar{d^{\not g}_f} - \bar{d_f}}{sd(d_f)} - \frac{\bar{d^g_f} - \bar{d_f}}{sd(d_f)}$$

where d_f represents all distance values with respect to feature f (the formula is not simplified for the sake of clarity). We emphasize that we normalized the difference scores for each feature separately. Had we normalized with respect to *all* the differences, we would only have transformed the original problem in a linear fashion.

Note that this formulation allows us to apply the definitions to both categorical and to numerical data, assuming only that the difference measure is numerical. See illustration in Figure 1.

For this work we used a difference function that finds the aggregated minimum Levenshtein distance between two sites as calculated by Gabmap (Nerbonne et al., 2011). However, we again emphasize that the benefit of this method in comparison to others proposed earlier is that it can be used with any feature type as long as one can define a numerical distance metric between the features. Regardless of the type of data set, some distance values between certain sites may not be possible to calculate, typically due to missing values. This may affect the scale and the reliability of the average distance calculations presented above. For the experiments reported below, we calculated average scores only if the missing values did not exceed 20% of the total values used in the calculation.

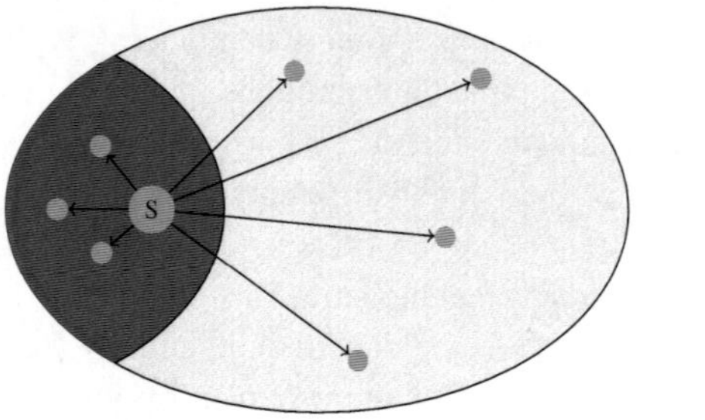

Figure 1: Illustration of the calculation of a distance function. Our proposal compares the mean distance of all pairs of sites within a group, including all those shown on the left (in blue) to the mean distance of the pairs of sites where the first is within the group and the second outside it.

Fisher's Linear Discriminant

The formulation we propose looks a good deal like the well-known Fisher's linear discriminant (FLD) (Schalkoff, 1992, 90ff), which maximizes the differences in means between two data sets with respect to (the sum of) their variances.

$$S = \frac{\sigma^2_{between}}{\sigma^2_{within}}$$

But FLD is defined for vectors, while we wish to generalize to cases where only *differences* are guaranteed to be numerical measures. The mean of categorical features, for example, is undefined. We might imagine applying something like FLD in the space of differences, but note that low variance does not necessarily correspond to a tightly knit group in difference space. If we measure the differences among all the pairs of sites in a candidate group, each of which realizes a given categorical feature differently, the mean difference of pairs will be one (unit) and the variance zero. Difference spaces are simply constructed differently.

Silhouette method

We also note relation of our approach to the SILHOUETTE method introduced by Rousseeuw (1987) used to evaluate clustering validity. The silhouette method is used to determine the optimal number of clusters for a given dataset. It starts from data that has already been clustered using any of the (hierarchical or flat) clustering techniques. For every object i in the data (these would be sites in clustering to detect dialect groups) it calculates the average dissimilarity to all other objects in the same cluster $a(i)$, and the average dissimilarity to all objects in all other clusters (for every cluster separately). After the distances to all other clusters are computed, the cluster with the smallest average distance ($b(i)$) to the object in question is selected as the most appropriate one for that object. The silhouette $s(i)$ is calculated as

$$s(i) = \frac{b(i) - a(i)}{max\{a(i), b(i)\}}$$

Values close to 1 indicate that the object is appropriately clustered, while negative values indicate that the object should have been clustered in its neighbouring cluster. By comparing silhouette values obtained by clustering into different numbers of groups, this technique indicates an optimal clustering.

We compare average distances within groups to average distance to objects outside groups with respect to individual features, making our proposal different. A second point of difference is that we aim not to score 'groupings', but rather how characteristic specific features are for a given grouping.

3 Experimental set up

The method we propose is tested on Dutch and German dialect data. We use Levenshtein algorithm in order to calculate the distances between the sites and Ward's clustering method to group the sites. In this section we give a brief description of the data and the clustering procedure.

Dutch data set

Dutch dialect data comes form the Goeman-Taeldeman-Van Reenen Project[1] that comprises 1876 items collected from more than 600 locations in the Netherlands and Flanders. The data was collected during the period 1979-1996, transcribed into IPA and later digitalized. It consists of inflected and uninflected words, word groups and short sentences. More on this project can be found in Goeman and Taeldeman (1996).

The data used in this paper is a subset of the GTRP data set and consist of the pronunciations of 562 words collected at 613 location in the Netherlands and Flanders. It includes only single word items that show phonetic variation. Multi-word items and items that show morphological, rather than phonetic variation, were excluded from the analysis. Items where multiple lexemes per site are possible were also excluded.[2]

German data set

German dialect data comes from the project 'Kleiner Deutscher Lautatlas — Phonetik' at the 'Forschungszentrum Deutscher Sprachatlas' in Marburg. In this project a number of sentences from Georg Wenker's huge collection of German dialects (1870s-1880s)[3] were recorded and transcribed in the late 1970s and early 1990s (Göschel, 1992). The aim of the project was to give an overview of the sound structure of modern German dialects.

In this paper we use a small subset of the data that consists of the transcriptions of 40 words. We have selected only words that are present at all or almost all 186 locations evenly distributed over Germany.

Distance matrices

The distances between each pair of sites within each of the two data sets were calculated using the Levenshtein algorithm (Levenshtein, 1966). This method is frequently used in dialect comparison to measure the differences between two sites (Nerbonne et al., 1996; Heeringa, 2004). It aligns two strings and calculates the number of mismatching segments in two strings. The total distance between two sites is the average distance between all compared strings collected at those two sites. For the method proposed in this paper, any other method whose output is a numerical distance metric between the features can be applied. The final result is a *site* $\times$ *site* distance matrix, that can later be analyzed by means of clustering or, alternatively, using a dimensionality reduction technique such multidimensional scaling.

We analyze two distance matrices using Ward's clustering algorithm, also known as the minimal variance algorithm. We use *MDS plots* (as implemented in Gabmap (Nerbonne et al., 2011)) as a visual basis to choose the optimal number for clusters for the two data sets. The choice of the

[1]http://www.meertens.knaw.nl

[2]The data set used in this paper can be downloaded from http://www.gabmap.nl/ app/examples/.

[3]See, too, the *Digitaler Wenker Atlas* (DiWA) project, http://www.3.diwa.info/

appropriate clustering algorithm is a difficult task as is the determination of the number of significant groups (Prokić and Nerbonne, 2008), but these questions are not the subjects of this paper. At the risk of repeating ourselves, we emphasize that our focus in this paper is not the choice of clustering method or the determination of the most significant (number of) groups. We do not even assume that the groups were obtained via clustering, only that candidate groups have somehow been identified. We focus then on finding the most characteristic features for a given group of sites. In the next section we present the results of applying our method to the Dutch and German data sets.

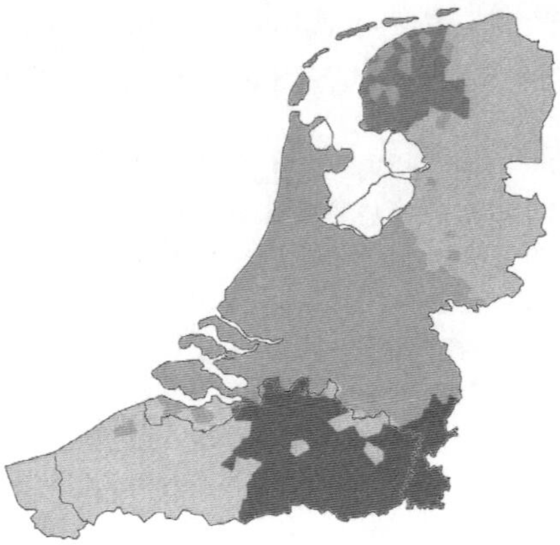

Figure 2: Six dialect groups in Dutch speaking area.

Evaluation

We evaluate success in the task of selecting items characteristic of an area by using MDS to analyze a distance matrix obtained from only that item. We then project the first, most important MDS dimension to a map asking whether the original group of sites indeed is identified. Note that in successful cases the area corresponding to the group may be shaded either as darker than the rest or as lighter. In either case the item (word) has served to characterize the region and the sites in it.

We also experimented with clustering to analyze the distances based on the pronunciations of the candidate characteristic shibboleths, but single word distances unsurprisingly yielded very unstable results. For that reason we use MDS.

4 Results

Dutch

We examine a clustering of the distance matrix for Dutch varieties with six clusters, which we present in Figure 2.

The clustering algorithm identified Frisian (dark green), Low Saxon (Groningen and Overijsel, light blue), Dutch Franconian varieties (pink), Limburg (dark blue), Belgian Brabant (red) and West Flanders (light green) dialect groups. For each feature (word) in our data set and for each group of sites (cluster) we calculated the differences within the given site and also with respect to each of the other five groups in order to determine which words differ the least within the given group and still differ a great deal with respect to the sites outside the group. The top five words for each group of sites are presented in Table 1.

The results obtained show that the same word could be prominent for more than one cluster; for example, the word *scheiden* is scored highly in two different dialect groups. In Figure 3 we present maps of Dutch language area that are based on the pronunciations of the best scoring words for each of the six groups of sites. For each word we calculated the Levenshtein distance and analyzed the resulting distance matrices using MDS. In maps in Figure 3 we present the first extracted dimension, which always explains most of the variation in the data.[4] We also supply the degree to which the extracted dimensions correlate with the distances in the input matrix.

Maps in Figure 3 reveal that the best scoring word does indeed identify the cluster in question. For example, the map in Figure 3(a) reveals that based on the pronunciation of word *vrijdag* the Frisian-speaking area is internally homogeneous and distinct from the rest of the sites. No other groups can be identified in the map. In Figure 3(b) we present the analysis of a distance matrix based on the pronunciation of the word *wonen* 'live' that was found to be relevant for the Low Saxon area. The map shows two areas, Low Saxon and West Flanders, where it was also among top 10 best scored words, as two distinct areas.[5]

[4]The only exception is Figure 3(b) where we present second dimension.

[5]These two areas are both known for pronouncing the *slot 'n* in final unstressed syllables of the form /ən/ as a syllabic nasal that has assimilated in place to the preceding consonant.

(a) *vrijdag* ($r = 0.78$), selected as most characteristic of the Frisian area.

(b) *wonen* ($r = 0.54$), characteristic both of Low Saxon (in the northeast) but also of West Flanders (southwest).

(c) *durven* ($r = 0.54$), characteristic of Franconian Dutch.

(d) *wegen* ($r = 0.59$), characteristic of Limburg.

(e) *gisteren* ($r = 0.60$), selected as characteristic of Belgian Brabant.

(f) *heet* ($r = 0.58$), selected as characteristic of West Flanders, but in fact not awfully successful in distinguishing exactly that area.

Figure 3: Dutch dialect area based on the pronunciation of words (a) *vrijdag*, (b) *wonen*, (c) *durven*, (d) *wegen*, (f) *heet* and (e) *gisteren* selected as characteristic of respective areas.

Frisian		Low Saxon		Franconian		Limburg		West Flanders		Belg.Brabant	
2.891217	vrijdag	1.881354	wonen	1.131973	durven	2.317413	wegen	1.605255	heet	1.968656	gisteren
2.808631	zoet	1.875302	dopen	1.101160	maanden	2.048480	schoenen	1.587253	weten	1.803535	gewoon
2.659577	geven	1.784224	scheiden	1.096989	metselen	2.015069	schaven	1.573224	weer	1.794680	gal
2.618426	draden	1.747136	bijten	1.073387	houden	1.979678	schapen	1.567049	keuren	1.764176	kleden
2.606748	dun	1.721321	worden	1.054981	dorsen	1.956787	scheiden	1.548940	horen	1.753901	wippen

Table 1: Five most characteristic words for each Dutch dialect variety.

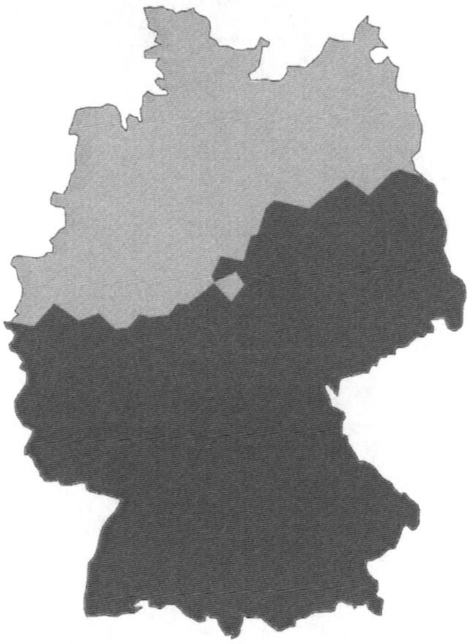

Figure 4: Two dialect groups in Germany.

German

We ran the same analysis for the German data set. In Figure 4 we present the two largest groups in the cluster analysis of the distances obtained using 40 words. We might have examined more groups, but we wished to examine results based on larger groups as well.

We focus on the top-level, two-way split that divides Germany into north and south.[6] These areas correspond with the traditional division into Low German on one hand, and Middle and High German on the other. Just as with the Dutch data, for every word in the data set and for each group of sites we calculate the distances with respect to the word in order to see how well the words characterize one of the two dialect groups. The results are presented in Table 2. Because we are examining a two-way split, it is not surprising that the same words sometimes characterize the areas (inversely).

In Figures 5(a) and 5(b) we present the MDS maps based on the distances derived from comparing the words *weisse* and *gefahre*, which were two best ranked words.

North		South	
1.057400	weisse	1.056600	gefahre
1.011804	gefahre	0.909610	gross
0.982128	bleib	0.825211	weisse
0.920354	Ochse	0.764463	Pfeffer
0.831812	gross	0.755694	baue

Table 2: Five most prominent words for two dialect groups in Germany. Because we examine a two-way split, some words characterize both areas.

The word *weisse* shows only small differences within the north, which is illustrated by the light-colored northern part of Germany in Figure 5(a). The map in Figure 5(b) shows an even clearer split highlighting the High German area based on the best ranked word found by our method. This word shows also low variation in the Low German area (second best scored), which is also clearly visible in Figure 5(b).

5 Conclusions

In this paper we have presented a method to detect the most characteristic features of a candidate group of linguistic varieties. The group might be one obtained from cluster analysis, but it might also be obtained from correspondence analysis (Cichocki, 2006), or it might simply be another group identified for theoretical or extra-linguistic reasons (geography or social properties).

The method is applicable to any feature type as long as one can define a numerical distance metric between the elements. In particular the method maybe applied to categorical data whose differences are individually zero or one, or to vowels characterized by the Euclidean distance between formant vectors (or pairs), and it may be applied to edit distance measures applied to phonetic transcriptions. The proposed method is therefore not constrained in its application to only the categorical features, as the proposal in Wieling & Nerbonne (2011) was.

Essentially the method seeks items that differ minimally within a group but differ a great deal

[6] In anticipation of worries about the analysis we hasten to add that more finely discriminated groups may also be distinguished. That is not our purpose here.

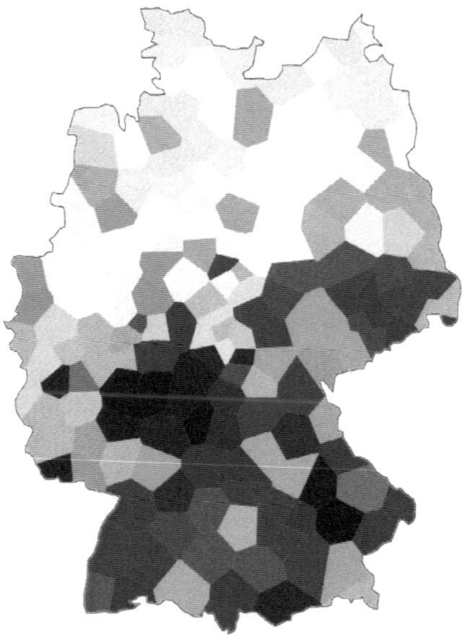

(a) *weisse* ($r = 0.63$)

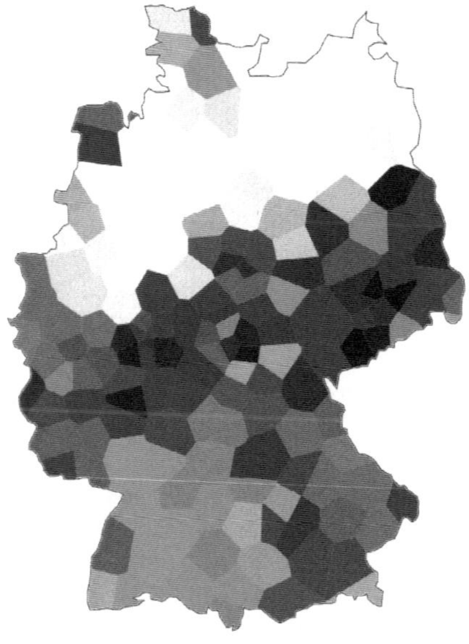

(b) *gefahre* ($r = 0.59$)

Figure 5: First MDS dimensions based on the pronunciation of words (a) *weisse* and (b) *gefahre*.

with respect to elements outside it. We crucially limited its application to elements that were instantiated at least 20% of the sites, and we used normalized z-scores in order to improve the comparability of the measurements.

We demonstrated the effectiveness of the proposed method on real dialect data by trying to identify the words that show low variation within a given dialect area, and high variation outside a given area. We evaluate the results of these experiments by visually examining the distances induced from single words. Although this indicated that the technique is performing well, we concede that alternative evaluations would be worth while, e.g. simply mapping the density of low distances between pairs in the distance matrix. This awaits future work.

The proposed method can be used in dialectometry to automatically identify characteristic features in dialect variation, while at the same time it offers traditional dialectologists insights into the details involved. Its application may also not be limited to dialectology (including dialectometry). It is a general method that can be applied in other branches of linguistics, such as historical linguistics or typology, that deal with language classification at various levels.

The method proposed in this paper might also find use in the evaluation of clustering, specifically in helping researchers to determine the optimal number of groups in a clustering solution. It might then result in a modification of the silhouette technique discussed earlier.

Application of computational methods in dialectology and historical linguistics is still not generally accepted. This state of affairs is due less to the questions that the groups of researchers are trying to answer, and more to the methods they are using to reach their goals. Bringing them together is a challenging task. The method we propose can analyse large amounts of data without losing sight of the linguistic details.

References

J.K. Chambers and Peter Trudgill. 1998. *Dialectology*. Cambridge University Press, Cambridge.

Wladyslaw Cichocki. 2006. Geographic variation in Acadian French /r/: What can correspondence analysis contribute? *Literary and Linguistic Computing*, 21(4):529–542. Special Issue, J.Nerbonne & W.Kretzschmar (eds.), *Progress in Dialectometry: Toward Explanation*.

Hans Goebl. 1982. *Dialektometrie: Prinzipien und Methoden des Einsatzes der Numerischen Taxonomie im Bereich der Dialektgeographie*. Österreichische Akademie der Wissenschaften, Wien.

Antonie Goeman and Johan Taeldeman. 1996. Fonologie en morfologie van de nederlandse dialecten. een nieuwe materiaalverzameling en twee nieuwe atlasprojecten. *Taal en Tongval*, 48:38–59.

Joachim Göschel. 1992. Das Forschungsinstitut für Deutsche Sprache "Deutscher Sprachatlas". Wissenschaftlicher Bericht, Das Forschungsinstitut für Deutsche Sprache, Marburg.

Wilbert Heeringa. 2004. *Measuring Dialect Pronunciation Differences using Levenshtein Distance*. Ph.D. thesis, Rijksuniversiteit Groningen.

Therese Leinonen. 2010. *An Acoustic Analysis of Vowel Pronunciation in Swedish Dialects*. Ph.D. thesis, University of Groningen.

Vladimir I. Levenshtein. 1966. Binary codes capable of correcting insertions, deletions and reversals. *Cybernetics and Control Theory*, 10(8):707–710. Russian orig. in *Doklady Akademii Nauk SSR* 163(4), 845–848, 1965.

John Nerbonne, Wilbert Heeringa, Erik van den Hout, Peter van der Kooi, Simone Otten, and Willem van de Vis. 1996. Phonetic distance between dutch dialects. In Gert Durieux, Walter Daelemans, and Steven Gillis, editors, *CLIN VI: Proc. from the Sixth CLIN Meeting*, pages 185–202. Center for Dutch Language and Speech, University of Antwerpen (UIA), Antwerpen.

John Nerbonne, Rinke Coleand, Charlotte Gooskens, Peter Kleiweg, and Therese Leinonen. 2011. Gabmap: A web application for dialectology. *Dialectologia*, Special issue II:65–89.

John Nerbonne. 2009. Data-driven dialectology. *Language and Linguistics Compass*, 3(1):175–198.

Jelena Prokić and John Nerbonne. 2008. Recognizing groups among dialects. *International Journal of Humanities and Arts Computing*, 2(1-2):153–172. DOI: 10.13366/E1753854809000366.

Peter J. Rousseeuw. 1987. Silhouettes: a graphical aid to the interpretation and validation of cluster analysis. *Journal of Computational and Applied Mathematics*, 20:53–65.

Robert Schalkoff. 1992. *Pattern Recognition: Statistical, Structural and Neural Approaches*. John Wiley, New York.

Jean Séguy. 1973. La dialectométrie dans l'atlas linguistique de gascogne. *Revue de Linguistique Romane*, 37(145):1–24.

Martijn Wieling and John Nerbonne. 2011. Bipartite spectral graph partitioning for clustering dialect varieties and detecting their linguistic features. *Computer Speech and Language*, 25:700–715. DOI:10.1016/j.csl.2010.05.004. Published online May 21, 2010.

Martijn Wieling. 2012. *A Quantitative Approach to Social and Geogrpahical Dialect Variation*. Ph.D. thesis, University of Groningen.

Estimating and visualizing language similarities using weighted alignment and force-directed graph layout

Gerhard Jäger
University of Tübingen, Department of Linguistics
gerhard.jaeger@uni-tuebingen.de

Abstract

The paper reports several studies about quantifying language similarity via phonetic alignment of core vocabulary items (taken from Wichman's Automated Similarity Judgement Program data base). It turns out that weighted alignment according to the Needleman-Wunsch algorithm yields best results.

For visualization and data exploration purposes, we used an implementation of the Fruchterman-Reingold algorithm, a version of force directed graph layout. This software projects large amounts of data points to a two- or three-dimensional structure in such a way that groups of mutually similar items form spatial clusters.

The exploratory studies conducted along these ways lead to suggestive results that provide evidence for historical relationships beyond the traditionally recognized language families.

1 Introduction

The *Automated Similarity Judgment Program* (Wichmann et al., 2010) is a collection of 40-item Swadesh lists from more than 5,000 languages. The vocabulary items are all given in a uniform, if coarse-grained, phonetic transcription.

In this project, we explore various ways to compute the pairwise similarities of these languages based on sequence alignment of translation pairs. As the 40 concepts that are covered in the data base are usually thought to be resistant against borrowing, these similarities provide information about genetic relationships between languages.

To visualize and explore the emerging patterns, we make use of *Force Directed Graph Layout*. More specifically, we use the CLANS[1] implementation of the Fruchterman-Reingold algorithm (Frickey and Lupas, 2004). This algorithm takes a similarity matrix as input. Each data point is treated as a physical particle. There is a repelling force between any two particles — you may think of the particles as electrically charged with the same polarity. Similarities are treated as attracting forces, with a strength that is positively related to the similarity between the corresponding data points.

All data points are arranged in a two- or three-dimensional space. The algorithm simulates the movement of the particles along the resulting force vector and will eventually converge towards an energy minimum.

In the final state, groups of mutually similar data items form spatial clusters, and the distance between such clusters provides information about their cumulative similarity.

This approach has proven useful in bioinformatics, for instance to study the evolutionary history of protein sequences. Unlike more commonly used methods like SplitsTree (or other phylogenetic tree algorithms), CLANS does not assume an underlying tree structure; neither does it compute a hypothetical phylogenetic tree or network. The authors of this software package, Tancred Frickey and Andrei Lupas, argue that this approach is advantageous especially in situations were a large amount of low-quality data are available:

> "An alternative approach [...] is the visualization of all-against-all pairwise

[1] **Cl**uster **AN**alysis of **S**equences; freely available from http://www.eb.tuebingen.mpg.de/departments/1-protein-evolution/software/clans

Proceedings of the EACL 2012 Joint Workshop of LINGVIS & UNCLH, pages 81–88,
Avignon, France, April 23 - 24 2012. ©2012 Association for Computational Linguistics

> similarities. This method can handle unrefined, unaligned data, including non-homologous sequences. Unlike phylogenetic reconstruction it becomes more accurate with an increasing number of sequences, as the larger number of pairwise relationships average out the spurious matches that are the crux of simpler pairwise similarity-based analyses." (Frickey and Lupas 2004, 3702)

This paper investigates two issues, that are related to the two topics of the workshop respectively:

- Which similarity measures over language pairs based on the ASJP data are apt to supply information about genetic relationships between languages?
- What are the advantages and disadvantages of a visualization method such as CLANS, as compared to the more commonly used phylogenetic tree algorithms, when applied to large scale language comparison?

2 Comparing similarity measures

2.1 The LDND distance measure

In Bakker et al. (2009) a distance measure is defined that is based on the Levenshtein distance (= edit distance) between words from the two languages to be compared. Suppose two languages, $L1$ and $L2$, are to be compared. In a first step, *the normalized Levenshtein distances* between all word pairs from $L1$ and $L2$ are computed. (Ideally this should be 40 word pairs, but some data are missing in the data base.) This measure is defined as

$$\mathrm{nld}(x, y) \doteq \frac{d_{Lev}(x, y)}{\max(l(x), l(y))}. \quad (1)$$

The normalization term ensures that word length does not affect the distance measure.

If $L1$ and $L2$ have small sound inventories with a large overlap (which is frequently the case for tonal languages), the distances between words from $L1$ and $L2$ will be low for non-cognates because of the high probability of chance similarities. If $L1$ and $L2$ have large sound inventories with little overlap, the distance between

```
h a n t     h a n t
| | | |     | | | |
h E n d     m a n o
```

Figure 1: Simple alignment

non-cognates will be low in comparison. To correct for this effect, Bakker et al. (2009) normalize the distance between two synonymous words from $L1$ and $L2$ by defining the normalized Levenshtein distance by the average distance between all words from $L1$ and $L2$ that are non synonymous ($39 \times 40 = 1,560$ pairs if no data are missing). The **NDLD** distance between $L1$ and $L2$ is defined as the average doubly normalized Levenshtein distance between synonymous word pairs from $L1$ and $L2$. (LDND is a distance measure rather than a similarity measure, but it is straightforward to transform the one type of measure into the other.)

In the remainder of this section, I will propose an improvement of LDND in two aspects:

- using weighted sequence alignment based on phonetic similarity, and
- correcting for the variance of alignments using an information theoretic distance measure.

2.2 Weighted alignment

The identity-based sequence alignment that underlies the computation of the Levenshtein distance is rather coarse grained because it does not consider different degrees of similarities between sounds. Consider the comparison of the English word *hand* (/hEnd/ in the ASJP transcription) to its German translation *hand* (/hant/) on the one hand and its Spanish translation *mano* (/mano/) on the other hand. As the comparison involves two identical and two non-identical sounds in each case (see Figure 1), the normalized Levenshtein distance is 0.5 in both cases. It seems obvious though that /hEnd/ is much more similar to /hant/ than to /mano/, i.e. it is much more likely to find an /a/ corresponding to an /E/ in words that are cognate, and and /d/ corresponding to a /t/, than an /h/ corresponding to an /m/ or a /t/ to an /o/.

There is a parallel here to problems in bioinformatics. When aligning two protein sequences, we want to align molecules that are evolutionarily related. Since not every mutation is equally likely, not all non-identity alignments are equally unlikely. The *Needleman-Wunsch* algorithm (Needleman and Wunsch, 1970) takes a similarity matrix between symbols as an input. Given two sequences, it computes the optimal global alignment, i.e. the alignment that maximizes the sum of similarities between aligned symbols.

Following Henikoff and Henikoff (1992), the standard approach in bioinformatics to align protein sequences with the Needleman-Wunsch algorithm is to use the BLOSUM (*Block Substitution Matrix*), which contains the *log odds* of amino acid pairs, i.e.

$$S_{ij} \propto \log \frac{p_{ij}}{q_i \times q_j} \quad (2)$$

Here S is the substitution matrix, p_{ij} is the probability that amino acid i is aligned with amino acid j, and q_i/q_j are the relative frequencies of the amino acids i/j.

This can straightforwardly be extrapolated to sound alignments. The relative frequencies q_i for each sound i can be determined simply by counting sounds in the ASJP data base.

The ASJP data base contains information about the family and genus membership of the languages involved. This provides a key to estimate p_{ij}. If two word x and y have the same meaning and come from two languages belonging to the same family, there is a substantial probability that they are cognates (like /hEnd/ and /hant/ in Figure 1). In this case, some of the sounds are likely to be unchanged. This in turn enforces alignment of non-identical sounds that are historically related (like /E/-/a/ and /d/-/T/ in the example).

Based on this intuition, I estimated p in the following way:[2]

- Pick a family F at random that contains at least two languages.

- Pick two languages $L1$ and $L2$ that both belong to G.

[2] A similar way to estimate sound similarities is proposed in Prokic (2010) under the name of *pointwise mutual information* in the context of a dialectometric study.

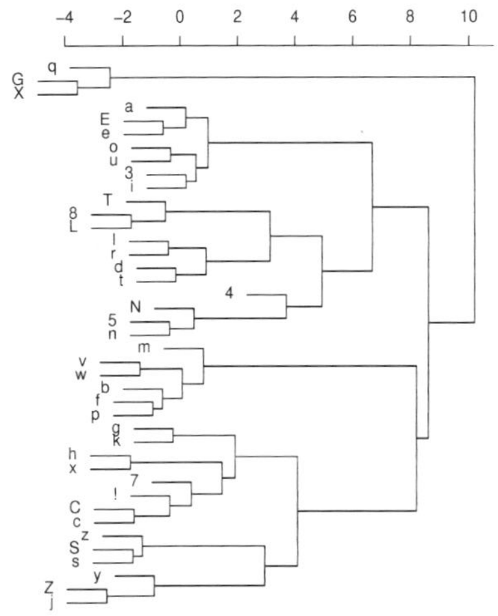

Figure 2: Sound similarities

- Pick one of the forty Swadesh concepts that has a corresponding word in both languages.

- Align these two words using the Levenshtein distance algorithm and store all alignment pairs.

This procedure was repeated 100,000 times. Of course most of the word pairs involved are not cognates, but it can be assumed in these cases, the alignments are largely random (except for universal phonotactic patterns), such that genuine cognate alignments have a sufficiently large effect.

Note that language families vary considerably in size. While the data base comprises more than 1,000 Austronesian and more than 800 Niger-Congo languages, most families only consist of a handful of languages. As the procedure described above samples according to families rather than languages, languages that belong to small families are over-represented. This decision is intentional, because it prevents the algorithm from overfitting to the historically contingent properties of Austronesian, Niger-Congo, and the few other large families.

The thus obtained log-odds matrix is visualized in Figure 2 using hierarchical clustering. The outcome is phonetically plausible. Articulatorily similar sounds — such as the vowels, the alveolar sound, the labial sounds, the dental sounds etc. — form clusters, i.e. they have high log-odds amongst each other, while the log-odds between sounds from different clusters are low.

Using weighted alignment, the similarity score for /hEnd/ $\sim$ /hant/ comes out as ≈ 4.1, while /hEnd/ $\sim$ /mano/ has a score of ≈ 0.2.

2.3 Language specific normalization

The second potential drawback of the LDND measure pertains to the second normalization step described above. The distances between translation pairs are divided by the average distance between non-translation pairs. This serves to neutralize the impact of the sound inventories of the languages involved — the distances between languages with small and similar sound inventories are generally higher than those between languages with large and/or different sound inventories.

Such a step is definitely necessary. However, dividing by the average distance does not take the effect of the variance of distances (or similarities) into account. If the distances between words from two languages have generally a low variance, the effect of cognacy among translation pairs is less visible than otherwise.

As an alternative, I propose the following similarity measure between words. Suppose s is some independently defined similarity measure (such as the inverse normalized Levenshtein distance, or the Needleman-Wunsch similarity score). For simplicity's sake, L_1 and L_2 are identified with the set of words from the respective languages in the data base:

$$s^i(x, y|L_1, L_2)$$
$$\doteq -log\frac{|\{(x',y') \in L_1 \times L_2 | s(x',y') \geq s(x,y)\}|}{|L_1| \times |L_2|}$$

The fraction gives the relative frequency of word pairs that are at least as similar to each other than x to y. If x and y are highly similar, this expression is close to 0. Conversely, if they are entirely dissimilar, the expression is close to 0.

The usage of the negative logarithm is motivated by information theoretic considerations. Suppose you know a word x from L_1 and you have to pick out its translation from the words in L_2. A natural search procedure is to start with the word from L_2 which is most similar to x, and then to proceed according to decreasing similarity. The number of steps that this will take (or, up to a constant factor, the relative frequency of word pairs that are more similar to each other than x to its translation) is a measure of the distance between x and its translation. Its logarithm corresponds (up to a constant factor) to the number of bits that you need to find x's translation. Its negation measures the amount of information that you gain about some word if you know its translation in the other language.

The information theoretic similarity between two languages is defined as the average similarity between its translation pairs.

2.4 Comparison

These considerations lead to four different similarity/distance measures:

- based on Levenshtein distance vs. based on Needleman-Wunsch similarity score, and
- normalization via dividing by average score vs. information theoretic similarity measure.

To evaluate these measures, I defined a gold standard based on the know genetic affiliations of languages:

$$\begin{aligned} gs(L_1, L_2) &\doteq 2 \text{ if } L_1 \text{ and } L_2 \\ &\quad\ \text{belong to the same genus} \\ gs(L_1, L_2) &\doteq 1 \text{ if } L_1 \text{ and } L_2 \\ &\quad\ \text{belong to the same family} \\ &\quad\ \text{but not the same genus} \\ gs(L_1, L_2) &\doteq 0 \text{ else} \end{aligned}$$

Three tests were performed for each metric. 2,000 different languages were picked at random and arranged into 1,000 pairs, and the four metrics were computed for each pair. First, the correlation of these metrics with the gold standard was computed. Second, a logistic regression model was fitted, where a language pair has the value 1 if the languages belong to the same genus, and 0 otherwise. Third, the same was repeated with families rather than genera. In both cases, the log-likelihood of another sample of 1,000 language pairs according to the thus fitted models was computed.

Table 1 gives the outcomes of these tests. The information theoretic similarity measure based on the Needleman-Wunsch alignment score performs best in all three test. It achieves the highest correlation with the gold standard (the correlation coefficient for LDND is negative because it is a distance metric while the other measures are

metric	*correlation*	*log-likelihood genus*	*log-likelihood family*
LDND	-0.62	-116.0	-583.6
Levenshtein^i	0.61	-110.5	-530.5
NW normalized	0.62	-108.1	-518.5
NW^i	$\mathbf{0.64}$	$\mathbf{-106.7}$	$\mathbf{-514.5}$

Table 1: Tests of the different similarity measures

similarity metrics; only the absolute value matters for the comparison), and it assigns the highest log-likelihood on the test set both for family equivalence and for genus equivalence. We can thus conclude that this metric provides most information about the genetic relationship between languages.

3 Visualization using CLANS

The pairwise similarity between all languages in the ASJP database (excluding creoles and artificial languages) was computed according to this metric, and the resulting matrix was fed into CLANS. The outcome of two runs, using the same parameter settings, are given in Figure 3. Each circle represents one language. The circles are colored according to the genus affiliation of the corresponding language. Figure 4 gives the legend.

In both panels, the languages organize into clusters. Such clusters represent groups with a high mutual similarity. With few exceptions, all languages within such a cluster belong to the same genus. Obviously, some families (such as Austronesian — shown in dark blue — and Indo-European — shown in brown — have a high coherence and neatly correspond to a single compact cluster. Other families such as Australian — shown in light blue — and Niger-Congo — shown in red — are more scattered.

As can be seen from the two panels, the algorithm (which is initialized with a random state) may converge to different stable states with different global configurations. For instance, Indo-European is located somewhere between Austronesian, Sino-Tibetan — shown in yellow —, Trans-New-Guinea (gray) and Australian in the left panel, but between Austronesian, Austro-Asiatic (orange) and Niger-Congo (red) in the right panel. Nonetheless, some larger patterns are recurrent across simulations. For instance, the Tai-Kadai languages (light green) always end up

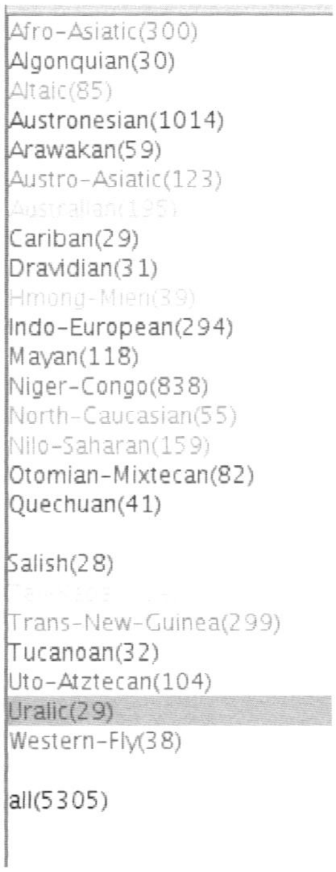

Figure 4: Legend for Figure 3

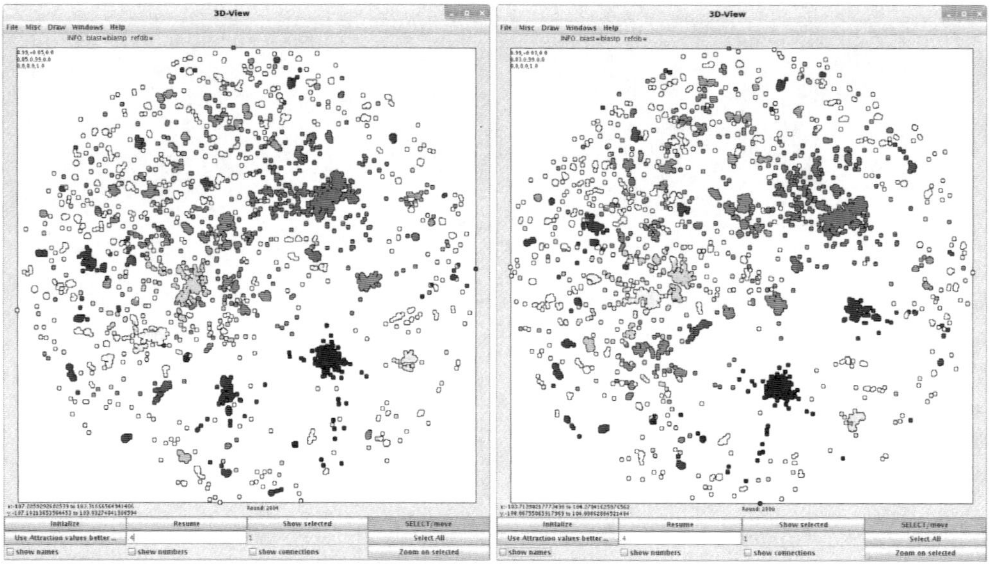

Figure 3: Languages of the world

in the proximity of the Austronesian languages. Likewise, the Nilo-Saharan languages (pink) do not always form a contiguous cluster, but they are always near the Niger-Congo languages.

It is premature to draw conclusions about deep genetic relationships from such observations. Nonetheless, they indicate the presence of weak but non-negligible similarities between these families that deserve investigation. Visualization via CLANS is a useful tool to detect such weak signals in an exploratory fashion.

4 The languages of Eurasia

Working with all 5,000+ languages at once introduces a considerable amount of noise. In particular the languages of the Americas and of Papua New Guinea do not show stable relationships to other language families. Rather, they are spread over the entire panel in a seemingly random fashion. Restricting attention to the languages of Eurasia (also including those Afro-Asiatic languages that are spoken in Africa) leads to more pronounced global patterns.

In Figure 5 the outcome of two CLANS runs is shown. Here the global pattern is virtually identical across runs (modulo rotation). The Dravidian languages (dark blue) are located at the center. Afro-Asiatic (brown), Uralic (pink), Indo-European (red), Sino-Tibetan (yellow), Hmong-Mien (light orange), Austro-Asiatic (orange), and Tai-Kadai (yellowish light green) are arranged

Figure 6: Legend for Figure 5

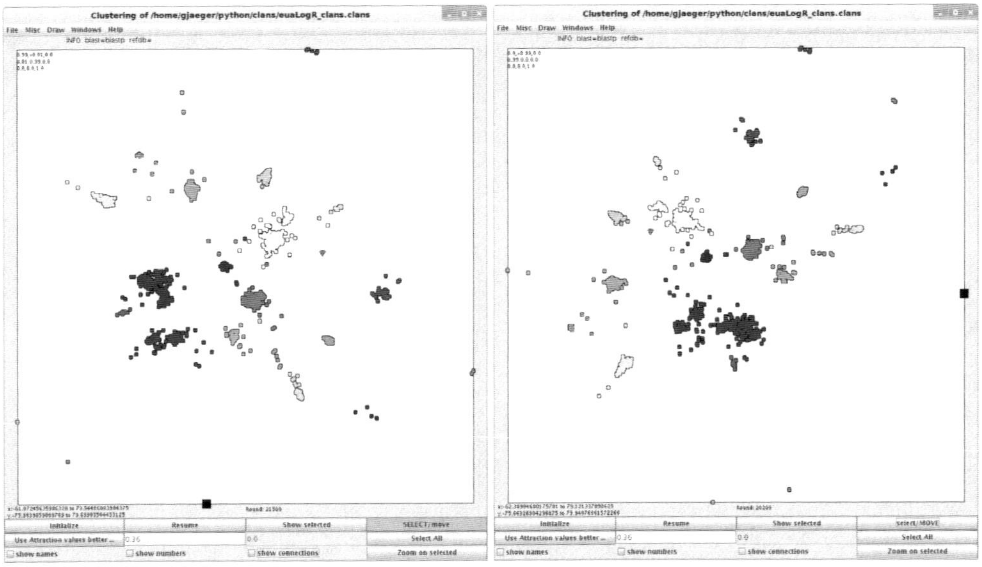

Figure 5: The languages of Eurasia

around the center. Japanese (light blue) is located further to the periphery outside Sino-Tibetan. Outside Indo-European the families Chukotko-Kamchatkan (light purple), Mongolic-Tungusic (lighter green), Turkic (darker green)[3] Kartvelian (dark purple) and Yukaghir (pinkish) are further towards the periphery beyond the Turkic languages. The Caucasian languages (both the North Caucasian languages such as Lezgic and the Northwest-Caucasian languages such as Abkhaz) are located at the periphery somewhere between Indo-European and Sino-Tibetan. Burushaski (purple) is located near to the Afro-Asiatic languages.

Some of these pattern coincide with proposals about macro-families that have been made in the literature. For instance the relative proximity of Indo-European, Uralic, Chukotko-Kamchatkan, Mongolic-Tungusic, the Turkic languages, and Kartvelian is reminiscent of the hypothetical Nostratic super-family. Other patterns, such as the consistent proximity of Japanese to Sino-Tibetan, is at odds with the findings of historical linguistics and might be due to language contact. Other patterns, such as the affinity of Burushaski to the Afro-Asiatic languages, appear entirely puzzling.

[3]According to the categorization used in ASJP, the Mongolic, Tungusic, and Turkic languages form the genus Altaic. This classification is controversial in the literature. In CLANS, Mongolic/Tungusic consistently forms a single cluster, and likewise does Turkic, but there is no indication that there is a closer relation between these two groups.

5 Conclusion

CLANS is a useful tool to aid automatic language classification. An important advantage of this software is its computational efficiency. Producing a cluster map for a 5,000 $\times$ 5,000 similarity matrix hardly takes more than an hour on a regular laptop, while it is forbidding to run a phylogenetic tree algorithm with this hardware and this amount of data. Next to this practical advantage, CLANS presents information in a format that facilitates the discovery of macroscopic patterns that are not easily discernible with alternative methods. Therefore it is apt to be a useful addition to the computational toolbox of modern data-oriented historical and typological language research.

Acknowledgments

I would like to thank Andrei Lupas, David Erschler, and Søren Wichmann for many inspiring discussions. Furthermore I am grateful for the comments I received from the reviewers for this workshop.

References

Dik Bakker, André Müller, Viveka Velupillai, Søren Wichmann, Cecil H. Brown, Pamela Brown, Dmitry Egorov, Robert Mailhammer, Anthony Grant, and Eric W. Holman. 2009. Adding typology to lexicostatistics: a combined approach to language classification. *Linguistic Typology*, 13:167–179.

Tancred Frickey and Andrei N. Lupas. 2004. Clans: a java application for visualizing protein families based on pairwise similarity. *Bioinformatics*, 20(18):3702–3704.

Steven Henikoff and Jorja G. Henikoff. 1992. Amino acid substitution matrices from protein blocks. *Proceedings of the National Academy of Sciences*, 89(22):10915–9.

Saul B. Needleman and Christian D. Wunsch. 1970. A general method applicable to the search for similarities in the amino acid sequence of two proteins. *Journal of Molecular Biology*, 48:443453.

Jelena Prokic. 2010. *Families and Resemblances*. Ph.D. thesis, Rijksuniversiteit Groningen.

Søren Wichmann, André Müller, Viveka Velupillai, Cecil H. Brown, Eric W. Holman, Pamela Brown, Sebastian Sauppe, Oleg Belyaev, Matthias Urban, Zarina Molochieva, Annkathrin Wett, Dik Bakker, Johann-Mattis List, Dmitry Egorov, Robert Mailhammer, David Beck, and Helen Geyer. 2010. The ASJP Database (version 13). http://email.eva.mpg.de/˜wichmann/ASJPHomePage.htm.

Explorations in creole research with phylogenetic tools

Aymeric Daval-Markussen
Research Centre for Grammar and Language Use, Aarhus University
aymemeric@gmail.com

Peter Bakker
Research Centre for Grammar and Language Use, Aarhus University
linpb@hum.au.dk

Abstract

The principal goal of this paper is to illustrate various ways in which phylogenetic tools can advantageously be put to use in investigating and visualizing the relationships of creole languages to other languages, both creoles and non-creoles. After introducing a test study on the English-based creoles, the major theories seeking to explain the emergence and development of creoles will be reviewed and assessed. The final part of the paper is concerned with the typological status of creoles, where various samples will be used to show that creoles form a typologically coherent group among the world's languages.

1. Introduction

Although the linguistic processes underlying creolization remain far from being fully understood, computational methods offer today the opportunity of uncovering complex mechanisms of language evolution on the basis of quantitative investigations. More sophisticated and powerful algorithms now available enable the visualization of patterns in a straightforward manner that was not possible before.

Creole languages emerged in situations of intense contact between several languages, more often than not in the context of massive forced population displacements as were typical of European slave-trading ventures. A diglossic situation with a high-prestige variety (the superstrate) and several low-prestige languages (the substrates) characterized the settings in which creoles developed. Therefore, creole languages can be said to have several parents, and possess as well many often recurring features that appear *ex nihilo*. Thus, the problem of determining relationships between creole languages and other creoles or unrelated languages has long haunted creolists and been recognized as one of the challenges in the field.

Following recent developments in creolistics, where phylogenetic networks were used to investigate questions inherent to the field (Bakker et al. 2011, Daval-Markussen 2011, Daval-Markussen and Bakker 2011), the aim of this paper is to argue that creole languages offer an unparalleled venue for exploratory research in language evolution, and that available computational tools now permit to graphically represent the relationships between the languages considered. In our demonstration, we will exemplify various ways in which phylogenetic networks may advantageously be used to visualize the results.

Following the argumentation in Daval-Markussen (2011: 6-13), only structural features will be taken into account in the present study, since the lexical stock of a creole is mainly derived from a single source language, and this would likely be reflected in the resulting graphs.

In the first part of the paper, phylogenetic tools are used to represent the relationships between 33 English-based creoles, for which 62 typological features were selected and encoded binarily[1]. The second part examines the various scenarios proposed to account for the emergence of creole languages in the light of phylogenetic networks. To this end, samples of various sizes and including creoles as well as non-creole languages (mostly languages involved in the emergence of creoles) were used in order to visualize the impact of the various languages present in the contact situation on the new vernaculars. The final part deals with the typological status of creoles, a topic hotly debated in creolistics (e.g. DeGraff 2003; McWhorter 1998, 2011). Basing our analysis on samples of languages selected from the *World Atlas of Linguistic Structures* (Dryer and

[1] These correspond to the structural features described in Daval-Markussen and Bakker (2011).

Proceedings of the EACL 2012 Joint Workshop of LINGVIS & UNCLH, pages 89–97,
Avignon, France, April 23 - 24 2012.

Haspelmath 2011, hereafter WALS), we will show that phylogenetic methods represent a unique tool for exploring the relationships between creole languages and other languages of the world and can provide invaluable insights into questions on language birth and evolution.

2. Classification

A number of studies have sought to classify English-based creoles on the basis of shared similarities (Hancock 1969, 1987; McWhorter 1995; Baker 1999 to mention just a few). The results presented in these studies are in accordance on several higher-level groupings (the West African, the Suriname, and the Eastern/Western Caribbean groups). We expect therefore to find similar groupings in our results, even though we are using different features and a different method.

The languages selected for this investigation are presented in Hancock's (1987) seminal study on the relationships between 33 Atlantic English-based creoles[2]. On the basis of these data, Hancock (1987: 324-325) attempted to construct a historical scenario explaining their distribution. Although he summarized the results in a tree structure, it is worth mentioning that Hancock indicated the influences between varieties with dotted lines, thus foreshadowing the approach advocated here, i.e. when investigating relationships between (especially creole) languages, lateral influences must be taken into account and somehow be graphically depicted.

The 33 languages were analyzed and 62 typological features attesting the presence vs. absence of a particular phenomenon were selected for binary encoding (see also the Supplementary Materials).

The data were used as input for the software SplitsTree v. 4.12.3 (Huson and Bryant 2006) and returned the network presented in Fig. 1. The geographic location of each variety is indicated with the following colors: blue = Leeward Is., brown = Pacific; green = Caribbean; grey = Suriname; pink = Windward Is.; red = West Africa; yellow = mainland US.

Several clusters are immediately evident in the network reproduced in Fig. 1. While the color codes help visualize the geographic distribution of the included languages, the varieties which appear closest to one another also correspond to

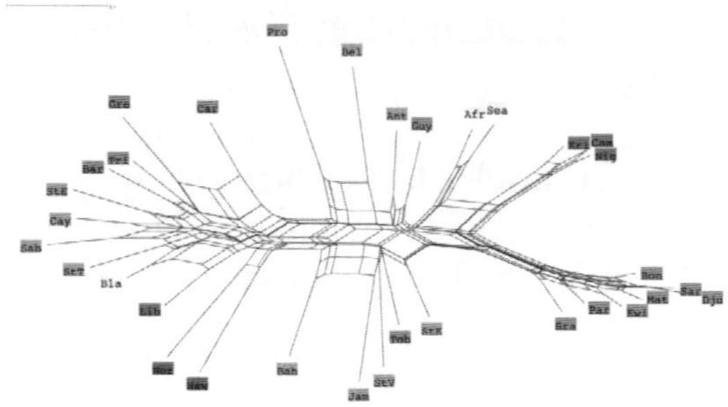

Figure 1: Phylogenetic network of 33 English-based creoles with 62 typological features

groupings identified by other authors (such as the Suriname creoles in grey in the lower right side of the graph). In several cases, we can observe disrupted groups, such as Afr/Sea and Bla (in yellow), or Kri/Nig/Cam and Lib (in red) in clusters which correspond to genealogical groupings (e.g. the Suriname creoles and the varieties of West Africa). The reason for these discrepancies is to be found in the histories of these vernaculars, which have developed apart from one another (see Daval-Markussen and Bakker 2011 for an overview). Besides, the results in Fig. 1 go against the conclusions of Donohue et al. (2011), who claim that the various clusterings observable in phylogenetic networks are due to the effects of areality and geography rather than to genealogy.

This indicates that phylogenetic networks can confidently be used to shed light on the relationships between creoles by presenting the results in such a visually appealing manner.

3. The challenges of creolistics

The present section focuses on the various explanations proposed to account for the similarities observed between creoles, an issue which has been central to creolistics ever since its beginnings. How creoles came about is still a matter of controversy, and in practice, most creolists agree on a working definition encompassing both the linguistic and sociohistorical aspects of creoles.

The main theories seeking to explain how creoles came into being claim that the languages that have played a major role in the creation of the nascent vernaculars were: i) the superstrate, or lexifier (the superstratist school); ii) the substrate languages spoken by the displaced populations (the substratist account); iii) only the superstrate and substrates provide the features available for competition and selection and

[2] The full list of languages and features used throughout the essay with the corresponding abbreviations is found in the Supplementary Materials.

nothing else (the Feature Pool hypothesis); and finally, iv) no language in particular and creole similarities are to be explained by restructuring universals, where similar solutions were found in order to optimize communication (the universalist approach). These approaches are not necessarily mutually exclusive (e.g. Mufwene 1986).

In order to determine whether the predictions made by the various theories accounting for the emergence and development of creoles are borne out by the facts, a sample of creoles and non-creole languages was carefully selected and binary oppositions were encoded according to the 97 morphosyntactic features presented in Holm and Patrick's *Comparative Creole Syntax* (Holm and Patrick 2007, henceforth CCS). The 18 creoles originally described in the Holm and Patrick volume were included, as well as languages known to be involved in the creation of the creoles. Apart from the 18 CCS creoles, we included 19 substrates, 7 lexifiers, as well as 8 non-creoles, selected because of their analytic character and relative low complexity so as to match the character of creoles (see Bakker et al. 2011).

In order to facilitate the interpretation of the figures, it should be kept in mind that the abbreviations used in each network provide the following information: a three-letter code was attributed to each language and written in upper-case for creoles and in lower-case for all non-creoles. A further distinction is made in all the abbreviations, where an initial capital letter (L, S or X) indicates whether the language is a lexifier, a substrate or a non-creole respectively, while a lower-case 'c' precedes all the abbreviations for the creoles.

In the following, with the help of phylogenetic networks, we will test the predictions made by each of the four major proposals seeking to account for the emergence and development of creoles.

3.1 The superstratist view

The main idea within the superstratist framework is that the structural similarities between creoles are due to the role played by the superstrate (or lexifier) language in the period of creole formation. Thus, in this view, creoles are mere continuations of the European languages which provided the bulk of their lexicon and are thus genetically related to their lexifiers. Moreover, according to Mufwene (e.g. 2000, 2008) and Chaudenson (1992, 2003), creolization results from normal language change under particular sociohistorical circumstances and is more a sociological process rather than a linguistic one, and therefore creoles are in this view indistinguishable from non-creoles structurally and typologically.

In order to test the validity of the superstratist approach, we produced a network

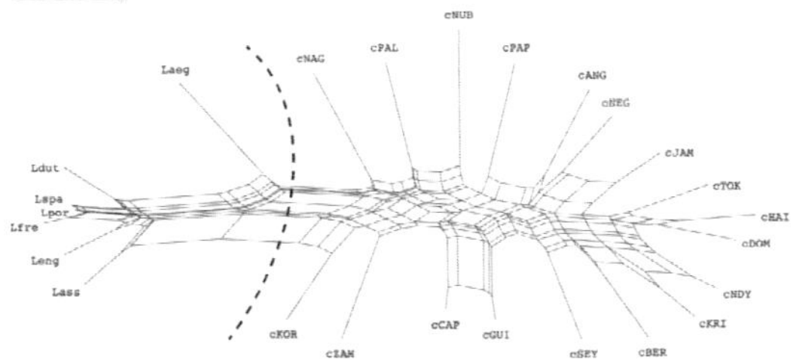

Figure 2: A network of 18 creoles and 7 lexifiers

including the 18 creoles of the CCS sample with the seven lexifiers involved in their creation. Fig. 2 shows the resulting network.

The seven lexifiers all cluster together on the left hand of the network, separated from the creoles by a curved line. All the Indo-European languages cluster neatly together, while Arabic (Laeg) shows up further removed, and the creoles all appear away from the lexifiers. Obviously, the visual interpretation of the network in Fig. 2 does not support the superstratist view, since the creoles do not group with their respective lexifiers, as otherwise expected. This strongly suggests that the superstrates have had a rather limited influence on the grammatical makeup of the incipient creoles at the time of restructuring.

3.2 The substratist position

The substratist school of thinking emphasizes the role of the substrate languages involved in the creation of a creole, which, in this view, was highly influenced by the languages of the enslaved populations (e.g. Holm 1989). Obvious influences are found in the lexicons of individual creoles in the form of borrowings and syntactic structures such as serial verb constructions have also been claimed to be inherited from substrate languages (e.g. Sebba 1987).

In order to assess the extent to which the substratist approach is able to account for the resemblances between creoles, we will examine a network including the 18 CCS creoles with a set of 19 languages which have been claimed to be substrate languages of the various creoles.

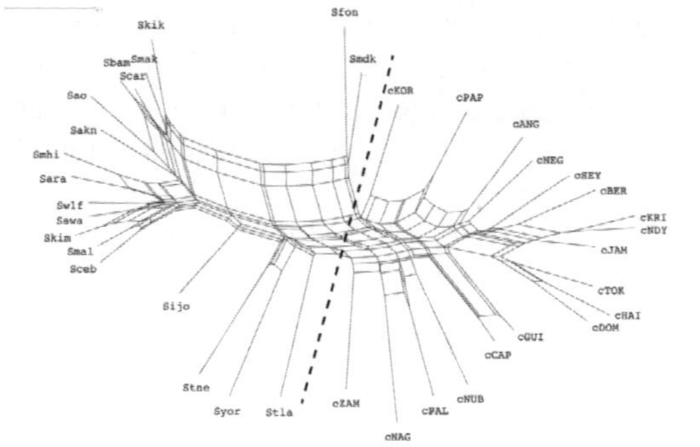

Figure 3: Phylogenetic network of 18 creoles and 19 substrates

The network in Fig. 3 shows an obvious clustering of all the creoles to the right of the dotted line, while all the substrates appear on the left side. Several West African languages often mentioned in the context of creoles are found in the vicinity of the creole cluster and form a transition zone between creoles and non-creoles. Fon (Sfon), Ijo (Sijo), Mandinka (Smdk), Temne (Stne) and Yoruba (Syor) are known to share some structures with creoles (they all use preverbal TMA markers for instance), and this is clearly reflected in the network, where they appear between the creole and non-creole clusters.

Similarly, Tolai (Stla) appears relatively close to the creoles without affecting its relative position to Tok Pisin (cTOK), hence suggesting that the substratist approach fails to fully account for the facts.

3.3 The feature pool approach

The main proponent of the feature pool approach is Mufwene (e.g. 2001, 2008 - see also Aboh and Ansaldo 2006), who advocates a view inspired by genetics and applied to language change. In this context, languages are conceived of as biological species, and processes of language change are explained through the lens of population genetics and Darwinian evolution. Hence, in this view, the roles of the dominant substrates and non-standard varieties of the lexifier are critical, since they provide the feature pool where particular items compete for selection, first in individual idiolects, and then in the wider linguistic community (Mufwene 2008).

In order to test the validity of the feature pool approach, two languages which are known substrates of Seychellois (cSEY), Makhuwa (Smak) and Malagasy (Smal), were specifically included, as well as a third substrate language, Swahili (Sswa), which was encoded for being a suggested substrate for another creole, Nubi Arabic (cNUB). In this sense, we voluntarily tipped the balance in favor of the languages that we know were present at the time when Seychellois emerged and must therefore have provided the feature pool from which the various items were available options for competition and selection in this framework.

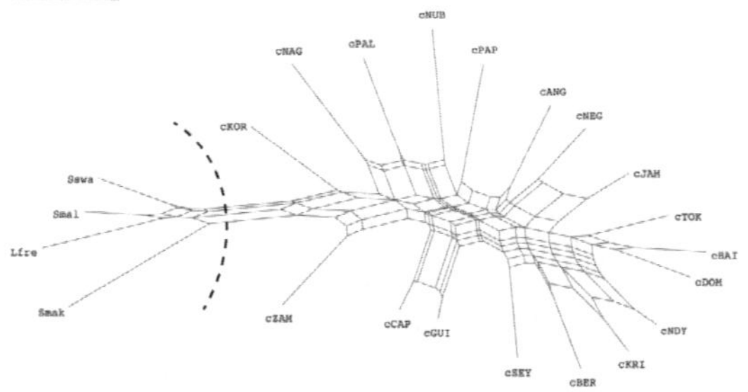

Figure 4: A network of 18 creoles, 3 substrates and one lexifier

The network in Fig. 4 shows that even though only languages involved in the creation of Seychellois were included, the creoles cluster together, which goes against the predictions of a feature pool view, according to which Seychellois would be expected to appear close to the languages that were involved in its formation. The topology of the creole cluster in this and previous networks remains strikingly similar, without affecting the position of Seychellois in the lower right side of the graph. This strongly suggests that the role of the languages involved in the formation of creoles is overstated in a feature pool approach.

3.4 The universalist view

Another hypothesis on creole formation posits that structural similarities between creoles are due to an innate biological propensity, to cognitive constraints or to universals of language restructuring. Thus, language creators drew on the same cognitive resources and universal linguistic processes when trying to solve the communicative problems they encountered, and which in turn resulted in the observed similarities between creolized vernaculars. Bickerton (1981, 1984) further claims that a language-acquisition device in the human brain is the source of creole similarities and regulates the outcome of imperfect language acquisition with the default (or unmarked) settings due to the limited input.

In order to assess the validity of the last hypothesis, that of a universalist account of creole formation, a sample of 52 languages including both substrates and lexifiers was used. Fig. 5 presents a network illustrating the relationships between these languages.

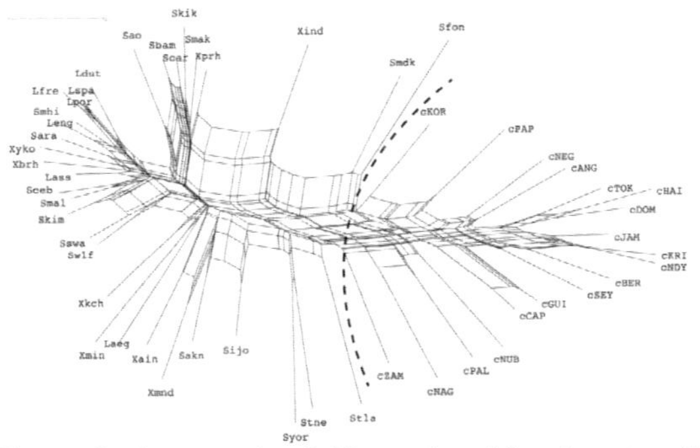

Figure 5: A network of 18 creoles, 19 substrates, 7 lexifiers and 8 non-creoles

In the graph in Fig. 5, the creole cluster is again clearly identifiable to the right of the dotted line. On closer inspection, the network reveals on the upper left a cluster including all the Indo-European languages, Assamese (Lass), Dutch (Ldut), English (Leng), French (Lfre), Marathi (Smhi), Portuguese (Lpor) and Spanish (Lspa). However, this cluster is disrupted by the presence of Arawak (Sara), Kolyma Yukaghir (Xyko) and Brahui (Xbrh). Another genealogical cluster comprising the Afro-Asiatic languages Egyptian Arabic (Laeg) and Mina (Xmin) is found in the lower left side of the graph.

The four Bantu languages that were included, Kikongo (Skik), Kimbundu (Skim), Makhuwa (Smak) and Swahili (Swa), appear in different clusters. Only Kimbundu and Swahili do show up in a cluster on the left in spite of their belonging to widely different branches of the Bantu family (respectively Bantu P and Bantu G in the Guthrie 1948 classification), whereas Kikongo and Kimbundu, which are both Bantu H, appear in opposite ends of the graph. Similarly, the other Niger-Congo languages of West Africa, Akan (Sakn), Bambara (Sbam), Fon (Sfon), Ijo (Sijo), Mandinka (Smdk), Temne (Stne), Wolof (Swlf) and Yoruba (Syor), all appear in different clusters, with the exception of Temne and Yoruba. As for the three Austronesian languages of the sample, Cebuano (Sceb) and Malagasy (Smal) appear in a cluster on the left, far from Tolai (Stla).

Thus, the software was able to detect a clear phylogenetic signal in only a few cases, which in itself is not surprising, since the features were originally selected as representative of the Atlantic creoles (Holm and Patrick 2007: vi). Hence, the results lend support to the universalist position. Besides, all the graphs presented so far also support the idea that creoles form a relatively homogeneous group of languages, in that the creoles are clearly visible and easily distinguishable from the other languages.

4. Creole typology

In this section, we will deal with the typological status of creoles. The issue has long been controversial in creolistics, and the debate has severely suffered from a paucity of systematic cross-linguistic empirical studies directly addressing the question. However, recent studies have shed new light on the matter with the help of phylogenetic tools (Cysouw 2009, Bakker et al. 2011, Daval-Markussen 2011). In the following section, we will show in a similar spirit that creoles pattern similarly in phylogenetic analyses, thus providing further support to the claim that creoles form a synchronically distinguishable sub-group among the world's languages.

4.1 Sampling and method

Traditionally, comparative work in creolistics has focused on subdomains of syntax and/or lexicon for individual languages and/or a restricted number of languages to compare with. In spite of an increasing awareness of the lack of comparative studies encompassing creoles other than the ones lexified by Indo-European languages (partly remedied for with the publication of Holm and Patrick's long-awaited *Comparative Creole Syntax* in 2007), a majority of investigations on creoles still focus on varieties derived from Indo-European superstrates, partly because of the rarity of creole with a non-European lexical base.

The question whether creoles are structurally distinguishable as a group against other languages of the world can be visualized with Neighbor-Joining trees (Saitou and Nei 1987), which have the advantage of quickly returning clear-cut groupings. Since in this part of the study, we are less concerned with pinpointing the reticulation events that shaped creoles than in establishing typological relationships, we have opted for using NJ trees in the remainder of this article.

The study conducted by Parkvall (2008) was the first to make use of quantitative cross-linguistic data for creoles, and the results presented strongly suggested that creoles are structurally distinguishable from non-creoles from a simplicity point of view. In his investigation of the complexity of creoles, Parkvall selected 43 features, 37 of which were taken directly from the WALS (Dryer and Haspelmath 2011), with a further six added by that author. These features were used to calculate the relative complexity of the 155 languages included in the WALS for which at least 30 features were known (see Parkvall 2008 for the selection criteria). He then added data on 30 creoles and pidgins with diverse lexifiers (2008: 278), some of which are also found in the CCS sample: Dominican, Guinea Bissau, Haitian, Jamaican, Nubi, Negerhollands, Palenquero and Tok Pisin, i.e. almost half of the Holm and Patrick sample. Parkvall interpreted his results as evidence that creoles are structurally less complex than other natural languages. Consequently, another conclusion reached by the author was that creoles form a typological group characterized by a relatively low level of structural complexity.

The dataset used by Parkvall (2008) also served to provide additional evidence that creoles do indeed form a typological group (Bakker et al. 2011) on the basis of a quantitative empirical analysis. The strongest piece of evidence Bakker et al.'s (2011) large-scale investigation presents relies on Parkvall's (2008) data: 34 creoles and pidgins distinctly cluster in a network including 155 non-creole languages of the world. However, the validity of the results is somewhat undermined by the fact that the data which allowed the authors to reach this conclusion were specifically selected on the basis of creole properties, in that Parkvall selected the features in WALS that could be quantified in terms of complexity (e.g. presence versus absence of a grammatical distinction, or less versus more of a particular phenomenon). Thus, one could object that the results do not really reflect what the authors claim them to (see also Kouwenberg 2010 for a critical assessment).

In order to provide additional, and this time irrefutable evidence, these results must be replicated with different samples and different features. This is what will be attempted in this section, first with the CCS languages and features used in the previous section, then with various samples of WALS languages and features.

4.2 Using the CCS features and languages

The morphosyntactic features described in Holm and Patrick (2007) are divided up into 20 overarching categories covering various areas (such as TMA systems, NPs or relativization strategies), which were reduced to 18 binary features by selecting for each category the feature(s) that were shared by most creoles. The major linguistic families are indicated with colors in order to facilitate the interpretation of

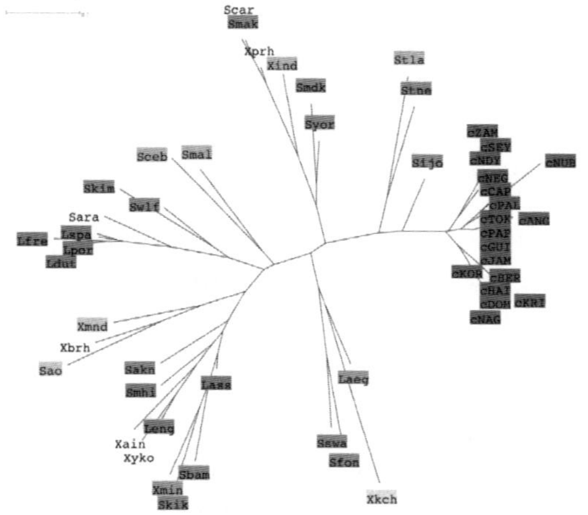

Figure 6: NJ tree of 50 languages with 18 binary features

the graphs (cobalt blue = creoles; cyan = Nilo-Saharan; dodger blue = Afro-Asiatic; green = Indo-European; light blue = Niger-Congo; olive = Austronesian; orange = Austro-Asiatic; pink = Altaic; purple = Uto-Aztecan; red = Australian; tangerine = Trans New Guinea; yellow = Sino-Tibetan).

A cluster consisting of all the creoles is immediately visible in the right end of the tree. The analysis producing these results is based on binary characters only attesting the presence vs. absence of a feature. Therefore, we will introduce in the next section new samples selected from a different database that allows the inclusion of finer-grained distinctions.

4.3 Using WALS to settle the matter

The database provided by the *World Atlas of Linguistic Structures* (Dryer and Haspelmath 2011) consists of descriptions of 144 typological features in a wide variety of languages of the world (2678 as of March 2012 in the constantly updated online version). In the following, different datasets will be extracted from the

WALS in order to further explore the relationships of creoles in the context of the world's linguistic diversity.

The features that are shared by at least 60% of the CCS languages were retained and used to produce several trees based following the multiple-state encoding of the WALS. In the following figures, the same color codes were applied to identify typological clusters.

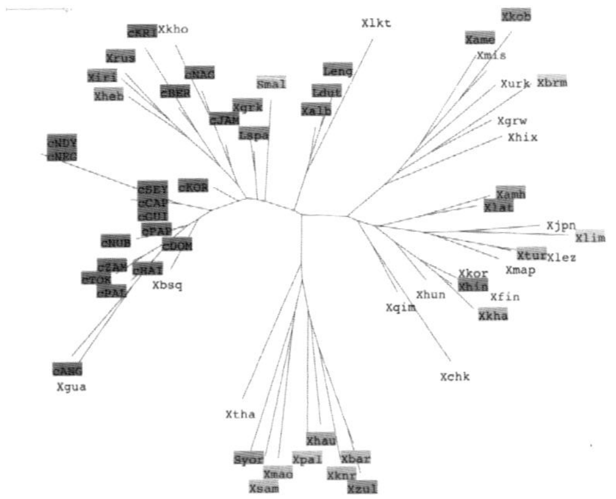

Figure 7: NJ tree of 61 languages with 9 multi-state features

The creole cluster is immediately evident on the left side of the graph in Fig. 7, but a closer look reveals several anomalies: two unrelated languages, Basque (Xbsq) and Guarani (Xgua), appear in the periphery of the core creole cluster, while further up the tree on the initial branch of the creole cluster, four non-creoles show up: the Indo-European Irish and Russian (Xiri and Xrus), the Afro-Asiatic language Hebrew (Xheb) and the Khoisan language Khoekhoe (Xkho).

In order to test the robustness of these results, a larger, more representative sample of the world's languages is required. A logical result of the operation of reducing the number of features increases the number of languages, therefore we gathered another sample of 76 languages based on 6 multi-character features, which returned the tree presented in Fig. 8.

The graph reveals a much denser creole cluster compared to the previous graphs, thus emphasizing the relative homogeneity of creoles as a group. However, several non-creoles appear within the creole cluster: Basque (Xbsq) and Khoekhoe (Xkho) in the core cluster, and four Indo-European languages, Dutch (Ldut), English (Leng), Greek (Xgrk) and Spanish (Lspa), the Uto-Aztecan language O'odham (Xood) and Hungarian (Xhun, Finno-Ugric) in its periphery.

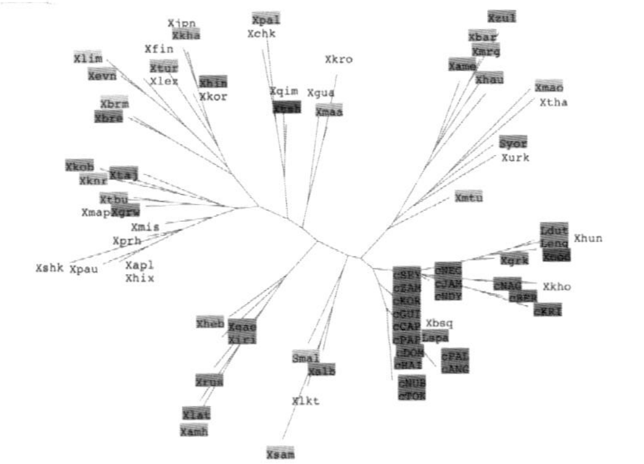

Figure 8: NJ tree of 76 languages with 6 multi-state features

In order to further increase the number of languages included, we have kept the 4 features which were shared by at least 80% of the CCS creoles. The resulting tree is presented in Fig. 9.

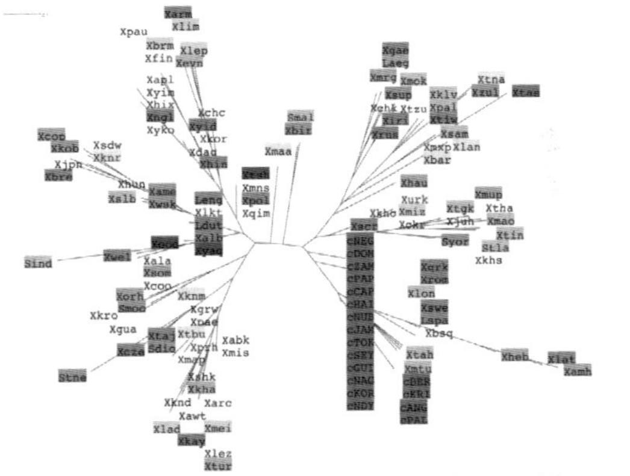

Figure 9: NJ tree of 134 languages with 4 multi-state features

In this final graph, the creole cluster is once again unequivocally identifiable. This time, a majority of the creoles (16 out of 18) are present on a single branch, while two creoles, Krio (cKRI) and Berbice Dutch (cBER) appear on an adjacent branch together with three Austronesian languages, Loniu (Xlon), Motu (Xmtu) and Tahitian (Xtah). The graph in Fig. 9 thus provides conclusive evidence as to the status of creoles: they do form a coherent group of languages that can be distinguished solely on synchronic grounds, as is clearly visible in this, and in previous graphs.

5. Conclusion

We have shown that the application of phylogenetic tools can help shed new light on the typological relationships between languages in general on the one hand, and, on the other hand, more specifically on the relationships between creoles and other languages, both creoles and non-creoles. The problem of the classification of creoles was shown to be a manageable task with the help of phylogenetic networks. The various theories seeking to account for the similarities between creoles were investigated with the help of phylogenetic networks, and it was found that the chosen analysis was advantageous in that it allowed to graphically represent the relationships between the various languages involved in the emergence of creoles. Finally, the controversial question of whether creoles form a distinguishable subgroup among the world's languages was similarly satisfactorily answered using phylogenetic trees. Moreover, we introduced different ways of depicting the results, where color codes were used so as to instantly identify linguistic patterns.

The availability of freely accessible online databases is constantly increasing, and the prospects for future research are many in the perspective of the interplay between computational methods and linguistics, and, more specifically, in the context of creole languages, as their emegence raise questions on the very nature of language evolution as well.

References

Enoch O. Aboh and Umberto Ansaldo. 2006. The role of typology in language creation. In Umberto Ansaldo, Stephen Matthews and Lisa Lim (eds.), *Deconstructing creole*, 39–66. Amsterdam/Philadelphia: Benjamins.

Philip Baker. 1999. "Investigating the origin and diffusion of shared features among the Atlantic English Creoles". In Philip Baker and Adrienne Bruyn (eds.), *St Kitts and the Atlantic Creoles. The texts of Samuel Augustus Mathews in perspective,* 315-364. London: Battlebridge.

Peter Bakker, Aymeric Daval-Markussen, Mikael Parkvall and Ingo Plag. 2011. Creoles are typologically distinct from non-creoles. In Parth Bhatt and Tonjes Veenstra (eds.), *Journal of Pidgin and Creole Languages.* 26(1): 5-42.

Derek Bickerton. 1981. *Roots of Language.* Ann Arbor: Karoma.

Derek Bickerton. 1984. The language bioprogram hypothesis. *The Behavioral and Brain Sciences.* 7: 173-188.

Robert Chaudenson. 1992. *Des îles, des hommes, des langues.* Paris: L'Harmattan.

Robert Chaudenson. 2003. *La créolisation: théorie, applications, implications.* Paris: L'Harmattan.

Michael Cysouw. 2009. APiCS, WALS, and the creole typological profile (if any). Paper presented at the 1st APiCS conference, Leipzig, 5-8 November 2009.

Aymeric Daval-Markussen and Peter Bakker. 2011. A phylogenetic networks approach to the classification of English-based Atlantic creoles. *English World-Wide.* 32(2).

Aymeric Daval-Markussen. 2011. Of networks and trees in contact linguistics: new light on the typology of creoles. MA thesis, Aarhus University.

Michel DeGraff. 2003. Against Creole Exceptionalism. *Language.* 79(2): 391-410.

Mark Donohue, Simon Musgrave, Bronwen Whitting, and Søren Wichmann. 2011. Typological feature analysis models linguistic geography. *Language.* 87(2): 369-383.

Matthew Dryer and Martin Haspelmath (eds.). 2011. *The World Atlas of Linguistic Structures Online.* Munich: Max Planck Digital Library. Available online at http://wals.info/. Accessed on 2012-01-15.

Malcolm Guthrie. 1948. *The classification of the Bantu languages.* London: Oxford University Press.

Ian F. Hancock. 1969. A provisional comparison of the English-based Atlantic Creoles. *African Language Review.* 8: 7-72.

Ian F. Hancock. 1987. A preliminary classification of the anglophone Atlantic creoles with syntactic data from thrity-three representative dialects. In Glenn G. Gilbert (ed.), *Pidgin and Creole languages. Essays in memory of John E. Reinecke,* 264-333. Honolulu: University of Hawaii Press.

John Holm. 1989. *Pidgins and Creoles. Vol. 2. Reference survey.* Cambrige: Cambridge University Press.

John Holm and Peter L. Patrick (eds.). 2007. *Comparative Creole Syntax.* London: Battlebridge.

Daniel H. Huson and David Bryant. 2006. Application of phylogenetic networks in evolutionary studies. *Molecular Biology and Evolution.* 23: 254-267.

Silvia Kouwenberg. 2010. Creole studies and linguistic typology: Part 2. *Journal of Pidgin and Creole Languages.* 25(2): 359-380.

John H. McWhorter. 1995. Sisters under the skin: a case for genetic relationship between the Atlantic English-based Creoles. *Journal of Pidgin and Creole Languages.* 10(2): 289-333.

John H. McWhorter. 1998. Identifying the creole prototype. Vindicating a typological class. *Language.* 74(4): 788–818.

John H. McWhorter. 2011. *Linguistic simplicity and complexity: Why do languages undress?* Berlin: Mouton de Gruyter.

Salikoko S Mufwene. 1986. The Universalist and Substrate Hypotheses Complement One Another. In Pieter Muysken and Norval Smith (eds.), *Substrata versus universals in creole genesis*, 129-162. Amsterdam/Philadelphia: John Benjamins.

Salikoko S. Mufwene. 2000. Creolization is a social, not a structural, process. In Ingrid Neumann-Holzschuh and Edgar Schneider (eds.), *Degrees of restructuring in creole languages*, 65-84. Amsterdam/Philadelphia: John Benjamins.

Salikoko S. Mufwene. 2001. *The Ecology of Language Evolution.* Cambridge: Cambridge University Press.

Salikoko S. Mufwene. 2008. *Language evolution: Contact, competition, and change.* London/New York: Continuum Press.

Mikael Parkvall. 2008. The simplicity of creoles in a cross-linguistic perspective. In Matti Miestamo, Kaius Sinnemäki, and Fred Karlsson (eds.), *Language Complexity. Typology, Contact, Change*, 265–285. Amsterdam/Philadelphia: John Benjamins.

Naruya Saitou and Masatoshi Nei. 1987. The neighbor-joining method: a new method for reconstructing phylogenetic trees. *Molecular Biology and Evolution.* 4(4): 406-425.

Mark Sebba. 1987. *The Syntax of Serial Verbs.* Amsterdam/Philadelphia: John Benjamins.

Tracking the dynamics of kinship and social category terms with AustKin II

Patrick McConvell
Australian National University
Canberra
Australia
Patrick.mcconvell@anu.edu.au

Laurent Dousset
CREDO – EHESS – AMU
3 place Victor Hugo
F-13003 Marseille
dousset@ehess.fr

Abstract

The first AustKin project (AustKin I) collected a large database of kinship terms from Aboriginal languages all over Australia, endeavouring to maintain standards of spelling, kin formulae and group identities, without losing the details of original sources used. An online geospatial interface has been used to map distributions of forms of terms and their polysemies or equations. The patterns of the latter provide identification of kinship systems as defined in ethnology. The project proposed and tested hypotheses about the evolution of such systems in Australia based on knowledge of the common polysemies and related changes. The next stage, AustKin II, builds on hypotheses from the current authors and others, testing these further by adding two more components to the database: the marriage rules and the social categories used by each group. Of the latter, section and subsection systems are unique to Australia. The aim is to gauge how these different systems fit together and propose how they evolved over time and how they influenced each other.

1.The AustKin project

1.1The design of the AustKin database.

The AustKin database documents words in the domain of kinship terminologies for 316 Australian languages or dialects (which could be grouped into about 200 languages, depending on criteria used). The 3i6 languages/dialects have an average of approximately two different wordlists each. from different ethnographic or historical sources for each language or dialect, with a total of over 22 000 words that belong to the domain of kinship.

Designing a database and an interface to such a database has revealed itself to be a complex matter since the number and diversity of variables that need to be taken into account are considerable. In summary, the following had to be taken into account:

A – Systemic variables
1) Kinship terminologies are not just words, but also relationships; and in particular they are related among each other.
2) A kinship terminology constitutes a system; but not all kinship terminologies belong to the same type of system.
3) Kinship terminologies change and they need to be placed against their chronological and historical background.

B – Sporadic variables
1) Kinship terminologies are recorded by humans, and often by non-linguists; they include errors.
2) Kinship terminologies are seldom complete, and need to be completed when possible through other sources.
3) Original Informants may not always have been local speakers.

Arriving at, or at least proposing, potential solutions to the B-type variables was not as difficult as it may appear. The solution chosen was to keep each kin term in its original form as it appears in the original source, while working with rewritten words (for instance those in an orthography standard for the whole database) linked to the original source, so as to be able to retrace every step of transformation and analysis

Proceedings of the EACL 2012 Joint Workshop of LINGVIS & UNCLH, pages 98–107,
Avignon, France, April 23 - 24 2012. ©2012 Association for Computational Linguistics

undertaken for each kinship term and system. The standard orthography used for comparison is based on common ground between practical orthographies in use, and can be entered on a normal keyboard, rather than for instance the Interenational Phonetic Alphabet.

We have also chosen to record as many as possible sets for each language and to investigate these in parallel. And further, the individual researchers had the opportunity to create a "canonical" set out of these various and often partial word lists for analytical purposes.

Here again, it was important to be able to trace steps and modifications. Therefore, each such canonical set is attributed to a participant of the team, and each participant of the team can create his or her own canonical set, or create other types of sets of words based on typologies or groupings the researcher is interested in.

1.2 Standardisation of kinterm meanings

Kinship terms can generally be described using the following elementary idiom, which is in one form or another applied in anthropology and linguistics, but which we have to some degree adapted to our needs.

Females:
M = Mother (one generation above, direct line)
Z = Sister (same generation, identical link to M or F)
D = Daughter (one generation below, direct line)
W = Wife (same generation, alliance, reciprocal of H)

Males:
F = Father (one generation above, direct line)
B = Brother (same gen., identical link to M or F)
S = Son (one generation below, direct line)
H =Husband (same generation, alliance, reciprocal of W)

Additionally, since this element is in some cases structurally significant, the following two codes are used to indicate relative age difference:
e = elder
y = younger

Also, for some terms, the gender of the propositus needs to be detailed: f=female; m = male. The 'propositus' refers to e.g. 'John' in 'John's father'. Thus, for example, a man's patrilateral female cross-cousin is a father's sister's daughter and is coded as mFZD. Terms for grandchildren require this distinction of gender of propositus to be made. For instance the reciprocal of MM is fDS or fDD, whereas the reciprocal of MF is mDS or mDD.

'Cross' in the term 'cross-cousin' means that there is difference in gender between the first two kin links in the kintype e.g. beween 'mother' and 'brother' in MBD and 'father' and 'sister' in FZD. The obverse is 'parallel', where the gender of the two links is the same, as in the parallel cousins MZD and FBD. In many kinship systems around the world, including in Australia, this is a fundamental distinction: for instance 'cross-cousins' can frequently marry, whereas parallel cousins are classed as siblings, and cannot marry. 'Cross' and 'parallel' are also used for other relations e.g. MF is a cross-grandparent and MM is a parallel grandparent.

The way of coding by letters concatenated into strings representing kintypes allows for the search and establishment of equivalences (also known as 'equations' or 'polysemies'). For example, if after searching for equivalences, the words for MBD and FZD are found to be identical in some languages, then we can assume that cross-cousins are not distinguished according to father's or mother's line. Such conclusions have important consequences for the identification, for example, of so-called skewed systems). In such systems, the equivalences are between vertically adjacent generations, for instance an MBD can be called M in an Omaha system, which identifies relatives linked vertically in the male line.

1.3 Kinterm polysemies and kinship systems

A well-used search function in the AustKin database is the polysemy search. This finds languages in which specific kin types are united in one kin term. So to take the examples already mentioned, we can use this function to find languages in which MBD=FZD, or MBD=M. These instances of polysemy can then be mapped on-line using the geo-spatial interface of AustKin. The actual forms of these terms can also be mapped using another search function and overlays of language families and subgroups used to get a preliminary idea of whether the forms and the polysemies are correlated with linguistic groupings.

These polysemies are the prime features which identify what we know as 'kinship systems'. MBD=FZD, for instance, is a symmetrical system of cross-cousin terminology and, as discussed in the section on AustKin II, tends to be associated with symmetrical cross-cousin marriage. On the other hand, if MBD ≠ FZD (the terms for the kin types are different) then this an asymmetrical system, associated with asymmetrical marriage in many cases.

MBD =M is a feature of an Omaha skewing system. Even in the case of skewing, it is often the case that there is variability between the use of separate or the same term depending on social and discourse contexts, remarked also for other types of systems in Australia (Dousset, 2002, 2003) as well as elsewhere in the world by Kronenfeld (2009). The database allows coding of such contexts of variation.

From Morgan (1997 [1871]) on, it has been remarked that there is a limited set of ways in which kinship terminologies vary, and there have been several attempts to codify these as named systems. The normal usage of the term 'kinship system' in anthropology emphasises patterns of equivalence as discussed in the above paragraphs Systems which have more than one diagnostic equation can be plotted using the AustKin database. The 'Kariera' system, named after a language group reputedly with this pattern in its full form, exhibits several equations and non-equations in the grandparental generation

MM=FFZ≠FM=MFZ; FF=MMB≠MF=FMB;

This type of system also usually has the symmetrical cross-cousin pattern FZD=MBD, FZS=MBS . However, adding additional criteria for these named types may not be best practice. Rather, one of the strategies we have followed in AustKin I research is to propose hypotheses about which are the most robust diagnostic patterns and then verify empirically in our database the extent to which other patterns can be predicted by the most diagnostic pattern of polysemy, e.g. the grandparental equations or non-equations cited above for 'Kariera' (McConvell and Hendery, to appear).

'Kariera' itself can be considered as a sub-type of the Dravidian system, found in many societies on all continents, where 'cross' and 'parallel' relatives are rigorously distinguished. However, in the Australian Kariera systems this characteristic of distinguishing cross and parallel is found strongly expressed in the grandparental generation, whereas elsewhere in the world this may not be the case.

Kariera is only one of the systems in Australia. Others include the 'Aranda' system in which

MM≠FFZ≠FM≠MFZ; FF≠MMB≠MF≠FMB

in other words, twice the number of distinctive terms. Other kinds of systems are those with asymmetrical cross-cousin terms (eg FZD≠MBD) and asymmetrical grandparent terms, which form a kind of half-way house between Kariera and Aranda, for instance

MM≠FFZ≠FM=MFZ; FF≠MMB≠MF=FMB

One system which neutralises the cross-parallel division found in Kariera is the so-called 'Aluridja' system. In some such systems the main feature is the neutralisation of distinctions between cross-cousins and parallel cousins/siblings. In some systems, such as in the Western Desert, the distinction between cross and parallel grandparents is also neutralised yielding a system like the modern European grandmother-grandfather terminology.

1.4 Reconstruction of proto-forms, proto meanings and proto-systems

While anthropological (ethnological) research on kinship has sometimes been comparative, producing synchronic typologies of systems, it has rarely focused on diachronic change and reconstruction. Even the work on transformations from Levi-Strauss to more recent significant work such as Godelier et al. (1998) has not tied transformations to times, places and lexical forms.

In linguistics, however, there has been a current of research on reconstructing kinship terms and systems (e.g. Blust, 1980; Whistler, 1980), but not in Australia. Our aim in the AustKin project has been to apply the comparative method to Australian kinship data using systematic querying of databases, and marry the results to anthropological work.

One of the key issues in kinship reconstruction is understanding and prediction of types of semantic change. A guiding principle has been that most semantic change happens via a stage of polysemy. In our database we can find instances of polysemy A=B which lie between meaning A and meaning B. So for instance we can map M=MBD and MB=MBS, two of the key Omaha equations. These show distributions of this polysemy (with different forms of kinship terms) in various areas (Figure 1, see McConvell, in press).

Figure 1: Omaha skewing polysemies in Northern Australia

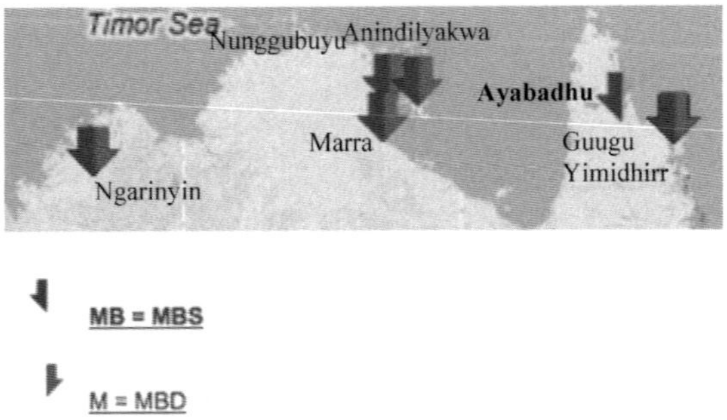

These polysemy patterns have implications for the change in meaning of terms and their reconstruction. Note that one of the languages with an Omaha skewing pattern in Figure 1 is Ayabadhu in eastern Cape York Peninsula. Now look at the distribution of cognates of the root for MB in Ayabadhu (*kaala*) in Figure 2. The MB meanings are all clustered around Cape York Peninsula in the Paman subgroup of Pama-Nyungan and to some extent south of there (the left-side blue half-arrows). However there are also cognates scattered north-west into Yolngu, in North-east Arnhem Land, west into Ngumpin-Yapa, south-east into Southern Queensland and Northern New South Wales. All these latter forms of the root (the right-side red half-arrows) have the meaning of (matrilateral) cross-cousin and/or spouse or sibling-in-law (the latter polysemy change is due to cross-cousin marriage).

The hypothesis to explain this striking pattern is that the original meaning is MB, as reconstructed in proto-Paman, but also, we suggest, in proto-Pama-Nyungan. The meaning change to MB's child (MBD/MBS) and subsequently extended to spouse through another common polysemy, is due to the existence of Omaha skewing in Paman languages, which is the bridge between the uncle and cousin/spouse meaning. This bridge remains intact in the form of a polysemy in some languages such as Ayabadhu.

Figure 2: distribution *kaal MB > MBS > spouse

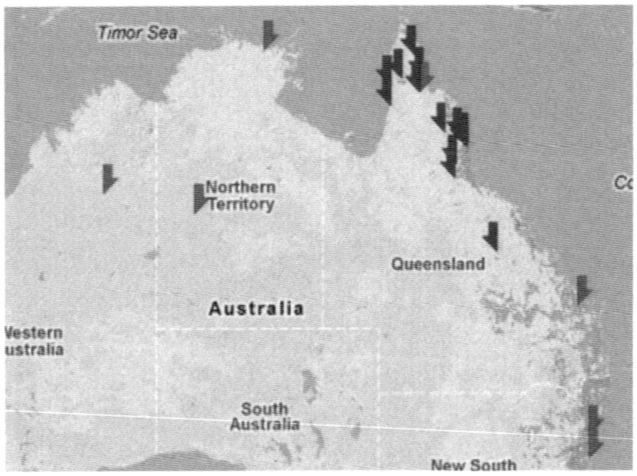

This method of reconstruction has now been applied to many of the kinship terms in our database, providing reconstructions of proto-forms and proto-meanings with accounts of semantic change which accord with the highly constrained types of polysemy we know of, and geographical distribution of the languages.

While kinship terms are usually inherited, there are a number of loan forms, and the source of these is recorded in the database. Two types of these have been examined in the project.

1. forms which are imported to fill a gap in a system when there is a change in kinship system, for instance the fact that all terms for FF in Ngumpin-Yapa are borrowed from different sources points to a change to an Aranda system from one with less grandparent terms

2. forms which are widely borrowed (*Wanderwörter*) tend to be affinal (in-law) terms or have a polysemy which includes an affinal sense. The examples of these examined seem to indicate a change in marriage arrangements and associated avoidance and joking relationships over time (McConvell, 2011).

2. The AustKin II project

We are now designing an AustKin II database, linked to the AustKin I but being able to store, handle and map two additional features of kinship and social organization: 1) marriage rules, including aspects of prescription, proscription (unmarriageability) , preferential and alternative marriages; and 2) category systems such as moieties, semi-moieties, sections and subsections. We aim to track and visualise how these systems interact with each other over time.

2.1 Marriage rules

In Aboriginal Australia, marriages take place between kinship categories or classes, not just between individuals, lineages, clans or moieties. A preferential or prescribed wife for a male propositus may be a MBD (mother's brother's daughter); or she may be a MMBDD (mother's mother's brother's daughter's daughter), or she may be a classificatory – not actual - DD (daughter's daughter) etc. In most cases, the hypothesis can be advanced that the kinship terminologies which are part of the AustKin I database are coherent with this new database that will record and map the marriage relationships.

Earlier attempts at typologies of kinship systems often included marriage rules in the definition of kinship systems. This would not be a wise precedent for us to follow. We know for instance that sometimes the marriage systems do not 'fit' exactly with the kinship terminologies. Because of our concern with change we also need to record such cases very carefully as they may represent 'phasing in' of a kinship terminology or marriage system not totally in harmony with each other due to time-lag between them, or competition between different systems exerting influence on a group. It is important to record marriage rules separately from kinship systems to compare them as independent factors.

In many cases there is a main 'straight' marriage partner recognized, and this person can be designated by a kin type e.g. MBD for a man. These are often classificatory rather than actual cross-cousins, and in some groups actual first cross-cousins are unmarriageable. For many systems though there is a hierarchy of preference for marriageable kin types. Among the Gurindji for instance, for a man the MMBDD is the 'first choice', but a cross-cousin MBD/FZD is second choice, and so on. There is a need then for a ranked coding of marriage options, using kin types, with other systems and cultural categories being brought in where necessary.

Some marriage systems may be a good deal more complex than this, even at the level of ideal rules, involving, for instance, preference for certain other clans or language groups, geographic exogamy, or contingent dispreference for marriage with families with whom marriage had been contracted in previous generations, generating a pattern Keen (2002) calls 'shifting webs'. Where these factors are systematic they should be allowed for in our coding protocols.

Beyond the 'ideal rules' of marriage, we do intend to make a foray into the actual marriages that have taken place over time, at least in some manageable sample data sets, and link the systemic analysis of terminologies and expressed rules to actual genealogies. There are now several such large genealogical databases available which some members of our team are working with, and which could provide the basis for such work. So far analysis has been done with these data sets using the Social Network Analysis tool *Pajek* (de Nooy et al., 2011), by Woodrow Denham and James Rose, research associates on this project.

One exercise could be comparison of predictions of ideal marriage rules with what had actually occurred, and if there is divergence, seeking reasons for that. Among the Gurindji it seems that preferred 'straight' marriage has been much less adhered to than among the neighbouring Warlpiri. Several possibilities exist for explaining such discrepancies. The Warlpiri are a larger population, and can presumably make marriages which address practical issues in choosing spouses at the same time as abiding by the strict rules. Also possibly there has been change in the marriage patterns among the Gurndji in the last two hundred years which increases optionality without abandoning the system. In the Western Desert, another example, there seem to be two at first sight contradictory strategies involved. One that aims to consolidate group membership through rules of repeated marriages between families; and another that aims at the diversification of the social network through the prohibition of these repetitions. This is a further topic to be investigated by examining marriage patterns in selected regions and possible conditioning factors.

There is often a strong connection between kinship terms and marriage rules. Because affinal terms are associated with kintypes which also have a 'consanguineal' meaning, there is often a polysemy between them – not only between spouse and cross-cousin in a Kariera system, but between WM (mother-in-law) and FZ also in a Kariera system, and other pairings. The change in meanings of terms provide evidence of change in marriage systems over time, for instance the old root *kaal- MB>MBS reflected in Warlpiri *kali-* as 'spouse, MMBDC'. There has been change from preference for cross-cousin spouse to a second-cousin spouse – the latter known to be associated with the 'Aranda' system.

Other connections between kin term polysemies and marriage rules can include the type mentioned earlier, that is, the equation FZD=MBD=W, that might imply bilateral cross-cousin marriage. However this and similar predictions should be tested empirically rather than taken for granted, and this is a task that the AustKin II database will be able to do. If the predictions are not borne out, then the proto-form or loan sources of the terms concerned can be investigated to determine if there has been historical change.

Other aspects which can be of importance in the relations between marriage and kinship terms, their origins and loan spread are avoidance and ritual behaviours. We will try to use coding systems from the Ethnographic Atlas (Murdock, 1967; Gray, 1998) for this where possible, but we may again need to modify these to our needs.

Figure 3: The general work plan for designing the marriage database and its interface

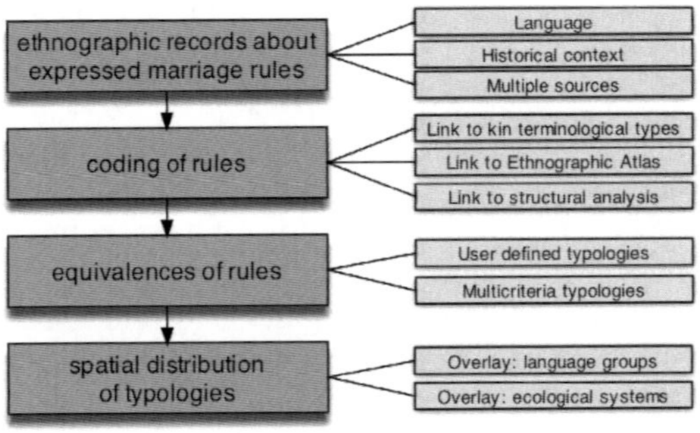

2.2 Sections and subsections

Sections and subsections and their development have been topics investigated over years by the present authors Dousset (2005 on spread of sections in the Western Desert) and McConvell (1985, 1997 on the origin and spread of subsections in north central Australia).

Sections and subsections are named sociocentric divisions, four and eight respectively. Each occurs in separate regions with a little overlap between them The sections are made up of a set pf classificatory or fictive parallel kin of the same or harmonic (+2 or -2) generations In subsections each section is divided into two, with those who are classificatory mother's mother('s siblings) and woman's daughter's children to each other separated into a different subsection from siblings and father's father('s siblings). They are categories which each individual derives from his or her parents, but the section or subsection term of the child are different from those of its parents. Sections and subsections are unique to Australia.

To illustrate a four-section system, take the Gamilaraay in northern NSW: each section has a different term for men and women: the sections are ordered into two named matrilineal moieties and two (unnamed) generation levels (see table, based on Wafer and Lissarrague (2008):454). The marriage rule is articulated in terms of section membership: a person's spouse should be from the opposite matrimoiety and the same generation level; e.g. a Gambuu man marries a Maadhaa woman and their children are Gabii and Gabudhaa, while a Buudhaa woman's husband is Marrii and their children are Yibaay and Yibadha.

Generation level/Matrimoiety	**Gubadhin -Yanguu**	**Dhilbi-Wudhurru**
1 Masculine 1 Feminine	Gambuu *Buudhaa*	Marrii *Maadhaa*
2 Masculine 2 Feminine	Yibaay *Yibadha*	Gabii *Gabudhaa*

In this case, and many others where there is a section system, the prescribed marriage is with a classificatory cross-cousin (a mother's brother's child or father's sister's child).

Regarding subsections, the 8 skin system, McConvell's work has shown clearly how important linguistic evidence is to plotting evolution and spread of such systems. He was able to explain the apparent gender prefixes in subsection terms of gender-less languages like Warlpiri (masculine *Japanangka* vs. feminine Napanangka) by tracing the origin of the terms to languages far to the north which earlier had gender prefixes of the right form (see also Harvey (2008)).

Unlike kinship terms, which tend to be mostly inherited, subsection terms, and probably most section terms, are diffused (loanwords). It seems unlikely that kinship terminologies, and social categories database, have parallel histories. More complex relationships are likely to be uncovered in this project.

Relative chronology of the spread of subsections from the origin area in the north was discovered by use of the 'linguistic stratigraphy' of sound changes in the subsection terms, compared to sound changes in other words. In some cases it may be possible to convert these relative chronologies into absolute chronologies by use of archaeological dating of material culture items, terms for which show related patterns of sound change, or perhaps datable contacts with overseas visitors who brought loanwords (like the Macassans) over the past few hundred years.

Both sections and subsections undergo permutations or rotations in some areas into which they diffused. For instance, in the Pilbara of Western Australia, in the systems shown in the tables below, Kariera (1) and Coastal Nyangumarta (2) have the same arrangement except that the term Milangka has replaced the older term Palyeri (Palyarri). However in Inland Nyuangumarts (3) the terms have switched around positions on the grid – Karimarra the classificatory mother or daughter of Panaka on the coast has become his/her spouse inland, and Purungu the reverse process has occurred

1. Kariera sections (Radcliffe-Brown ,1913)

A	Banaka	B	Burung
C	Karimera	D	Palyeri

2. Coastal Nyangumarta sections (O'Grady & Mooney, 1973)

A	Panaka	B	Purungu
C	Karimarra	D	Milangka

3. Inland Nyangumarta sections (O'Grady & Mooney, 1973)

A	Panaka	B	Karimarra
C	Purungu	D	Milangka

In part of the Western Desert a partial merger of two section systems took place yielding what was known as a 6-section system (but see Doussset 2005 for a different interpretation). A more dramatic merger of two sections systems with a particular pattern of marriage alliance yielded the original subsection system (McConvell, 1985, 1997).

McConvell (1985) also analyses the various permutations of subsection terms in Arnhem Land as a historical sequence and advances the idea that 'bottlenecks' allow for such changes to occur, where unorthodox marriages occur among fringe isolated groups leading to change in the systems. This kind of hypothesis will be investigated further in AustKin II.

It is important for the AustKin II project to have a clear method of coding the meaning and structure of section and subsection systems. The Pilbara examples above illustrate the method introduced by Radcliffe-Brown, in which each position in the grid has a letter A-D (and a number 1-2 in the case of subsections). This system potentially indicates two things:

(a) the (pseudo-) kinship relationships between the sections A-B (spouse, cross-cousin etc); A-C (mother-child, MB-niece/nephes etc) and so on.

(b) the 'pragmatic equivalence' between two sections/subsections with the same alphanumeric code in different language groups, that is that A refers to the same category of people in wider dealing between groups, withut necessarily using a linguistically related form

It is necessary to include the Radcliffe-Brown (1930-31) coding in the database simply because this is the most widely used standard. However while criterion (b) is clear from the literature in some cases, in others it is less so and requires fine grained historical and ethnological research – bearing in mind also that these systems are no longer in use in many areas and not well remembered. Pragmatic equivalence is a key to understanding how systems work, however, since they are inherently wide-scale linking together people in large marriage and socioeconomic networks.

Other coding schemas or types of representations will have to be included, such as those proposed by Cresswell (1975) or Service (1960). However, in addition to the coding of sections and subsections in an optimal way, we also need to code for moieties and other social institutions and category systems such as clans. Matrimoieties and patrimoieties are found in different areas, sometimes close together. Berndt (2000) represents such social classifications across Australia in a map, but the lack of ability to show layering and overlaps of different kinds of systems is a drawback with such representations (cf. McConvell's maps in Peterson et al. (2005):91).

Moreover, moieties have clans (matriclans or patriclans) affiliated to them. Both moieties and clans often carry totemic animal names. Testart (1978) has argued, from evidence of associated clan species, that the matrimoieties historically preceded the patrimoieties and that there was a transformation of matrimoieties into patrimoieties.

Figure 4: The general work plan for setting up the social category database

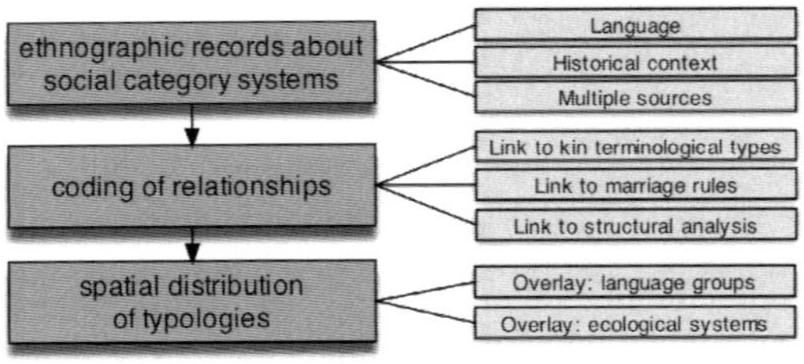

2.3 Analysis of synchronic and diachronic relationships between kin, skins and marriage

In relation to Australia here has been a tradition of combining kinship terminology, marriage rules and social categories (sections and subsections) into a unitary 'kinship system' in which these elements are inextricably connected by close functional cohesion. This perception of how Australian systems operate became especially influential due to analyses of section systems by anthropologists exploring componential approaches such as Burling (1962), Often this nglects the relative independence and differing histories of these elements.

More significantly for our project, such an approach does not facilitate comparison and the tracing of diachronic interactions of kinship terminology, marriage and social categories which we have identified as a major goal.

We need to design the AustKin II database so that these elements are in separate modules but their relationships can be tracked both visualization by historical-geographical maps and subject to statistical analysis showing how closely the elements match with each other. We already have standard assumptions which we can recast as hypotheses and pay close attention to the mismatches and deviations.

Beyond these three components there is also a demographic one, in particular how actual marriage patterns relate to maintenance and change of marriage rules, kinship systems and social categories. The possibility of 'bottlenecks' leading to change in social category systems has been mentioned– this relates both to marriage patterns, general interaction and perhaps population size and density.

A number of writers have proposed hypotheses relating different types of social categories to differing ecological conditions (e.g, Yengoyan, 1976, cf. McKnight, 1981). Ecological determinist hypotheses generally do not work well, and are flawed by their synchronic and ahistorical nature – when what is needed is understanding of movements which drive diffusion of such systems.

Hypotheses such as Keen (1982, 2004) linking polygyny to types of marriage and associated age structure and marriage network flows in different areas of Arnhem Land are more promising. The work done in AustKin I developing a diachronic dimension for Yolngu kinship in North-east Arnhem land (McConvell & Keen, 2011) can now be put together with the correlational work by Keen to explore the dynamics of how kinship, marriage and demography influence each other over time.

Another more wide ranging hypothesis to which we pay attention is that of White and Denham (2009), where the functional advantage of types of kinship systems such as Omaha skewing and social categories like sections and subsections lies in their driving force towards exogamy, rescuing small groups from otherwise almost certain demographic collapse. Simulations could play a role in testing these kinds of hypotheses.

If our historical reconstruction work can begin to find relative or even absolute dates for these institutional changes, we can contribute to debate which has gone on for some time over whether the type of society of recent times in Australia is very ancient or whether there was a major change, perhaps related to 'intensification' (economic and population growth) identified by archaeologists in the Holocene. It has been argued that this led to more stable groupings and ethnicities, based on specific types of kinship, marriage and social organisation.

The hypothesis of the origin and spread of subsections now has a secure foundation, but requires much more detailed work of the kind outlined for the AustKin II project. The question of the origin of sections, the older system from which subsections evolved by merger of two section systems, is still at an earlier stage .

3.Technology

As is the case with AustKin I (Dousset et al., 2010), AustKin II will be based on a rather classic LAMP environment (Linux-Apache-MySQL-PHP) to assure portability, redeployment and simultaneous multiuser tasking. Data itself is stored in a highly flat and atomized manner in multiple small-scale tables linked to each other through multiple relationships. Groupings, filtering, sorting, recombination, or hierarchical relationships are reconstructed through the PHP scripts on the fly and if necessary stored in other database tables to ensure as strictly as possible a clear distinction between interpretation or analysis and the raw data itself. In AustKin II, this model will allow us to reconstruct data following different modes of representation and Coding (Radcliffe-Brown, Cresswell, Service etc.) without actually modifying the raw data itself.

Figure 5: Simplified relationships between tables in AustKin I, model for AustKin II

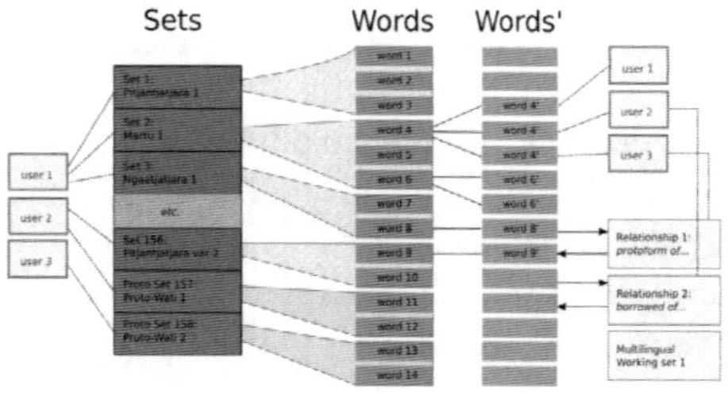

4. Conclusions

The study of the evolution of Australian kinship systems and the relationship between them and marriage and social category ('skins') systems is significant not just for Australia. It has been claimed by Allen (1998) that the primordial world social organization was based on a 'tetradic' structure similar to sections, from which evolved Dravidian-Kariera systems. Hage (2003) claimed to have found 'Kariera' systems in proto-languages in many part of the world.

If the earliest kinship systems we can detect in Australia by our reconstruction methods are Kariera, then this adds some weight to the world primordial (or very early) Dravidian-Kariera hypothesis, but is by no means convincing, as we are probably dealing with proto-languages of not much more than 5000 years in age. A similar problem of relative short age also besets the idea that Australian sections may be relics of a very early human type of social organization. It may be that sections are in fact younger than the proto-languages e.g. proto-Pama-Nyungan) and this is something AustKin II may be able to find out.In order to give credible answers to such questions we should not indulge in speculation, as so many have. We have some good methods in linguistics and ethnology and these have to be put to work systematically.

We have made a good start with AustKin I and its database of Australian indigenous kinship terminology, which enables us to reconstruct systems going back some thousands of years and visualize the distributions of patterns and changes. The next step, AustKin II, brings this together with other modules in a database dealing with marriage and the social category systems, especially sections and subsections. With these tools in hand we will explore the co-evolution of these systems - their interaction with each other over time.

References

Nicholas Allen. 1998. The prehistory of Dravidian-type terminologies. In Maurice Godelier, Thomas Trautmann & F. Tjon Sie Fat (eds.) *Transformations of kinship*, 314-331.

Ronald Berndt. 2000. *The World of the First Australians.* Canberra: Aboriginal Studies Press.

Robert Blust. 1980. Early Austronesian Social Organization: The Evidence of Language. *Current Anthropology,* 21(2):205-47.

Robbins Burling. 1962. A structural restatement of Njamal kinship terminology. *Man,* 62:122-124.

R. Cresswell. 1975. La parenté, Cresswell R. (ed.) *Elements d'Ethnologie*, 2: 132-174. Paris: Armand Collin.

Wouter De Nooy, Andrej Mrvar and Vladimir Batagelj. 2011. *Exploratory Social Network Analysis with Pajek.* Cambridge: Cambridge University Press.

Laurent. Dousset. 2002. Accounting for context and substance: the Australian Western Desert kinship system. *Anthropological Forum*, 12(2):193-204.

Laurent Dousset. 2003. On the misinterpretation of the Aluridja kinship system type (Australian Western Desert). *Social Anthropology*, 11(1): 43-61.

Laurent Dousset. 2005. *Assimilating identities: Social Networks and the Diffusion of Sections.* Sydney: Oceania Monograph 57.

Laurent Dousset. 2011. *Australian Aboriginal Kinship: an introductory handbook with particular emphasis on the Western Desert.* Pacific-credo Publications.

Laurent Dousset. In press. Horizontal and vertical skewing: similar objectives, two solutions. In Thomas R. Trautmann and Peter M. Whiteley (eds) *Crow-Omaha: New Light on a Classic Problem of Kinship Analysis*. Arizona University Press.

Laurent Dousset, Rachel Hendery, Claire Bowern, Harold Koch & Patrick McConvell. 2010. Developing a database for Australian Indigenous kinship terminology: The AustKin project, *Australian Aboriginal Studies,* 2010(1):42-56.

Maurice Godelier, Thomas Trautmann and F. Tjon Sie Fat (eds.). 1998. *Transformations of kinship*. Washington DC: Smithsonian.

J. Patrick Gray. 1998. Ethnographic Atlas Codebook. *World Cultures,* 10(1):86-136.

Per Hage. 2003. The ancient Maya kinship system. *Journal of Anthropological Research.* 59:5-21.

Mark Harvey. 2008. *Proto-Mirndi.* Canberra: Pacific Linguistics.

Doug Jones and Bojka Milicic (eds.). 2010. *Kinship, language and prehistory: Per Hage and the Renaissance in Kinship Studies.* Salt Lake City: University of Utah Press.

Ian Keen. 1982. How Some Murngin Men Marry Ten Wives: The Marital Implications of Matrilateral Cross-Cousin Structures. *Man,* 17(4): 620-642.

Ian Keen. 2002. Seven Aboriginal marriage systems and their correlates. *Anthropological Forum,* 12(2):145-157.

Ian Keen. 2004. *Aboriginal Economy and Society: Australia at the threshold of Colonisation.* Melbourne: Oxford University Press.

David Kronenfeld. 2009. *Fanti kinship and the analysis of kinship terminologies.* Champagne: University of Illinois Press.

Patrick McConvell. 1985. The Origin of Subsections in Northern Australia. *Oceania,* 56:1-33.

Patrick McConvell. In press. Omaha skewing in Australia: overlays, dynamism and change. In Thomas R. Trautmann and Peter M. Whiteley (eds) *Crow-Omaha: New Light on a Classic Problem of Kinship Analysis.* Arizona University Press.

Patrick McConvell. 1997. Long lost relations: Pama-Nyungan and Northern kinship. In Patrick McConvell and Nicholas Evans (eds.) *Archeology and Linguistics: Aboriginal Australia in Global Perspective,* 207-236.

Patrick McConvell and Nicholas Evans (eds.). 1997. *Archaeology and Linguistics: Aboriginal Australia in Global Perspective.* Melbourne: Oxford University Press.

Patrick McConvell and Rachel Hendery. To appear. What is a Kariera kinship system?

Patrick McConvell and Ian Keen. 2010. The transition from Kariera to an asymmetrical system: Cape York Peninsula to North-east Arnhem Land. In Doug Jones and Bojka Milicic (eds.) *Kinship, language and prehistory: Per Hage and the Renaissance in Kinship Studies,* 99-132.

Patrick McConvell, Ian Keen and Rachel Hendery (eds.). In press. *Kinship change and reconstruction.* Salt Lake City: University of Utah Press.

David McKnight. 1981. Distribution of Australian Aboriginal 'Marriage Classes': Environmental and Demographic Influences. *Man (N.S.),* 16: 75-89.

Lewis Henry Morgan. 1997. *Systems of consanguinity and affinity of the Human Family.* Lincoln & London: University of Nebraska Press [Smithsonian Institution volume 17 [1871].

George P. Murdock. 1967. *Ethnographic Atlas.* Pittsburgh: Pittsburgh University Press.

Geoffrey O'Grady and Kathleen Mooney. 1973. Nyangumarda Kinship Terminology. *Anthropological Linguistics,* 15(1):1-23.

Nicolas Peterson and Patrick McConvell. 2005. Social Organisation. In Bill Arthur and Frances Morphy (eds.) *Macquarie Atlas of Indigenous Australia,* 88-112. Sydney:Macquarie.

Alfred Reginald Radcliffe-Brown. 1913. Three Tribes of Western Australia. *Journal of the Royal Anthropological Institute*, 43:143-19

Alfred Reginald Radcliffe-Brown. 1930-31. The social organization of Australian tribes. *Oceania,* 1(1-4): 34-63; 206-46; 322-41; 426-56.

Elman R. Service. 1960. Sociocentric Relationship Terms and the Australian Class System, G.E. Dole & R.L. Carneiro (eds.) *Essays in the Science of Culture in Honour of Leslie G. White,* 416-436. New York: Thomas Crowell.

Alain Testart. 1978. *Des Classifications dualistes en Australie.* Paris: Maison des Sciences de l'homme.

Thomas Trautmann, and Peter Whiteley (eds.). In press. *Crow-Omaha: New Light on a Classic Problem of Kinship Analysis.* Tucson: University of Arizona Press.

James Wafer, Amanda Lissarague and Jean Harkins. 2008. *A handbook of Aboriginal languages of New South Wales and the Australian Capital Territory.* Nambucca Heads: Muurbay.

Kenneth Whistler. 1980. *Proto-Wintun Kin Classification: a case study of reconstruction of a complex semantic system.* Ph.D dissertation, University of California Berkeley.

Douglas White and Woodrow Denham. 2007. The Indigenous Marriage Paradox. Paper for SASci meeting , San Antonio.

Aram Yengoyan. I976. Structure, event and ecology in Aboriginal Australia: a comparative viewpoint. In Nicolas Peterson (eds.) *Tribes and boundaries in Australia,* 121-140. Canberra: Australian Institute of Aboriginal Studies.

Using context and phonetic features in models of etymological sound change

Hannes Wettig[1], **Kirill Reshetnikov**[2] and **Roman Yangarber**[1]
[1]Department of Computer Science
University of Helsinki, Finland
First.Last@cs.helsinki.fi
[2]Institute of Linguistics
Academy of Sciences
Moscow, Russia

Abstract

This paper presents a novel method for aligning etymological data, which models context-sensitive rules governing sound change, and utilizes phonetic features of the sounds. The goal is, for a given corpus of cognate sets, to find the best alignment at the sound level. We introduce an imputation procedure to compare the goodness of the resulting models, as well as the goodness of the data sets. We present evaluations to demonstrate that the new model yields improvements in performance, compared to previously reported models.

1 Introduction

This paper introduces a context-sensitive model for alignment and analysis of etymological data. Given a raw collection of etymological data (the *corpus*)—we first aim to find the "best" alignment at the sound or symbol level. We take the corpus (or possibly several different corpora) for a language family as *given*; different data sets are typically conflicting, which creates the need to determine which is more correct. Etymological data sets are found in digital etymological databases, such as ones we use for the Uralic language family. A database is typically organized into *cognate sets*; all elements within a cognate set are posited (by the database creators) to be derived from a common origin, which is a word-form in the ancestral proto-language.

Etymology encompasses several problems, including: discovery of sets of cognates—genetically related words; determination of genetic relations among groups of languages, based on linguistic data; discovering *regular sound correspondences* across languages in a given language family; and reconstruction of forms in the proto-languages.

Computational methods can provide valuable tools for the etymological community. The methods can be judged by how well they model certain aspects of etymology, and by whether the automatic analysis produces results that match theories established by manual analysis.

In this work, we allow *all* the data—and only the data—to determine what rules underly it, rather than relying on external (and possibly biased) rules that try to explain the data. This approach will provide a means of measuring the quality of the etymological data sets in terms of their internal consistency—a dataset that is more consistent should receive a higher score. We seek methods that analyze the data automatically, in an unsupervised fashion, to determine whether a complete description of the correspondences can be discovered automatically, directly from raw etymological data—cognate sets within the language family. Another way to state the question is: what alignment rules are "inherently encoded" in the given corpus itself.

At present, our aim is to analyze given etymological datasets, rather than to construct new ones from scratch. Because our main goal is to develop methods that are as objective as possible, the models make no *a priori* assumptions or "universal" principles—e.g., no preference to align vowel with vowels, or a symbol with itself. The models are not aware of the *identity* of a symbol across languages, and do not try to preserve identity, of symbols, or even of features—rather they try to find maximally regular correspondences.

In Section 2 we describe the data used in our experiments, and review approaches to etymological alignment over the last decade. We formalize the problem of alignment in Section 3, give the

Proceedings of the EACL 2012 Joint Workshop of LINGVIS & UNCLH, pages 108–116,
Avignon, France, April 23 - 24 2012.

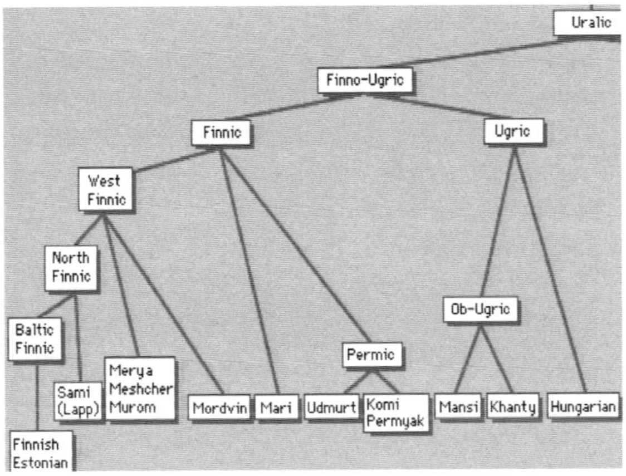

Figure 1: Finno-Ugric branch of Uralic language family (the data used in the experiments in this paper)

technical details of our models in Section 4. We present results and discussion in Sections 5 and 6.

2 Data and Related Work

We use two large Uralic etymological resources. The StarLing database of Uralic, (Starostin, 2005), based on (Rédei, 1988 1991), contains over 2500 cognate sets. *Suomen Sanojen Alkuperä* (SSA), "The Origin of Finnish Words", a Finnish etymological dictionary, (Itkonen and Kulonen, 2000), has over 5000 cognate sets, (about half of which are only in languages from the Balto-Finnic branch, closest to Finnish). Most importantly, for our models, SSA gives "dictionary" word-forms, which may contain extraneous morphological material, whereas StarLing data is mostly stemmed.

One traditional arrangement of the Uralic languages[1] is shown in Figure 1. We model etymological processes using these Uralic datasets.

The methods in (Kondrak, 2002) learn regular one-to-one sound correspondences between pairs of related languages in the data. The methods in (Kondrak, 2003; Wettig et al., 2011) find more complex (one-to-many) correspondences. These models operate on one language pair at a time; also, they do not model the *context* of the sound changes, while most etymological changes are conditioned on context. The MCMC-based model proposed in (Bouchard-Côté et al., 2007) explicitly aims to model the context of changes, and operates on more than a pair of languages.[2]

We should note that our models at present operate at the phonetic level only, they leave semantic judgements of the database creators unquestioned. While other work, e.g. (Kondrak, 2004), has attempted to approach semantics by computational means as well, our model uses the given cognate set as the fundamental unit. In our work, we do not attempt the problem of discovering cognates, addressed, e.g., in, (Bouchard-Côté et al., 2007; Kondrak, 2004; Kessler, 2001). We begin instead with a set of etymological data (or more than one set) for a language family *as given*. We focus on the principle of *recurrent sound correspondence*, as in much of the literature, including (Kondrak, 2002; Kondrak, 2003), and others.

As we develop our alignment models at the sound or symbol level, in the process of evaluation of these models, we also arrive at modeling the relationships among groups of languages within the family. Construction of phylogenies is studied extensively, e.g., by (Nakhleh et al., 2005; Ringe et al., 2002; Barbançon et al., 2009). This work differs from ours in that it operates on manually pre-selected sets of *characters*, which capture divergent features of languages within the family, whereas we operate on the raw, *complete* data.

There is extensive work on alignment in the machine-translation (MT) community, and it has been observed that methods from MT alignment may be projected onto alignment in etymology. The intuition is that translation sentences in MT correspond to cognate words in etymology, while words in MT correspond to sounds in etymology. The notion of *regularity* of sound change in etymology, which is what our models try to capture, is loosely similar to contextually conditioned correspondence of translation words across languages. For example, (Kondrak, 2002) employs MT alignment from (Melamed, 1997; Melamed, 2000); one might employ the IBM models for MT alignment, (Brown et al., 1993), or the HMM model, (Vogel et al., 1996). Of the MT-related models, (Bodrumlu et al., 2009) is similar to ours in that it is based on MDL (the Minimum Description Length Principle, introduced below).

[1]Adapted from Encyclopedia Britannica and (Anttila, 1989)

[2]Using this method, we found that the running time did not scale well for more than three languages.

3 Aligning Pairs of Words

We begin with pairwise alignment: aligning pairs of words, from two related languages in our corpus of cognates. For each word pair, the task of alignment means finding exactly which symbols correspond. Some symbols may align with "themselves" (i.e., with similar or identical sounds), while others may have undergone changes during the time when the two related languages have been evolving separately. The simplest form of such alignment at the symbol level is a pair $(\sigma : \tau) \in \Sigma \times T$, a single symbol σ from the *source alphabet* Σ with a symbol τ from the *target alphabet* T. We denote the sizes of the alphabets by $|\Sigma|$ and $|T|$.

To model *insertions* and *deletions*, we augment both alphabets with a special empty symbol—denoted by a dot—and write the augmented alphabets as $\Sigma_.$ and $T_.$. We can then align word pairs such as *vuosi—al* (meaning "year" in Finnish and Xanty), for example as any of:

v	*u*	*o*	*s*	*i*		*v*	*u*	*o*	*s*	*i*	
|	|	|	|	|		|	|	|	|	|	etc...
a	*l*	.	.	.		.	*a*	.	*l*	.	

The alignment on the right then consists of the symbol pairs: (v:.), (u:a), (o:.), (s:l), (i:.).

4 Context Model with Phonetic Features

The context-aware alignment method we present here is built upon baseline models published previously, (Wettig et al., 2011), where we presented several models that do not use phonetic features or context. Similarly to the earlier ones, the current method is based on the *Minimum Description Length* (MDL) Principle, (Grünwald, 2007).

We begin with a raw set of (observed) data—the not-yet-aligned word pairs. We would like to find an alignment for the data—which we will call the *complete* data—complete with alignments, that make the most sense globally, in terms of embodying regular correspondences. We are after the regularity, and the more regularity we can find, the "better" our alignment will be (its goodness will be defined formally later). MDL tells us that the more regularity we can find in the data, the fewer bits we will need to encode it (or compress it). More regularity means lower entropy in the distribution that describes the data, and lower entropy allows us to construct a more economical code. That is, if we have no knowledge about any regularly of correspondence between symbols, the joint distribution over all possible pairs of symbols will be very flat (high entropy). If we know that certain symbol pairs align frequently, the joint distribution will have spikes, and lower entropy. In (Wettig et al., 2011) we showed how starting with a random alignment a good joint distribution can be learned using MDL. However the "rules" those baseline models were able to learn were very rudimentary, since they could not use any information in the context, and we know that many regular correspondences are conditioned by context.

We now introduce models that leverage information from the context to try to reduce the uncertainty in the distributions further, lowering the coding cost. To do that, we will code sounds in terms of their phonetic features: rather than coding the symbols (sounds) as atomic, we code them as vectors of phonetic features. Rather than aligning symbol pairs, we align the corresponding features of the symbols. While coding each feature, the model can make use of features of other sounds in its context (environment), through a special decision tree built for that feature.

4.1 Features

We will code each symbol, to be aligned in the complete data, as a feature vector. First we code the **Type** feature, with values: K (consonant), V (vowel), dot, and *word boundary*, which we denote as $\#$. Consonants and vowels have their own sets of features, with 2–8 values per feature:

	Consonant articulation	
M	**Manner**	plosive, fricative, glide, ...
P	**Place**	labial, dental, ..., velar
X	**Voiced**	–, +
S	**Secondary**	–, affricate, aspirate, ...
	Vowel articulation	
V	**Vertical**	high–low
H	**Horizontal**	front–back
R	**Rounding**	–, +
L	**Length**	1–5

4.2 Contexts

While coding any symbol, the model will be allowed to query a fixed, finite set of *candidate contexts*. A context is a triplet (L, P, F), where L is the level—either source or target,—and P is one of the positions that the model may query—relative to the position currently being coded; for example, we may allow positions as in Fig. 2. F is one of the possible features found at that position. Therefore, we will have about 2 levels * 8 positions * 2–6 features $\approx$ 80 candidate contexts that can be queried by the model, as explained below.

I	itself,
–P	previous position
–S	previous non-dot symbol
–K	previous consonant
–V	previous vowel
+S	previous or self non-dot symbol
+K	previous or self consonant
+V	previous or self vowel

Figure 2: An example of a set of possible positions in the context—relative to the position currently being coded—that can be queried by the context model.

4.3 The Two-Part Code

We code the complete (i.e., aligned) data using a *two-part code*, following the MDL Principle. We first code which particular model instance we select from our *class* of models, and then code the data, given the defined model. Our model class is defined as: a set of decision trees (forest), with one tree to predict each feature on each level. The model instance will define the particular structures for each of the trees.

The forest consists of 18 decision trees, one for each feature on the source and the target level: the type feature, 4 vowel and 4 consonant features, times 2 levels. Each node in such tree will either be a leaf, or will be split by querying one of the candidate contexts defined above. The cost of coding the structure of the tree is one bit for every node—to encode whether this node was split (is an internal node) or is a leaf—plus $\approx \log 80$ times the number of internal nodes—to encode *which* particular context was chosen to split that node. We will explain how the best context to split on is chosen in Sec. 4.6.

Each feature and level define a tree, e.g., the "voiced" (**X**) feature of the source symbols corresponds to the source-**X** tree. A node N in this tree holds a distribution over the values of **X** of only those symbol instances in the complete data that have reached in N by following the context queries, starting from the root. The tree structure tells us precisely which path to follow—completely determined by the context. For example, when coding a symbol α based on another symbol found in the context of α—at some level (say, target), some position (say, –K), and one of its features (say, **M**)—the next edge down the tree is determined by that feature's value; and so on, down to a leaf. For an example of an actual decision tree learned by the model, see Fig. 5.

To compute the code length of the complete data, we only need to take into account the distributions at *the leaves*. We could choose from a variety of coding methods; the crucial point is that the chosen code will assign a particular number—the *cost*—to every possible alignment of the data. This code-length, or cost, will then serve as the *objective function*—i.e., it will be the value that the algorithm will try to optimize. Each reduction in cost will correspond directly to reduction in the entropy of the probability distribution of the symbols, which in turn corresponds to more certainty (i.e., regularity) in the correspondences among the symbols, and to improvement in the alignment. This is the link to our goal, and the reason for introducing code lengths—it gives us a single number that describes the quality of an alignment.

We use *Normalized Maximum Likelihood* (NML), (Rissanen, 1996) as our coding scheme. We choose NML because it has certain optimality properties. Using NML, we code the distribution at each leaf node separately, and summing the costs of all leaves gives the total cost of the aligned data—the value of our objective function.

Suppose n instances end up in a leaf node N, of the λ-level tree, for feature F having k values (e.g., consonants satisfying N's context constraints in the source-**X** tree, with $k = 2$ values: $-$ and $+$), and the values are distributed so that n_i instances have value i (with $i \in \{1, \ldots, k\}$). Then this requires an NML code-length of

$$\begin{aligned} L_{NML}(\lambda; F; N) &= -\log P_{NML}(\lambda; F; N) \\ &= -\log \frac{\prod_i \left(\frac{n_i}{n}\right)^{n_i}}{C(n,k)} \end{aligned} \tag{1}$$

Here $\prod_i \left(\frac{n_i}{n}\right)^{n_i}$ is the maximum likelihood of the multinomial data at node N, and the term

$$C(n,k) = \sum_{n'_1+\ldots+n'_k=n} \prod_i \left(\frac{n'_i}{n}\right)^{n'_i} \tag{2}$$

is a normalizing constant to make P_{NML} a probability distribution.

In the MDL literature, e.g., (Grünwald, 2007), the term $-\log C(n,k)$ is called the *stochastic complexity* or the *(minimax) regret* of the model, (in this case, the multinomial model). The NML distribution provides the unique solution to the minimax problem posed in (Shtarkov, 1987),

$$\min_{\hat{P}} \max_{\mathbf{x^n}} \log \frac{P(\mathbf{x^n}|\hat{\mathbf{\Theta}}(\mathbf{x^n}))}{\hat{P}(\mathbf{x^n})} \quad (3)$$

where $\hat{\Theta}(\mathbf{x^n}) = \arg\max_{\Theta} \mathbf{P}(\mathbf{x^n})$ are the *maximum likelihood parameters* for the data $\mathbf{x^n}$. Thus, P_{NML} minimizes the worst-case regret, i.e., the number of excess bits in the code as compared to the best model in the model class, with hind-sight. For details on the computation of this code length see (Kontkanen and Myllymäki, 2007).

Learning the model from the observed data now means aligning the word pairs and building the decision trees in such a way as to minimize the two-part code length: the sum of the model's code length—to encode the structure of the trees,—and the data's code length—to encode the aligned word pairs, using these trees.

4.4 Summary of the Algorithm

The full learning algorithm runs as follows:

We start with an initial *random* alignment for each pair of words in the corpus, i.e., for each word pair choose some random path through the matrix depicted in Figure 3.

From then on we alternate between two steps: **A.** re-build the decision trees for all features on source and target levels, and **B.** re-align all word pairs in the corpus. Both of these operations monotonically decrease the two-part cost function and thus compress the data.

We continue until we reach convergence.

4.5 Re-alignment Procedure

To align source word $\vec{\sigma}$ consisting of symbols $\vec{\sigma} = [\sigma_1 ... \sigma_n]$, $\vec{\sigma} \in \Sigma^*$ with target word $\vec{\tau} = [\tau_1 ... \tau_m]$ we use dynamic programming. The tree structures are considered fixed, as are the alignments of all word pairs, except the one currently being aligned—which is subtracted from the counts stored at the leaf nodes.

We now fill the matrix V, left-to-right, top-to-bottom. Every possible alignment of $\vec{\sigma}$ and $\vec{\tau}$ corresponds to exactly one path through this matrix: starting with cost equal to 0 in the top-left cell, moving only downward or rightward, and terminating in the bottom-right cell. In this Viterbi-like matrix, every cell corresponds to a partially completed alignment: reaching cell (i,j) means having read off i symbols of the source word and j symbols of the target. Each cell $V(i,j)$—marked X in the Figure—stores the cost of the *most probable* path so far: the most probable way to have scanned $\vec{\sigma}$ through symbol σ_i and $\vec{\tau}$ through τ_j:

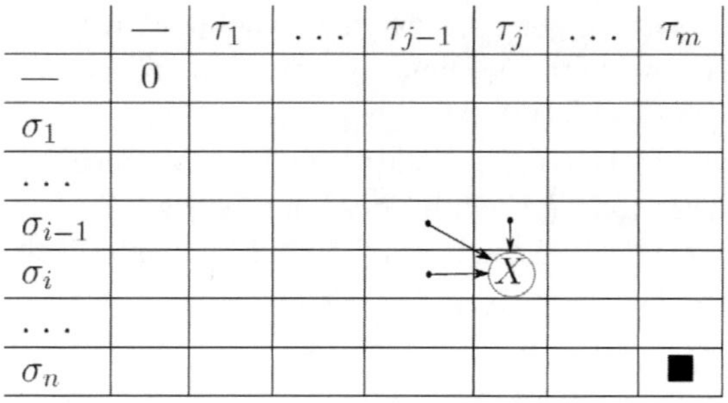

Figure 3: Dynamic programming matrix V, to search for the most probable alignment

$$V(i,j) = \min \begin{cases} V(i,j-1) & +L(.:\tau_j) \\ V(i-1,j) & +L(\sigma_i:.) \\ V(i-1,j-1) & +L(\sigma_i:\tau_j) \end{cases}$$

Each term $V(\cdot,\cdot)$ has been computed earlier by the dynamic programming; the term $L(\cdot)$—the cost of aligning the two symbols, inserting or deleting—is determined by the change in *data* code length it induces to add this event to the corresponding leaf in all the feature trees it concerns.

In particular, the cost of the most probable *complete* alignment of the two words will be stored in the bottom-right cell, $V(n,m)$, marked ■.

4.6 Building Decision Trees

Given a complete alignment of the data, we need to build a decision tree, for each feature on both levels, yielding the lowest two-part cost. The term "decision tree" is meant in a probabilistic sense here: instead of a single value, at each node we store a *distribution* of the corresponding feature values, over all instances that reach this node. The distribution at a leaf is then used to code an instance when it reaches the leaf in question. We code the features in some fixed, pre-set order, and source level before target level.

We now describe in detail the process of building the tree for feature **X**, for the source level, (we will need do the same for all other features, on both levels, as well). We build this tree as follows. First, we collect all instances of consonants on the source level, and gather the the counts for feature **X**; and build an initial count vector; suppose it is:

value of **X**:	+	−
	1001	1002

This vector is stored at the *root* of the tree; the cost of this node is computed using NML, eq. 1.

Next, we try to split this node, by finding such a context that if we query the values of the feature in that context, it will help us reduce the entropy in this count vector. We check in turn all possible candidate contexts, (L, P, F), and choose the best one. Each candidate refers to some symbol found on the source (σ) or the target (τ) level, at some relative position P, and to one of that symbol's features F. We will condition the split on the possible values of F. For each candidate, we try to split on its feature's values, and collect the resulting alignment counts.

Suppose one such candidate is (σ, –V, **H**), i.e., (source-level, previous vowel, Horizontal feature), and suppose that the **H**-feature has two values: *front/back*. The vector at the root node (recall, this tree is for the **X**-feature) would then split into two vectors, e.g.:

value of **X**:	+	−
X | **H**=*front*	1000	1
X | **H**=*back*	1	1001

This would likely be a very good split, since it reduces the entropy of the distribution in each row almost to zero. The criterion that guides the choice of the best candidate to use for splitting a node is the sum of the *code lengths* of the resulting split vectors, and the code length is proportional to the entropy.

We go through all candidates exhaustively, and greedily choose the one that yields the greatest reduction in entropy, and drop in cost. We proceed recursively down the tree, trying to split nodes, and stop when the total tree cost stops decreasing.

This completes the tree for feature **X** on level σ. We build trees for all features and levels similarly, from the current alignment of the complete data.

We augment the set of possible values at every node with two additional special branches: $\neq$, meaning the symbol at the queried position is of the wrong type and does not have the queried feature, and $\#$, meaning the query ran past the beginning of the word.

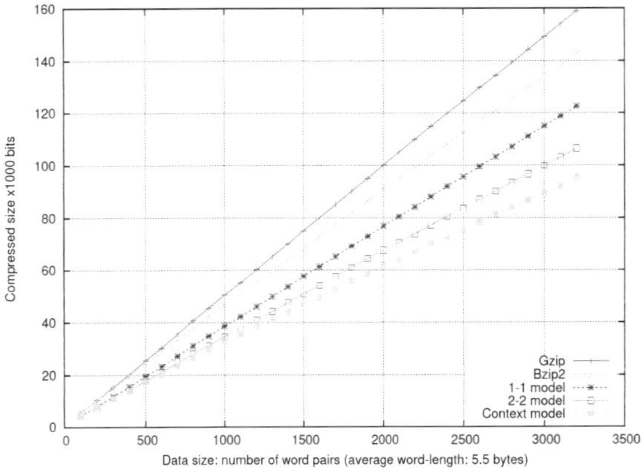

Figure 4: Comparison of compression power: Finnish-Estonian data from SSA, using the context model vs. the baseline models and standard compressors.

5 Evaluation and Results

One way to evaluate the presented models would require a *gold-standard* aligned corpus; the models produce alignments which could be compared to the gold-standard alignments, and we could measure performance quantitatively, e.g., in terms of accuracy. However, building a gold-standard aligned corpus for the Uralic data proved to be extremely difficult. In fact, it quickly becomes clear that this problem is at least as difficult as building a full reconstruction for all internal nodes in the family tree (and probably harder), since it requires full knowledge of all sound correspondences within the family. It is also compounded by the problem that the word-forms in the corpus may contain morphological material that is etymologically unrelated: some databases give "dictionary" forms, which contain extraneous affixes, and thereby obscure which parts of a given word form stand in etymological relationship with other members in the cognates set, and which do not. We therefore introduce other methods to evaluate the models.

Compression: In figure 4, we compare the context model, and use as baselines the standard data compressors, Gzip and Bzip, as well as the more basic models presented in (Wettig et al., 2011), (labeled "1x1 and "2x2"). We test the compression of up to 3200 Finnish-Estonian word pairs, from SSA. Gzip and Bzip compress data

	fin	*khn*	*kom*	*man*	*mar*	*mrd*	*saa*	*udm*	*ugr*
est	**0.26**	0.66	0.64	0.65	0.61	0.57	0.57	0.62	0.62
fin		0.63	0.64	0.65	0.59	0.56	0.50	0.62	0.63
khn			0.65	**0.58**	0.69	0.64	0.67	0.66	0.66
kom				0.63	0.68	0.66	0.70	**0.39**	0.66
man					0.68	0.65	0.72	0.62	0.62
mar						0.65	0.69	0.65	0.66
mrd							0.58	0.66	0.63
saa								0.67	0.70
udm									0.65

Table 1: Pairwise normalized edit distances for Finno-Ugric languages, on StarLing data (symmetrized by averaging over the two directions of imputation).

by finding regularities in it (i.e., frequent substrings). The comparison with Gzip is a "sanity check": we would like to confirm whether our models find more regularity in the data than would an off-the-shelf data compressor, that has no knowledge that the words in the data are etymologically related. Of course, our models know that they should align pairs of consecutive lines. This test shows that learning about the "vertical" correspondences achieves much better compression rates—allows the models to extract greater regularity from the data.

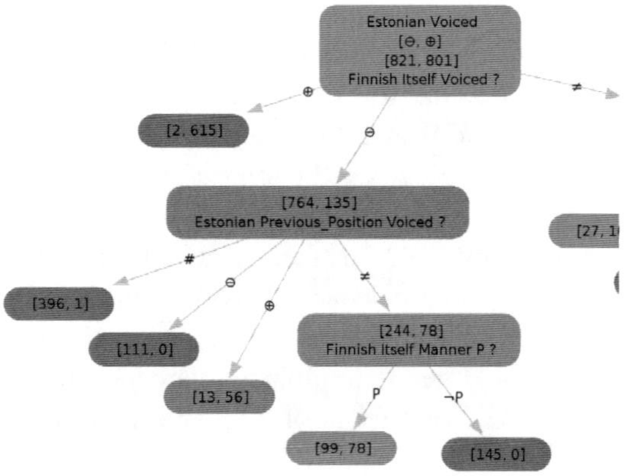

Figure 5: *Part of a tree, showing the rule for voicing of medial plosives in Estonian, conditioned on Finnish.*

Rules of correspondence: One our main goals is to model rules of correspondence among languages. We can evaluate the models based on how good they are at discovering rules. (Wettig et al., 2011) showed that aligning multiple symbols captures some of the context and thereby finds more complex rules than their 1-1 alignment model.

However, certain alignments, such as *t∼t/d*, *p∼p/b*, and *k∼k/g* between Finnish and Estonian, cannot be explained by the multiple-symbol model. This is due to the rule of *voicing of word-medial plosives* in Estonian. This rule could be expressed in terms of Two-level Morphology, (Koskenniemi, 1983) as: a voiceless plosive in Finnish, *may correspond* to voiced in Estonian, if not word-initial.[3] The context model finds this rule, shown in Fig. 5. This tree codes the *Target-level* (i.e., Estonian) *Voiced* consonant feature. In each node, the counts of corresponding feature values are shown in brackets. In the root node—prior to knowing anything about the environment—there is almost complete uncertainty (i.e., high entropy) about the value of *Voiced* feature of an Estonian consonant: 821 voiceless to 801 voiced in our data. Redder nodes indicate higher entropy, bluer nodes—lower entropy. The query in the root node tells us to check the context *Finnish Itself Voiced* for the most informative clue about whether the current Estonian consonant is voiced or not. Tracing the options down left to right from the root, we obtain the rules. The leftmost branch says, if the Finnish is voiced ($\oplus$), then the Estonian is almost certainly voiced as well—615 voiced to 2 voiceless in this case. If the Finnish is voiceless (Finnish Itself Voiced $= \ominus$), it says voicing *may occur*, but only in the red nodes—i.e., only if preceded by a voiced consonant on Estonian level (the branch marked by $\oplus$, 56 cases), or—if previous position is *not a consonant* (the $\neq$ branch indicates that the candidate's query does not apply: i.e., the sound found in that position is not a consonant)—it can be voiced only if the corresponding Finnish is a plosive (P, 78 cases). The blue nodes in this branch say that otherwise, the Estonian consonant almost certainly remains voiceless.

The context models discover numerous complex rules for different language pairs. For example, they learn a rule that initial Finnish *k* "changes" (corresponds) to *h* in Hungarian, if it is followed by a back vowel; the correspondence between Komi trills and Udmurt sibilants; etc.

Imputation: We introduce a novel test of the quality of the models, by using them to *impute* unseen data, as follows. For a given model, and a language pair (L_1, L_2)—e.g., (Finnish, Estonian)—hold out one word pair, and train the model on the remaining data. Then show the model the hidden Finnish word and let it guess

[3] In fact, phonetically, in modern spoken Estonian, the consonants that are written using the symbols *b,d,g* are not technically voiced, but that is a finer point, we use this rule for illustration of the principle.

the corresponding Estonian. Imputation can be done for all models with a simple dynamic programming algorithm, similar to the Viterbi-like search used during training. Formally, given the hidden Finnish string, the imputation procedure selects from all possible Estonian strings the most probable Estonian string, given the model. We then compute an edit distance between the imputed sting and the true withheld Estonian word (e.g., using the Levenshtein distance). We repeat this procedure for all word pairs in the (L_1, L_2) data set, sum the edit distances and normalize by the total size of the (true) L_2 data—this yields the Normalized Edit Distance $NED(L_2|L_1, M)$ between L_1 and L_2, under model M.

Imputation is a more intuitive measure of the model's quality than code length, with a clear practical interpretation. NED is also the ultimate test of the model's quality. If model M imputes better than M'—i.e., $NED(L_2|L_1, M) < NED(L_2|L_1, M')$—then it is difficult to argue that M could be in any sense "worse" than M'—it has learned more about the regularities between L_1 and L_2, and it knows more about L_2 given L_1. The context model, which has much lower cost than the baseline, almost always has lower NED. This also yields an important insight: it is an encouraging indication that optimizing the code length is a good approach—the algorithm does *not* optimize NED directly, and yet the cost correlates strongly with NED, which is a simple and intuitive measure of the model's quality.

6 Discussion

We have presented a novel feature-based context-aware MDL model, and a comparison of its performance against prior models for the task of alignment of etymological data. We have evaluated the models by examining the the rules of correspondence that they discovers, by comparing compression cost, imputation power and language distances induced by the imputation. The models take only the etymological data set as input, and require no further linguistic assumptions. In this regard, they is as objective as possible, given the data. The data set itself, of course, may be highly subjective and questionable.

The objectivity of models given the data now opens new possibilities for comparing entire data sets. For example, we can begin to compare the Finnish and Estonian datasets in SSA vs. StarLing, although the data sets have quite different characteristics, e.g., different size—3200 vs. 800 word pairs, respectively—and the comparison is done impartially, relying solely on the data provided. Another direct consequence of the presented methods is that they enable us to quantify uncertainty of entries in the corpus of etymological data. For example, for a given entry x in language L_1, we can compute exactly the probability that x would be imputed by any of the models, trained on all the remaining data from L_1 plus any other set of languages in the family. This can be applied equally to any entry, in particular to entries marked dubious by the database creators.

We can use this method to approach the question of comparison of "competing" etymological datasets. The cost of an optimal alignment obtained over a given data set serves as a measure of its internal consistency.

We are currently working to combine the context model with 3- and higher-dimensional models, and to extend these models to perform diachronic imputation, i.e., reconstruction of protoforms. We also intend to test the models on databases of other language families.

Acknowledgments

We are very grateful to the anonymous reviewers for their thoughtful and helpful comments. We thank Suvi Hiltunen for the implementation of the models, and Arto Vihavainen for implementing some of the earlier models. This research was supported by the Uralink Project, funded by the Academy of Finland and by the Russian Fund for the Humanities.

References

Raimo Anttila. 1989. *Historical and comparative linguistics*. John Benjamins.

François G. Barbançon, Tandy Warnow, Don Ringe, Steven N. Evans, and Luay Nakhleh. 2009. An experimental study comparing linguistic phylogenetic reconstruction methods. In *Proceedings of the Conference on Languages and Genes*, UC Santa Barbara. Cambridge University Press.

Tugba Bodrumlu, Kevin Knight, and Sujith Ravi. 2009. A new objective function for word alignment. In *Proc. NAACL Workshop on Integer Linear Programming for NLP*.

Alexandre Bouchard-Côté, Percy Liang, Thomas Griffiths, and Dan Klein. 2007. A probabilistic approach to diachronic phonology. In *Proceedings of the 2007 Joint Conference on Empirical Methods in Natural Language Processing and Computational Natural Language Learning (EMNLP-CoNLL)*, pages 887–896, Prague, June.

Peter F. Brown, Vincent J. Della Pietra, Stephen A. Della Pietra, and Robert. L. Mercer. 1993. The mathematics of statistical machine translation: Parameter estimation. *Computational Linguistics*, 19(2):263–311.

Peter Grünwald. 2007. *The Minimum Description Length Principle*. MIT Press.

Erkki Itkonen and Ulla-Maija Kulonen. 2000. *Suomen Sanojen Alkuperä (The Origin of Finnish Words)*. Suomalaisen Kirjallisuuden Seura, Helsinki, Finland.

Brett Kessler. 2001. *The Significance of Word Lists: Statistical Tests for Investigating Historical Connections Between Languages*. The University of Chicago Press, Stanford, CA.

Grzegorz Kondrak. 2002. Determining recurrent sound correspondences by inducing translation models. In *Proceedings of COLING 2002: 19th International Conference on Computational Linguistics*, pages 488–494, Taipei, August.

Grzegorz Kondrak. 2003. Identifying complex sound correspondences in bilingual wordlists. In A. Gelbukh, editor, *Computational Linguistics and Intelligent Text Processing (CICLing-2003)*, pages 432–443, Mexico City, February. Springer-Verlag Lecture Notes in Computer Science, No. 2588.

Grzegorz Kondrak. 2004. Combining evidence in cognate identification. In *Proceedings of the Seventeenth Canadian Conference on Artificial Intelligence (Canadian AI 2004)*, pages 44–59, London, Ontario, May. Lecture Notes in Computer Science 3060, Springer-Verlag.

Petri Kontkanen and Petri Myllymäki. 2007. A linear-time algorithm for computing the multinomial stochastic complexity. *Information Processing Letters*, 103(6):227–233.

Kimmo Koskenniemi. 1983. *Two-level morphology: A general computational model for word-form recognition and production*. Ph.D. thesis, University of Helsinki, Finland.

I. Dan Melamed. 1997. Automatic discovery of non-compositional compounds in parallel data. In *The Second Conference on Empirical Methods in Natural Language Processing*, pages 97–108, Hissar, Bulgaria.

I. Dan Melamed. 2000. Models of translational equivalence among words. *Computational Linguistics*, 26(2):221–249.

Luay Nakhleh, Don Ringe, and Tandy Warnow. 2005. Perfect phylogenetic networks: A new methodology for reconstructing the evolutionary history of natural languages. *Language (Journal of the Linguistic Society of America)*, 81(2):382–420.

Károly Rédei. 1988–1991. *Uralisches etymologisches Wörterbuch*. Harrassowitz, Wiesbaden.

Don Ringe, Tandy Warnow, and A. Taylor. 2002. Indo-European and computational cladistics. *Transactions of the Philological Society*, 100(1):59–129.

Jorma Rissanen. 1996. Fisher information and stochastic complexity. *IEEE Transactions on Information Theory*, 42(1):40–47, January.

Yuri M. Shtarkov. 1987. Universal sequential coding of single messages. *Problems of Information Transmission*, 23:3–17.

Sergei A. Starostin. 2005. Tower of babel: Etymological databases. http://newstar.rinet.ru/.

Stephan Vogel, Hermann Ney, and Christoph Tillmann. 1996. HMM-based word alignment in statistical translation. In *Proceedings of 16th Conference on Computational Linguistics (COLING 96)*, Copenhagen, Denmark, August.

Hannes Wettig, Suvi Hiltunen, and Roman Yangarber. 2011. MDL-based Models for Alignment of Etymological Data. In *Proceedings of RANLP: the 8th Conference on Recent Advances in Natural Language Processing*, Hissar, Bulgaria.

LexStat: Automatic Detection of Cognates in Multilingual Wordlists

Johann-Mattis List
Institute for Romance Languages and Literature
Heinrich Heine University Düsseldorf, Germany
listm@phil.uni-duesseldorf.de

Abstract

In this paper, a new method for automatic cognate detection in multilingual wordlists will be presented. The main idea behind the method is to combine different approaches to sequence comparison in historical linguistics and evolutionary biology into a new framework which closely models the most important aspects of the comparative method. The method is implemented as a Python program and provides a convenient tool which is publicly available, easily applicable, and open for further testing and improvement. Testing the method on a large gold standard of IPA-encoded wordlists showed that its results are highly consistent and outperform previous methods.

1 Introduction

During the last two decades there has been an increasing interest in automatic approaches to historical linguistics, which is reflected in the large amount of literature on phylogenetic reconstruction (e.g. Ringe et al., 2002; Gray and Atkinson, 2003; Brown et al., 2008), statistical aspects of genetic relationship (e.g. Baxter and Manaster Ramer, 2000; Kessler, 2001; Mortarino, 2009), and phonetic alignment (e.g. Kondrak, 2002; Prokić et al., 2009; List, forthcoming).

While the supporters of these new automatic methods would certainly agree that their greatest advantage lies in the increase of repeatability and objectivity, it is interesting to note that the most crucial part of the analysis, namely the identification of cognates in lexicostatistical datasets, is still almost exclusively carried out manually. That this may be problematic was recently shown in a comparison of two large lexicostatistical datasets produced by different scholarly teams where differences in item translation and cognate judgments led to topological differences of 30% and more (Geisler and List, forthcoming). Unfortunately, automatic approaches to cognate detection still lack the precision of trained linguists' judgments. Furthermore, most of the methods that have been proposed so far only deal with bilingual as opposed to multilingual wordlists.

The LexStat method, which will be presented in the following, is a convenient tool which not only closely renders the most important aspects of manual approaches but also yields transparent decisions that can be directly compared with the results achieved by the traditional methods.

2 Identification of Cognates

2.1 The Comparative Method

In historical linguistics, cognacy is traditionally determined within the framework of the *comparative method* (Trask, 2000, 64-67). The final goal of this method is the reconstruction of proto-languages, yet the basis of the reconstruction itself rests on the identification of cognate words or morphemes within genetically related languages. Within the comparative method, cognates in a given set of language varieties are identified by applying a recursive procedure. First an initial list of putative cognate sets is created by comparing semantically and phonetically similar words from the languages to be investigated. In most of the literature dealing with the comparative method, the question of which words are most suitable for the initial compilation of cognate lists is not explicitly addressed, yet it seems obvious that the comparanda should belong to the basic vocabulary of the languages. Based on this *cognate list*, an ini-

Proceedings of the EACL 2012 Joint Workshop of LINGVIS & UNCLH, pages 117–125,
Avignon, France, April 23 - 24 2012. ©2012 Association for Computational Linguistics

tial list of putative sound correspondences (*correspondence list*) is created. Sound correspondences are determined by aligning the cognate words and searching for sound pairs which repeatedly occur in similar positions of the presumed cognate words. After these initial steps have been made, the cognate list and the correspondence list are modified by

1. adding and deleting cognate sets from the cognate list depending on whether or not they are consistent with the correspondence list, and

2. adding and deleting sound correspondences from the correspondence list, depending on whether or not they find support in the cognate list.

These steps are repeated until the results seem satisfying enough such that no further modifications, neither of the cognate list, nor of the correspondence list, seem to be necessary.

The specific strength of the comparative method lies in the *similarity measure* which is applied for the identification of cognates: Sequence similarity is determined on the basis of *systematic sound correspondences* (Trask, 2000, 336) as opposed to similarity based on surface resemblances of phonetic segments. Thus, comparing English *token* [təʊkən] and German *Zeichen* [tsaɪçən] 'sign', the words do not really sound similar, yet their cognacy is assumed by the comparative method, since their phonetic segments can be shown to correspond regularly within other cognates of both languages.[1] Lass (1997, 130) calls this notion of similarity *genotypic* as opposed to a *phenotypic* notion of similarity, yet the most crucial aspect of correspondence-based similarity is that it is *language-specific*: Genotypic similarity is never defined in general terms but always with respect to the language systems which are being compared. Correspondence relations can therefore only be established for individual languages, they can never be taken as general statements. This may seem to be a weakness, yet it turns out that the genotypic similarity notion is one of the most crucial strengths of the comparative method: Not only does it allow us to dive deeper in the history of languages in cases where phonetic change has corrupted the former identity of cognates to such an extent that no sufficient surface similarity is left, it also makes it easier to distinguish borrowed from commonly inherited items, since the former usually come along with a greater degree of phenotypic similarity.

2.2 Automatic Approaches

In contrast to the language-specific notion of similarity that serves as the basis for cognate detection within the framework of the comparative method, most automatic methods seek to determine cognacy on the basis of surface similarity by calculating the phonetic distance or similarity between phonetic sequences (words, morphemes).

The most popular distance measures are based on the paradigm of sequence alignment. In alignment analyses two or more sequences are arranged in a matrix in such a way that all corresponding segments appear in the same column, while empty cells of the matrix, resulting from non-corresponding segments, are filled with gap symbols (Gusfield, 1997, 216). Table 1 gives an example for the alignment of German *Tochter* [tɔxtər] 'daughter' and English *daughter* [dɔːtər]: Here, all corresponding segments are inserted in the same columns, while the velar fricative [x] of the German sequence which does not have a corresponding segment in the English word is represented by a gap symbol.

German	t	ɔ	x	t	ə	r
English	d	ɔː	-	t	ə	r

Table 1: Alignment Analysis

In order to retrieve a distance or a similarity score from such an alignment analysis, the matched *residue pairs*, i.e. the segments which appear in the same column of the alignment, are compared and given a specific score depending on their similarity. How the phonetic segments are scored depends on the respective *scoring function* which is the core of all alignment analyses. Thus, the scoring function underlying the *edit distance* only distinguishes identical from non-identical segments, while the scoring function used in the ALINE algorithm of Kondrak (2002) assigns individual similarity scores for the matching of phonetic segments based on phonetic features.

[1] Compare, for example, English *weak* [wiːk] vs. German *weich* [vaɪç] 'soft' for the correspondence of [k] with [ç], and English *tongue* [tʌŋ] vs. German *Zunge* [tsʊŋə] 'tongue' for the correspondence of [t] with [ts].

Using alignment analyses, cognacy can be determined by converting the distance or similarity scores to normalized distance scores and assuming cognacy for distances beyond a certain threshold. The normalized edit distance (NED) of two sequences A and B is usually calculated by dividing the edit distance by the length of the smallest sequence. The normalized distance score of algorithms which yield similarities (such as the ALINE algorithm) can be calculated by the formula of Downey et al. (2008):

(1) $$1 - \frac{2S_{AB}}{S_A + S_B},$$

where S_A and S_B are the similarity scores of the sequences aligned with themselves, and S_{AB} is the similarity score of the alignment of both sequences. For the alignment given in Table 1, the normalized edit distance is 0.6, and the ALINE distance is 0.25.

A certain drawback of most of the common alignment methods is that their scoring function defines segment similarity on the basis of phenotypic criteria. The similarity of phonetic segments is determined on the basis of their phonetic features and not on the basis of the probability that their segments occur in a correspondence relation in genetically related languages. An alternative way to calculate phonetic similarity which comes closer to a genotypic notion of similarity is to compare phonetic sequences with respect to their *sound classes*. The concept of sound classes goes back to Dolgopolsky (1964). The original idea was "to divide sounds into such groups, that changes within the boundary of the groups are more probable than transitions from one group into another" (Burlak and Starostin, 2005, 272)[2].

In his original study, Dolgopolsky proposed ten fundamental sound classes, based on an empirical analysis of sound-correspondence frequencies in a sample of 400 languages. Cognacy between two words is determined by comparing the first two consonants of both words. If the sound classes are identical, the words are judged to be cognate. Otherwise no cognacy is assumed. Thus, given the words German *Tochter* [tɔxtər] 'daughter' and English *daughter* [dɔːtər], the sound class representation of both sequences will be TKTR and TTR, respectively. Since the first two consonants of both words do not match regarding their sound classes, the words are judged to be non-cognate.

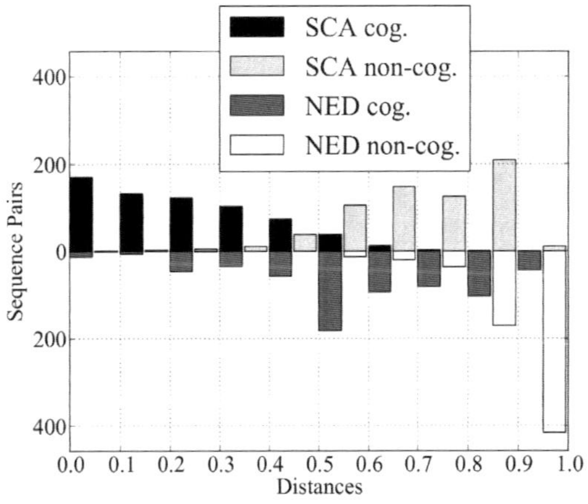

Figure 1: SCA Distance vs. NED

In recent studies, sound classes have also been used as an internal representation format for pairwise and multiple alignment analyses. The method for sound-class alignment (SCA, cf. List, forthcoming) combines the idea of sound classes with traditional alignment algorithms. In contrast to the original proposal by Dolgopolsky, SCA employs an extended sound-class model which also represents tones and vowels along with a refined scoring scheme that defines specific transition probabilities between sound classes. The benefits of the SCA distance compared to NED can be demonstrated by comparing the distance scores the methods yield for the comparison of the same data. Figure 1 contrasts the scores of NED with SCA distance for the alignment of 658 cognate and 658 non-cognate word pairs between English and German (see Sup. Mat. A). As can be seen from the figure, the scores for NED do not show a very sharp distinction between cognate and non-cognate words. Even with a "perfect" threshold of 0.8 that minimizes the number of false positive and false negative decisions there are still 13% of incorrect decisions. The SCA scores, on the other hand, show a sharper distinction between scores for cognates and non-cognates. With a threshold of 0.5 the percentage of incorrect decisions decreases to 8%.

There are only three recent approaches known to the author which explicitly deal with the task of cognate detection in multilingual wordlists. All methods take multilingual, semantically aligned

[2] My translation, original text: "[...] выделить такие группы звуков, что изменения в пределах группы более вероятны, чем переводы из одной группы в другую".

wordlists as input data. Bergsma and Kondrak (2007) first calculate the longest common subsequence ratio between all word pairs in the input data and then use an integer linear programming approach to cluster the words into cognate sets. Unfortunately, their method is only tested on a dataset containing alphabetic transcriptions; hence, no direct comparison with the method proposed in this paper is possible. Turchin et al. (2010) use the above-mentioned sound-class model and the cognate-identification criterion by Dolgopolsky (1964) to identify cognates in lexicostatistical datasets. Their method is also implemented within LexStat, and the results of a direct comparison will be reported in section 4.3. Steiner et al. (2011) propose an iterative approach which starts by clustering words into tentative cognate sets based on their alignment scores. These preliminary results are then refined by filtering words according to similar meanings, computing multiple alignments, and determining recurrent sound correspondences. The authors test their method on two large datasets. Since no gold standard for their test set is available, they only report intermediate results, and their method cannot be directly compared to the one proposed in this paper.

3 LexStat

LexStat combines the most important aspects of the comparative method with recent approaches to sequence comparison in historical linguistics and evolutionary biology. The method employs automatically extracted language-specific scoring schemes for computing distance scores from pairwise alignments of the input data. These language-specific scoring schemes come close to the notion of sound correspondences in traditional historical linguistics.

The method is implemented as a part of the LingPy library, a Python library for automatic tasks in quantitative historical linguistics.[3] It can either be used in Python scripts or directly be called from the Python prompt.

The input data are analyzed within a four-step approach: (1) sequence conversion, (2) scoring-scheme creation, (3) distance calculation, and (4) sequence clustering. In stage (1), the input sequences are converted to sound classes and their sonority profiles are determined. In stage (2), a permutation method is used to create language-specific scoring schemes for all language pairs. In stage (3) the pairwise distances between all word pairs, based on the language-specific scoring schemes, are computed. In stage (4), the sequences are clustered into cognate sets whose average distance is beyond a certain threshold.

3.1 Input and Output Format

The method takes multilingual, semantically aligned wordlists in IPA transcription as input. The input format is a CSV-representation of the way multilingual wordlists are represented in the STARLING software package for lexicostatistical analyses.[4] Thus, the input data are specified in a simple tab-delimited text file with the names of the languages in the first row, an ID for the semantic slots (*basic vocabulary items* in traditional lexicostatistic terminology) in the first column, and the language entries in the columns corresponding to the language names. The language entries should be given either in plain IPA encoding. Additionally, the file can contain headwords (items) for semantic slots corresponding to the IDs. Synonyms, i.e. multiple entries in one language for a given meaning are listed in separate rows and given the same ID. Table 2 gives an example for the possible structure of an input file.

ID	Items	German	English	Swedish
1	hand	hant	hænd	hand
2	woman	fraʊ	wʊmən	kvina
3	know	kɛnən	nəʊ	çɛna
3	know	vɪsən	–	veːta

Table 2: LexStat Input Format

The output format is the same as the input format except that each language column is accompanied by a column indicating the cognate judgments made by LexStat. Cognate judgments are displayed by assigning a cognate ID to each entry. If entries in the output file share the same cognate ID, they are judged to be cognate by the method.

3.2 Sequence Conversion

In the stage of sequence conversion, all input sequences are converted to sound classes, and their

[3]Online available under `http://lingulist.de/lingpy/`.

[4]Online available under `http://starling.rinet.ru/program.php`; a closer description of the software is given in Burlak and Starostin (2005, 270-275)

respective sonority profiles are calculated. LexStat uses the SCA sound-class model by default, yet other sound class models are also available.

The idea of sonority profiles was developed in List (forthcoming). It accounts for the well-known fact that certain types of sound changes are more likely to occur in specific prosodic contexts. Based on the sonority hierarchy of Geisler (1992, 30), the sound segments of phonetic sequences are assigned to different prosodic environments, depending on their prosodic context. The current version of SCA distinguishes seven different prosodic environments.[5] The information regarding sound classes and prosodic context are combined, and each input sequence is further represented as a sequence of tuples, consisting of the sound class and the prosodic environment of the respective phonetic segment. During the calculation, only those segments which are identical regarding their sound class as well as their prosodic context are treated as identical.

3.3 Scoring-Scheme Creation

In order to create language specific scoring schemes, a *permutation method* is used (Kessler, 2001). The method compares the *attested distribution* of residue pairs in phonetic alignment analyses of a given dataset to the *expected distribution*.

The attested distribution of residue pairs is derived from global and local alignment analyses of all word pairs whose distance is beyond a certain threshold. The threshold is used to reflect the fact that within the comparative method, recurrent sound correspondences are only established with respect to presumed cognate words, whereas non-cognate words or borrowings are ignored. Taking only the best-scoring word pairs for the calculation of the attested frequency distribution increases the accuracy of the approach and helps to avoid false positive matches contributing to the creation of the scoring scheme. Alignment analyses are carried out with help of the SCA method.

While the attested distribution is derived from alignments of semantically aligned words, the expected distribution is calculated by aligning word pairs without regard to semantic criteria. This is achieved by repeatedly shuffling the wordlists and aligning them with help of the same methods which were used for the calculation of the attested distributions. In the default settings, the number of repetitions is set to 1000, yet many tests showed that even the number of 100 repetitions is sufficient to yield satisfying results that do not vary significantly.

Once the attested and the expected distributions for the segments of all language pairs are calculated, a language-specific score $s_{x,y}$ for each residue pair x and y in the dataset is created using the formula

$$\text{(2)} \quad s_{x,y} = \frac{1}{r_1 + r_2}\left(r_1 \log_2\left(\frac{a_{x,y}^2}{e_{x,y}^2}\right) + r_2 d_{x,y}\right),$$

where $a_{x,y}$ is the attested frequency of the segment pair, $e_{x,y}$ is the expected frequency, r_1 and r_2 are scaling factors, and $d_{x,y}$ is the similarity score of the original scoring function which was used to retrieve the attested and the expected distributions.

Formula (2) combines different approaches from the literature on sequence comparison in historical linguistics and biology. The idea of squaring the frequencies of attested and expected frequencies was adopted from Kessler (2001, 150), reflecting "the general intuition among linguists that the evidence of phoneme recurrence grows faster than linearly". Using the binary logarithm of the division of attested and expected frequencies of occurrence is common in evolutionary biology to retrieve similarity scores ("log-odds scores") which are apt for the computation of alignment analyses (Henikoff and Henikoff, 1992). The incorporation of the alignment scores of the original language-independent scoring-scheme copes with possible problems resulting from small wordlists: If the dataset is too small to allow the identification of recurrent sound correspondences, the language-independent alignment scores prevent the method from treating generally probable and generally improbable matchings alike. The ratio of language-specific to language-independent alignment scores is determined by the scaling factors r_1 and r_2.

As an example of the computation of language-specific scoring schemes, Table 3 shows attested and expected frequencies along with the resulting similarity scores for the matching of word-initial and word-final sound classes in the KSL testset (see Sup. Mat. B and C). The word-initial and word-final classes T = [t, d], C = [ʦ], S = [ʃ, s, z]

[5] The different environments are: # (word-initial, cons.), V (word-initial, vow.), C (ascending sonority, cons.), v (maximum sonority, vow.), c (descending sonority, cons.), $ (word-final, cons.), and > (word-final, vow.).

English	German	Att.	Exp.	Score
#[t,d]	#[t,d]	3.0	1.24	6.3
#[t,d]	#[ʦ]	3.0	0.38	6.0
#[t,d]	#[ʃ,s,z]	1.0	1.99	-1.5
#[θ,ð]	#[t,d]	7.0	0.72	6.3
#[θ,ð]	#[ʦ]	0.0	0.25	-1.5
#[θ,ð]	#[s,z]	0.0	1.33	0.5
[t,d]$	[t,d]$	21.0	8.86	6.3
[t,d]$	[ʦ]$	3.0	1.62	3.9
[t,d]$	[ʃ,s]$	6.0	5.30	1.5
[θ,ð]$	[t,d]$	4.0	1.14	4.8
[θ,ð]$	[ʦ]$	0.0	0.20	-1.5
[θ,ð]$	[ʃ,s]$	0.0	0.80	0.5

Table 3: Attested vs. Expected Frequencies

in German are contrasted with the word-initial and word-final sound classes T = [t, d] and D = [θ, ð] in English. As can be seen from the table, the scoring scheme correctly reflects the complex sound correspondences between English and German resulting from the High German Consonant Shift (Trask, 2000, 300-302), which is reflected in such cognate pairs as English *town* [taʊn] vs. German *Zaun* [ʦaun] 'fence', English *thorn* [θɔːn] vs. German *Dorn* [dɔrn] 'thorn', English *dale* [deɪl] vs. German *Tal* 'valley' [taːl], and English *hot* [hɔt] vs. German *heiß* [haɪs] 'hot'. The specific benefit of representing the phonetic segments as tuples consisting of their respective sound class along with their prosodic context also becomes evident: The correspondence of English [t] with German [s] is only attested in word-final position, correctly reflecting the complex change of former [t] to [s] in non-initial position in German. If it were not for the specific representation of the phonetic segments by both their sound class and their prosodic context, the evidence would be blurred.

3.4 Distance Calculation

Once the language-specific scoring scheme is computed, the distances between all word pairs are calculated. Here, LexStat uses the "end-space free variant" (Gusfield, 1997, 228) of the traditional algorithm for pairwise sequence alignments which does not penalize gaps introduced in the beginning and the end of the sequences. This modification is useful when words contain prefixes or suffixes which might distort the calculation. The alignment analysis requires no further parameters such as gap penalties, since they have already been calculated in the previous step. The similarity scores for pairwise alignments are converted to distance scores following the approach of Downey et al. (2008) which was described in section 2.2.

Word Pair	SCA	LexStat
German *Schlange* [ʃlaŋə] English *Snake* [sneɪk]	0.44	0.67
German *Wald* [valt] English *wood* [wʊd]	0.40	0.64
German *Staub* [ʃtaup] English *dust* [dʌst]	0.43	0.78

Table 4: SCA Distance vs. LexStat Distance

The benefits of the language-specific distance scores become obvious when comparing them with general ones. Table 4 gives some examples for non-cognate word pairs taken from the KSL testset (see Sup. Mat. B and C). While the SCA distances for these pairs are all considerably low, as it is suggested by the surface similarity of the words, the language-specific distances are all much higher, resulting from the fact that no further evidence for the matching of specific residue pairs can be found in the data.

3.5 Sequence Clustering

In the last step of the LexStat algorithm all sequences occurring in the same semantic slot are clustered into cognate sets using a flat cluster variant of the UPGMA algorithm (Sokal and Michener, 1958) which was written by the author. In contrast to traditional UPGMA clustering, this algorithm terminates when a user-defined threshold of average pairwise distances is reached.

	Ger.	Eng.	Dan.	Swe.	Dut.	Nor.
Ger. [frau]	0.00	0.95	0.81	0.70	0.34	1.00
Eng. [wʊmən]	0.95	0.00	0.78	0.90	0.80	0.80
Dan. [kvenə]	0.81	0.78	0.00	0.17	0.96	0.13
Swe. [kviːa]	0.70	0.90	0.17	0.00	0.86	0.10
Dut. [vrɑuʊ]	0.34	0.80	0.96	0.86	0.00	0.89
Nor. [kʊinə]	1.00	0.80	0.13	0.10	0.89	0.00
Clusters	1	2	3	3	1	3

Table 5: Pairwise Distance Matrix

Table 5 shows pairwise distances of German, English, Danish, Swedish, Dutch, and Norwegian entries for the item WOMAN taken from the GER dataset (see Sup. Mat. B) along with the resulting cluster decisions of the algorithm when setting the threshold to 0.6.

4 Evaluation

4.1 Gold Standard

In order to test the method, a gold standard was compiled by the author. The gold standard consists of 9 multilingual wordlists conforming to the input format required by LexStat (see Supplementary Material B). The data was collected from different publicly available sources. Hence, the selection of language entries as well as the manually conducted cognate judgments were carried out independently of the author. Since not all the original sources provided phonetic transcriptions of the language entries, the respective alphabetic entries were converted to IPA transcription by the author. The datasets differ regarding the treatment of borrowings. In some datasets they are explicitly marked as such and treated as non-cognates, in other datasets no explicit distinction between borrowing and cognacy is drawn. Information on the structure and the sources of the datasets is given in Table 6.

File	Family	Lng.	Itm.	Entr.	Source
GER	Germanic	7	110	814	Starostin (2008)
ROM	Romance	5	110	589	Starostin (2008)
SLV	Slavic	4	110	454	Starostin (2008)
PIE	Indo-Eur.	18	110	2057	Starostin (2008)
OUG	Uralic	21	110	2055	Starostin (2008)
BAI	Bai	9	110	1028	Wang (2006)
SIN	Sinitic	9	180	1614	Hóu (2004)
KSL	varia	8	200	1600	Kessler (2001)
JAP	Japonic	10	200	1986	Shirō (1973)

Table 6: The Gold Standard

4.2 Evaluation Measures

Bergsma and Kondrak (2007) test their method for automatic cognate detection by calculating the *set precision* (PRE), the *set recall* (REC), and the *set F-score* (FS): The set precision p is the proportion of cognate sets calculated by the method which also occurs in the gold standard. The set recall r is the proportion of cognate sets in the gold standard which are also calculated by the method, and the set F-score f is calculated by the formula

$$f = 2\frac{pr}{p+r}. \tag{3}$$

A certain drawback of these scores is that they only check for completely identical decisions regarding the clustering of words into cognate sets while neglecting similar tendencies. The similarity of decisions can be evaluated by calculating the *proportion of identical decisions* (PID) when comparing the test results with those of the gold standard. Given all pairwise decisions regarding the cognacy of word pairs inherent in the gold standard and in the testset, the differences can be displayed using a contingency table, as shown in Table 7.

	Cognate Gold Standard	**Non-Cognate Gold Standard**
Cognate Testset	true positives	false positives
Non-Cognate Testset	false negatives	true negatives

Table 7: Comparing Gold Standard and Testset

The PID score can then simply be calculated by dividing the sum of true positives and true negatives by the total number of decisions. In an analogous way the *proportion of identical positive decisions* (PIPD) and the *proportion of identical negative decisions* (PIND) can be calculated by dividing the number of true positives by the sum of true positives and false negatives, and by dividing the number of false positives by the sum of false positives and true negatives, respectively.

4.3 Results

Based on the new method for automatic cognate detection, the 9 testsets were analyzed by LexStat, using a gap penalty of -2 for the alignment analysis, a threshold of 0.7 for the creation of the attested distribution, and 1:1 as the ratio of language-specific to language-independent similarity scores. The threshold for the clustering of sequences into cognate sets was set to 0.6. In order to compare the output of LexStat with other methods, three additional analyses of the datasets were carried out: The first two analyses were based on the calculation of SCA and NED distances of all language entries. Based on these scores all words were clustered into cognate sets using the flat cluster variant of UPGMA with a threshold of 0.4 for SCA distances and a threshold of 0.7 for NED, since these both turned out to yield the best results for these approaches. The third analysis was based on the above-mentioned approach by Turchin et al. (2010). Since in this approach all decisions regarding cognacy are either positive or negative, no specific cluster algorithm had to be applied.

Score	LexStat	SCA	NED	Turchin
PID	0.85	0.82	0.76	0.74
PIPD	0.78	0.75	0.66	0.56
PIND	0.93	0.90	0.86	0.94
PRE	0.59	0.51	0.39	0.39
REC	0.68	0.57	0.47	0.55
FS	0.63	0.55	0.42	0.46

Table 8: Performance of the Methods

The results of the tests are summarized in Table 8. As can be seen from the table, LexStat outperforms the other methods in almost all respects, the only exception being the proportion of identical negative decisions (PIND). Since non-identical negative decisions point to false positives, this shows that – for the given settings of LexStat – the method of Turchin et al. (2010) performs best at avoiding false positive cognate judgments, but it fails to detect many cognates correctly identified by LexStat.[6] Figure 2 gives the separate PID scores for all datasets, showing that LexStat's good performance is prevalent throughout all datasets. The fact that all methods perform badly on the PIE dataset may point to problems resulting from the size of the wordlists: if the dataset is too small and the genetic distance of the languages too large, one may simply lack the evidence to prove cognacy without doubt.

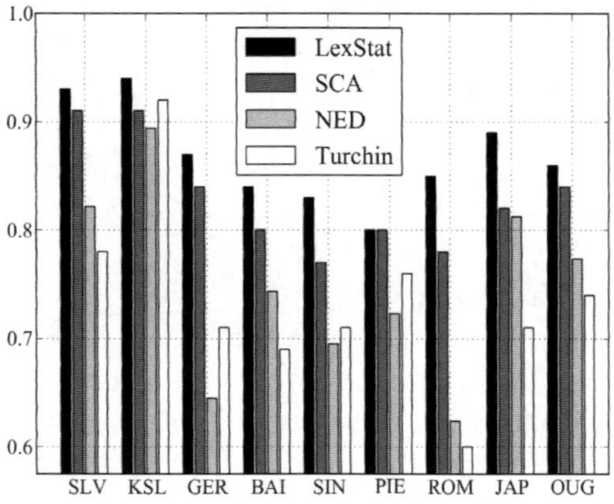

Figure 2: PID Scores of the Methods

[6]LexStat can easily be adjusted to avoid false positives by lowering the threshold for sequence clustering. Using a threshold of 0.5 will yield a PIND score of 0.96, yet the PID score will lower down to 0.82.

The LexStat method was designed to distinguish systematic from non-systematic similarities. The method should therefore produce less false positive cognate judgments resulting from chance resemblances and borrowings than the other methods. In the KSL dataset borrowings are marked along with their sources. Out of a total of 5600 word pairs, 72 exhibit a loan relation, and 83 are phonetically similar (with an NED score less then 0.6) but unrelated. Table 9 lists the number and the percentage of false positives resulting from undetected borrowings or chance resemblances for the different methods (see also Sup. Mat. D). While LexStat outperforms the other methods regarding the detection of chance resemblances, it is not particularly good at handling borrowings. LexStat cannot *per se* deal with borrowings, but only with language-specific as opposed to language-independent similarities. In order to handle borrowings, other methods (such as, e.g., the one by Nelson-Sathi et al., 2011) have to be applied.

	LexStat	SCA	NED	Turchin
Borr.	36 / 50%	44 / 61%	35 / 49%	38 / 53%
Chance R.	14 / 17%	35 / 42%	74 / 89%	26 / 31%

Table 9: Borrowings and Chance Resemblances

5 Conclusion

In this paper, a new method for automatic cognate detection in multilingual wordlists has been presented. The method differs from other approaches in so far as it employs language-specific scoring schemes which are derived with the help of improved methods for automatic alignment analyses. The test of the method on a large dataset of wordlists taken from different language families shows that it is consistent regardless of the languages being analyzed and outperforms previous approaches.

In contrast to the black box character of many automatic analyses which only yield total scores for the comparison of wordlists, the method yields transparent decisions which can be directly compared with the traditional results of the comparative method. Apart from the basic ideas of the procedure, which surely are in need of enhancement through reevaluation and modification, the most striking limit of the method lies in the data: If the wordlists are too short, certain cases of cognacy are simply impossible to be detected.

References

William H. Baxter and Alexis Manaster Ramer. 2000. Beyond lumping and splitting. Probabilistic issues in historical linguistics. In Colin Renfrew, April McMahon, and Larry Trask, editors, *Time depth in historical linguistics*, pages 167–188. McDonald Institute for Archaeological Research, Cambridge.

Shane Bergsma and Grzegorz Kondrak. 2007. Multilingual cognate identification using integer linear programming. In *RANLP Workshop on Acquisition and Management of Multilingual Lexicons*, Borovets, Bulgaria.

Cecil H. Brown, Eric W. Holman, Søren Wichmann, Viveka Velupillai, and Michael Cysouw. 2008. Automated classification of the world's languages. *Sprachtypologie und Universalienforschung*, 61(4):285–308.

Svetlana A. Burlak and Sergej A. Starostin. 2005. *Sravnitel'no-istoričeskoe jazykoznanie* [Comparative-historical linguistics]. Akademia, Moscow.

Aron B. Dolgopolsky. 1964. Gipoteza drevnejšego rodstva jazykovych semej Severnoj Evrazii s verojatnostej točky zrenija [A probabilistic hypothesis concerning the oldest relationships among the language families of Northern Eurasia]. *Voprosy Jazykoznanija*, 2:53–63.

Sean S. Downey, Brian Hallmark, Murray P. Cox, Peter Norquest, and Stephen Lansing. 2008. Computational feature-sensitive reconstruction of language relationships: Developing the ALINE distance for comparative historical linguistic reconstruction. *Journal of Quantitative Linguistics*, 15(4):340–369.

Hans Geisler and Johann-Mattis List. forthcoming. Beautiful trees on unstable ground. Notes on the data problem in lexicostatistics. In Heinrich Hettrich, editor, *Die Ausbreitung des Indogermanischen. Thesen aus Sprachwissenschaft, Archäologie und Genetik*. Reichert, Wiesbaden.

Hans Geisler. 1992. *Akzent und Lautwandel in der Romania*. Narr, Tübingen.

Russell D. Gray and Quentin D. Atkinson. 2003. Language-tree divergence times support the Anatolian theory of Indo-European origin. *Nature*, 426(6965):435–439.

Dan Gusfield. 1997. *Algorithms on strings, trees and sequences*. Cambridge University Press, Cambridge.

Steven Henikoff and Jorja G. Henikoff. 1992. Amino acid substitution matrices from protein blocks. *PNAS*, 89(22):10915–10919.

Jīng Hóu, editor. 2004. *Xiàndài Hànyǔ fāngyán yīnkù [Phonological database of Chinese dialects]*. Shànghǎi Jiàoyù, Shanghai.

Brett Kessler. 2001. *The significance of word lists. Statistical tests for investigating historical connections between languages*. CSLI Publications, Stanford.

Grzegorz Kondrak. 2002. *Algorithms for language reconstruction*. Dissertation, University of Toronto, Toronto.

Roger Lass. 1997. *Historical linguistics and language change*. Cambridge University Press, Cambridge.

Johann-Mattis List. forthcoming. SCA: Phonetic alignment based on sound classes. In Marija Slavkovik and Dan Lassiter, editors, *New directions in logic, language, and computation*. Springer, Berlin and Heidelberg.

Cinzia Mortarino. 2009. An improved statistical test for historical linguistics. *Statistical Methods and Applications*, 18(2):193–204.

Shijulal Nelson-Sathi, Johann-Mattis List, Hans Geisler, Heiner Fangerau, Russell D. Gray, William Martin, and Tal Dagan. 2011. Networks uncover hidden lexical borrowing in Indo-European language evolution. *Proceedings of the Royal Society B*, 278(1713):1794–1803.

Jelena Prokić, Martijn Wieling, and John Nerbonne. 2009. Multiple sequence alignments in linguistics. In *Proceedings of the EACL 2009 Workshop on Language Technology and Resources for Cultural Heritage, Social Sciences, Humanities, and Education*, pages 18–25, Stroudsburg, PA. Association for Computational Linguistics.

Donald Ringe, Tandy Warnow, and Ann Taylor. 2002. Indo-european and computational cladistics. *Transactions of the Philological Society*, 100(1):59–129.

Hattori Shirō. 1973. Japanese dialects. In Henry M. Hoenigswald and Robert H. Langacre, editors, *Diachronic, areal and typological linguistics*, pages 368–400. Mouton, The Hague and Paris.

Robert. R. Sokal and Charles. D. Michener. 1958. A statistical method for evaluating systematic relationships. *University of Kansas Scientific Bulletin*, 28:1409–1438.

George Starostin. 2008. Tower of Babel. An etymological database project. Online ressource. URL: `http://starling.rinet.ru`.

Lydia Steiner, Peter F. Stadler, and Michael Cysouw. 2011. A pipeline for computational historical linguistics. *Language Dynamics and Change*, 1(1):89–127.

Robert L. Trask, editor. 2000. *The dictionary of historical and comparative linguistics*. Edinburgh University Press, Edinburgh.

Peter Turchin, Ilja Peiros, and Murray Gell-Mann. 2010. Analyzing genetic connections between languages by matching consonant classes. *Journal of Language Relationship*, 3:117–126.

Feng Wang. 2006. *Comparison of languages in contact*. Institute of Linguistics Academia Sinica, Taipei.

Author Index